D1567771

Russian Armored Cars 1930-2000

James Kinnear

Darlington Productions, Inc.

FRONT COVER

Center: BA-10s in Vyborg, 1944. All of these vehicles are traveling with the
engine covers open, as was common in hot weather.

Bottom: A BP M-97 armored car at the Bronnitsy Proving Ground, Moscow,
Summer 1999. Photo by Aleksandr Koshavtsev

BACK COVER

Top: FAI-M on display in Moscow, 1999. This FAI-M is the restored FAI-M
which was, for a short time, displayed at the Central Armed Forces
Museum in Moscow. The vehicle was restored by the "Ekipazh" military
history group which has recovered other wartime Russian tanks in
addition to the FAI-M.

Middle: Three color camouflage scheme on a BA-6, Karelian Isthmus, 1941.

Middle: A turretless BRDM-2 (ex 9P148 ATGM vehicle) guarding a road check
point near Moscow during the first Chechen war.

Bottom: A GAZ-3937-10 negotiating a slope during field trials.

Published and distributed by
Darlington Productions, Inc
P.O. Box 5884
Darlington, Maryland 21034
410-457-5400
410-457-5480 fax
www.darlingtonproductions.com

ISBN 1-892848-05-8

Contact Darlington Productions for more information on other military titles or magazines.

Table of Contents

PREFACE

My interest in Russian armored cars originated with a small book by John Milsom, published in the "Armour in Profile" series in the early 1970s, which briefly described the history of Russian armored cars of the Second World War period. That book inspired my interest, and later research, into Russian armored vehicles, which has continued to the present day.

Until the downfall of the Soviet Union in 1991, the amount of archival material available to researchers in the West was relatively limited. For the wartime period, vehicle identification relied heavily on German intelligence reports with attendant German designations for vehicles as identified and destroyed or captured in battle. This book is written primarily from original Russian sources recently made available, and attempts to describe both the vehicles and their developments from the original Russian perspective. Russian designations are used throughout the book, with western military designations where appropriate, particularly when these reporting designations are better known to readers in the West.

This book concentrates on those vehicles which were designed in Russia and have served with the Soviet and Russian armed forces over the years. It does not attempt to describe in detail variants developed outside the Former Soviet Union in the former Warsaw Pact countries, or to cover in depth the foreign service of exported vehicles, as that would in itself require a complete volume.

I am indebted to a small group of Russian enthusiasts for their help with providing archival material and photographic references. Additionally, they also assisted in correcting some of my Western perspectives on Russian AFV design practice and history. In particular, I wish to thank Andrey Aksenov and Alexsandr Koshavtsev, who spent many hours helping with the preparation of this book and corrected numerous mistakes and misconceptions. Several of the drawings in this book were provided by Nikolai Polikarpov, and these are credited where appropriate. Steve Zaloga has, as always, been extremely generous with providing additional information and filling gaps in photographic references from his extensive database on Russian military equipment. Thanks also go to David Fletcher and his staff at the Tank Museum in Bovington, England, for allowing me to research their fascinating photographic collection. Appreciation is also extended to Mikhail Baryatinsky, Jochen Vollert, Trevor Larkum, Maxim Kolomiets, and Mikhail Svirin, who provided additional information and several rare reference photographs which complete the book. Where known, the original Russian press photographers have been credited with their work throughout the book. Some photographs are not as clear and sharp as I would prefer, but have been used where they illustrate rare vehicles of which better photographs are not available.

This book is the result of several years of research and interest. Few books written on Russian military equipment now remain accurate long after publication, due to constant new information being unearthed from long hidden and secret Soviet-era archival material. However, the use of Russian original sources throughout this text should provide the reader with an up-to-date and accurate account of an extensive but hitherto little researched subject.

This book was written in Russia and Ukraine over the years 1997-2000.

Jim Kinnear

1
Russian Armored Cars
A Historical Perspective

Before the First World War, the Russian Army utilized a combination of imported armored car designs and a small number of indigenous vehicles. The country did not, however, at this time possess the industrial base to series produce armored cars. There were several small automotive plants in Russia, but these were restricted to the production of limited numbers of light vehicles.

Interest in armored vehicles was forced on Russia as a result of the 1904-05 Russo-Japanese war, which proved a major learning experience for Russian forces at sea and on land. The war showed the backwardness of Russian tactics and also demonstrated the value of mechanized machine gun support for breakthrough operations. As a direct result of this wartime experience, several armored car designs were developed and prototypes tested for the Russian War Ministry, but series production of Russian armored cars was still some years in the future.

The first armored car designed in Russia was developed in 1905 by the Georgian engineer M.A.Nakashidze. His design for a machine gun armed vehicle with 4-8mm of armor, combat weight of 3,000kg, and a road speed of 50km/hour was accepted by the Russian War Ministry for service with the Russian Army. However, as no Russian plant was considered capable of producing the vehicle, manufacture was subcontracted to the French company Charron, Girardot, and Voigt, which completed and delivered nine vehicles to the Russian Army. At least one other vehicle was mysteriously "lost" en route to Russia through Germany and was subsequently evaluated by the German Army.

Several military plants began the development of armored cars during the period immediately following the Russo-Japanese War, including the Izhorskiy plant at Kolpino, near St. Petersburg, which had formerly specialized in the production of armor plate for naval vessels. The Izhorskiy plant produced its first armored car in 1906 and after many years of small scale production, the plant was to become the primary manufacturer of Russian armored cars during the 1930s.

In 1908, the Russko-Baltiysky (Russo-Balt) light vehicle plant in Riga, Latvia developed and produced its first indigenously designed armored car. The plant produced limited numbers of chassis for armored cars in Riga from 1908 until 1915, when parts of the plant (which also produced aircraft assemblies) were split and evacuated to Fili, Taganrog, and locations in the St. Petersburg region. The part of the plant relocated to Fili (now part of Moscow) was subsequently converted to specialize in the manufacture and repair of armored cars, tanks, and other vehicles. The plant was later renamed as the "First Brone-Tanko Avtomobilniy Zavod (BTAZ)." The Izhorskiy plant manufactured the armored bodies for these vehicles, which were assembled at the relocated Russko-Baltiysky plant after 1915. The most common early production model armored car was the Russo-Balt M, armed with three 7.62mm M-1905 "Maxim" machine guns, though 37mm main armament could also be installed. The vehicle was particularly slow, with a maximum speed of only 20km/hour, but was otherwise capable and well armed and mounted on a strong chassis.

The first Russian half track was designed in the garage of Tsar Nicholas 2 in 1909 and was produced at the Russko-Baltiysky plant from 1913. On this chassis, the first Russian series-produced half-track armored car was developed and produced; this vehicle also being commonly referred to as the Russo-Balt. To put armored car manufacture at this time in perspective, during the six-year period 1908-14, the Russko-Baltiysky plant produced only 450 vehicles in total, of which only a small number were armored cars.

At the beginning of the First World War, the major armored car manufacturers of the 1930s were in their formative years. Nearly all armored cars used in the Russian Army were foreign designs; principally imported from Great Britain and Italy as a result of a series of Russian War Office contracts issued in 1913. Some of the first foreign vehicles imported were sold to Russia by the firms Packard, White, Benz, Jeffrey, and Garford. These vehicles proved particularly unsuitable for Russian conditions, with weak chassis and light construction that did not survive well on Russian roads. Lacking available alternatives, Russian armored car designers nevertheless made maximum use of imported chassis, there being significant development of armored cars after 1914 using locally developed armored bodies mounted on these imported chassis. Late in 1914, the Putilov Plant in St. Petersburg began production of an 8,000kg armored car armed with a 76.2mm field gun. The new Putilov-Garford armored car was designed by F.F. Lender, who placed the 76.2mm gun in a rear turret. This provided a good arc of fire, with additional machine gun armament being provided for close support. It was later claimed by Russia as the world's first wheeled self propelled gun. The Putilov Garford was built in small numbers and made a significant contribution during the First World War and the Russian Civil War, which followed the 1917 Revolution. The vehicle, with its impressive 76.2mm armament, was often used to engage armored trains and served with the Red Army into the 1930s as a railway artillery vehicle, with its wheels converted to run on the Russian rail system.

Small numbers of vehicles were also produced during this period at the Izhorskiy plant. The Putilovsky, Izhorsky, and Obukhovsky (later Bolshevik) plants, which were all located in the St. Petersburg area, were to form the industrial center of Russian armored car production in the following decade. At this time, the Putilov plant was by far the largest producer of armored cars, to be overtaken by the Izhorsky plant in the 1930s when the Putilov plant was converted to heavy tank production.

In the meantime, St. Petersburg was renamed Petrograd in 1914 and again renamed, this time to Leningrad, in 1924. The renaming of cities, which was popular after 1917, was also applied to factories. The Putilovsky plant became the Krasniy Putilovsky (Red Putilovsky) plant in 1917, and was redesignated as the Kirovsky plant in 1934 in honor of Sergei Mironovitch Kirov, the then-current head of the Leningrad Communist Party.

During the First World War, before the major armored car manufacturers of the 1930s became established, many enterprising private individuals also designed armored vehicles on imported chassis in an attempt to have their projects accepted for lucrative military contracts. Many Russian armored car designs developed in the period 1914-18 included innovative features which were not included in series-produced vehicles until many years later. Noteworthy developments included the engineer Poplavko's Poplavko-Jeffery (AB-9) armored car of 1915 with its 4x4 chassis, twin engines, twin driver's positions, five forward and five reverse gears, and 16mm frontal armor. The Renault Mgebrov, designed in 1914 with its highly faceted armor for maximum ballistic protection and the incorporation of armored glass was also an interesting design concept. The futuristic-looking Renault Mgebrov was manufactured in small numbers from the spring of 1916. During the same period, 1915-17, N.N.

Filitov's Tricycle armored car, 1916. The Filitov armored car was one of many vehicles privately developed for lucrative Russian War Ministry contracts during the years 1916-1918. Approximately twenty were built and served with the Russian army.

Lebedenko designed several armored cars in the town of Dmitrov, near Moscow. In 1915 Colonel Gulkevitch designed a 40 tonne armored car on the imported Lombard chassis armed with a field gun intended for heavy fire support for infantry. Gulkevitch's design was impractical and not developed beyond conceptual stage, however he was particularly interested in the advantages of half-tracks for crossing obstacles, including barbed wire defenses. He went on to significantly modify his original plans and developed his designs into the first Russian half-track armored car for which the Putilov plant provided the armored body.

Though their ideas were not generally developed beyond prototype or limited series production stage at the time, these designers would play a prominent part in the development of future series-produced armored cars, while many of the ideas, such as the twin engines used on the Poplavko-Jeffery AB-9, were to be incorporated many years later in post World War Two vehicles such as the BTR-60 APC series.

In the autumn of 1914, the Putilovsky plant halted production of transport vehicles and reorganized as a specialized armored car manufacturer. In 1916, on government orders, it began production of Austin Putilov half-track armored cars with their distinctive twin offset turrets, which maximized the armament's arc of fire. The Austin Putilovets combined a half-track designed by the French engineer Kegresse (who worked in St. Petersburg on contract to the Russian government) on an Austin chassis armored by the Putilovsky plant. The vehicle was developed in the spring of 1916 and extensively field trialled during the months of August and September the same year. The vehicle excelled in trials and was immediately accepted for service in the Russian Army. The Austin-Putilov, with its two 7.62mm M-1910 machine guns, 8mm armor, and 25km/hour road speed was officially referred to as a half track armoured car,but the vehicles were often referred to as "poltanka" (literally "half-tank") in service. The vehicle is also referred to as the "Austin Kegresse" or "Putilov Kegresse". Later in 1916, the Putilov plant developed a new turret which provided an element of anti-aircraft fire capability.

The year 1916 was another important year for foreign procurement, with armored car purchase contracts being completed with the British firms Austin, Lanchester, Sheffield Simplex, Armstrong Whitworth, and Jarrott. Small numbers of vehicles were also purchased from Fiat of Italy and the French company Renault, while the purchasing expeditions also procured MkV and Whippet tanks from Great Britain and Renault FT tanks from France. Russia was gathering the knowledge and experience which would be refined in the development of indigenous vehicles in the years ahead, incorporating the

best of ideas from these imported designs.

Despite extensive overseas procurement from 1916, a significant gap followed in both foreign purchases and domestic manufacture, and by October 1918, the fledgling Red Army possessed a total of only 150 armored cars; this number remaining stable for several years. By 1918 there were thirty-eight armored "groups" in service with a total of 150 armored cars; each group consisting of four vehicles and one hundred supporting infantry. By 1919 there were fifty such groups, and this had risen to only fifty-one by 1920. Towards the end of the First World War in 1918, the Izhorskiy plant at Kolpino produced only 115 armored cars; the first post-World War One armored cars to enter Russian Army service being produced primarily by the relocated Russko-Baltiysky plant.

During the Civil War which followed the Russian Revolution, armored cars were the principle AFV on the battlefield. After the Civil War, Russia was left with only a handful of serviceable armored cars and a modernization program was desperately needed. This could not be achieved, however, until the Russian automotive industry was sufficiently advanced to support such a radical indigenous manufacturing program. The development of armored car (and tank) production from a cottage industry to mass production was dependent on the existance of a modern motor industry, which came about in Russia at the end of the 1920s.

On 7th November 1924, the AMO F-15 truck, a Russian development of the FIAT F-15 design, was paraded on Red Square, Moscow. The AMO F-15 was the first series-produced Russian truck. It was important in signalling the beginnings of a Russian heavy automobile industry, and with it the ability to use new series-produced chassis on which to mount armored car bodies. There was, however, no significant production of armored cars in Russia between 1918 and 1927. The BA-27 did not enter production until the beginning of the first Five Year Plan in 1927 as part of a major and long overdue program to mechanize the Russian Army.

In December 1929, the formal process of mechanizing the Russian Army began and mechanized brigades were formed, each with 220 tanks and 56 armored cars. In line with the overall mechanization plan, some thirty models of armored car were designed and produced during the period 1927-40. In the 1930s Russian armored cars were divided into two types; light and heavy, the difference in classification being in armament rather than weight. The light classification was used for armored cars armed with machine guns, while heavy armoured cars were generally those armed with a 37mm or 45mm tank gun. There were a small number of Russian "medium" armored cars, such as the BA-27M, but these were generally classified as heavy for operational purposes.

BA-10Ms on summer maneuvers, 1939. (Tank Museum, Bovington, UK. Ref: 2454/F4)

The first series-produced armored car produced in Russia was the BA-27, produced by the Izhorskiy plant on the AMO F-15 chassis from 1927, with later production batches of the BA-27 being built on the Ford AA chassis. A total of one hundred BA-27 vehicles were built. In 1931, Izhorskiy began production of the D-8 and D-12 on the light Ford/GAZ-A chassis, and later the same year began production of the heavy BA-I, the first in a series of BA heavy armored cars which remained in production until 1940. With series production of armored cars underway (albeit with limited numbers produced), the early 1930s were to represent the era of modern armored car and tank development in Russia in parallel with most other industrialized nations around the world.

The chassis for most armored cars of the 1930s were built by the KIM plant in Moscow and the Gorkiy plant in Nizhny Novgorod. The latter plant was originally known as the Nizhny Novgorod Automobile plant (NAZ), but was renamed as the Gorkiy Automobile Plant (GAZ) in the mid-1930s. These chassis were shipped to the armored car manufacturers (primarily the Izhorskiy and the smaller but longer established Vyksinskiy plant), where the armored bodies were mounted on the chassis and final assembly was undertaken. Prior to 1931, the imported Ford Timken chassis was used for some Russian armored cars. While this chassis was available thereafter, the provision of series production technology to the USSR by Henry Ford in 1931-32 gave a major boost to Russian armored car production. It provided ready made chassis for both light (Ford/GAZ-A and Ford/GAZ-AA-based) and heavy (GAZ-AAA-based) armored cars. ZiS was

also later to provide 6x4 chassis for limited production heavy armored cars.

During the early 1930s "operational" use of Russian armored cars was, for the most part, restricted to exercises conducted primarily in the Kiev Military District. Small numbers of Russian armored cars (especially the FAI, BA-3, and BA-6) were used during the Spanish Civil War, and experience gained during this conflict was incorporated into future designs which had better ballistic protection, particularly with regard to armor slope. The battles of the Khalkin Gol against Japan in the summer of 1939 were also a significant learning experience, with 345 Russian armored cars and 495 tanks engaged in combat operations during the conflict. Russian armored cars were also used in the invasion of Poland, the Baltic Republics, and Finland before the outbreak of total war against Germany in June 1941. Most armored cars were destroyed or abandoned within weeks of the outbreak of war with Germany, though some stationed in the Far East Military District at the time of war's outbreak appeared only later on the Russian "Western" front. A small number of captured vehicles were used by German Army.

Post-war, GAZ became the predominant armored car design bureau and manufacturer, with the GAZ plant producing the majority of Soviet and Russian wheeled AFVs from 1946 to the present day. This included the BTR-40, BRDM, and BRDM-2 armored cars and the BTR-60, BTR-70, and BTR-80 series of wheeled APCs. In 1972, a modern plant was established at Arzamas, south of Gorkiy (which was renamed Nizhny Novgorod in 1991) and in 1980 the Arzamas plant began concentrating on

BTR-80 and other AFV designs. The vehicles produced by GAZ and latterly Arzamas were used in large numbers by the Soviet Army and widely exported to former Warsaw Pact countries and other client states worldwide. They proved reliable in service and relatively simple to maintain. Today, even the elderly BTR-40 remains in service with some armies, some fifty years after its original introduction into Soviet Army service.

In 2000, worldwide defense needs have changed entirely from only ten years ago, when the needs of Warsaw Pact and NATO countries were supported by massive military spending and defense equipment production. Russia today is looking towards export markets, and new armored cars are being introduced with multipurpose military and paramilitary capability, in an attempt to widen the potential market in an era of reduced worldwide requirement for conventional armored vehicles.

2
Light Armored Cars
1930-1945

D-8

D-12

FAI

FAI-M

GAZ-TK

BA-20

BA-20M

LB-23

BA-21

LB-62

LB-NATI

BA-64

BA-64B

After the Civil War, Russia was left with only a handful of serviceable armored cars and a modernization program was desperately needed. This could not be achieved, however, until the Russian automotive industry was sufficiently advanced to support such a radical indigenous development program.

On the 7th November 1924, the AMO F-15 truck, a Russian development of a Fiat design, was paraded in Red Square. The introduction of this small Russian-developed and manufactured truck signalled the beginning of the Russian heavy automotive industry and with it the ability to use new chassis on which armored car bodies could be mounted for military purposes. This manufacturing potential was given a considerable boost with the establishment of a new plant in Nizhny Novgorod in 1931-32.

D-8 Light Armored Car

N.I. Dyrenkov was a senior design engineer at the KIM plant in Moscow when in 1930 the plant began production of the new Ford-A chassis, which was also at that time being readied for production at the giant "Gudok Oktyabrya" or "October Horn" (later GAZ) plant at Nizhny Novgorod. Dyrenkov had a long-term personal interest in armored car development and had read the U.S. journal *Army Ordnance*, in which articles on U.S. armored

D-8 armored car. Russian drawing showing rear armament installation.

cars and their tactical use had inspired him. The arrival of the new Ford-A chassis allowed him to develop his ideas and paper design studies into vehicles suitable for series production.

Dyrenkov made a prolonged visit to the Izhorskiy armor plant while the Ford-A chassis was being readied for production at the KIM plant in Moscow. He was very impressed with the capabilities of the Izhorskiy plant and his visit confirmed his thoughts on having his designs produced at Izhorskiy on the Ford-A chassis produced by KIM. In the mid-1930s, upon his return to the KIM plant, Dyrenkov began work on a new small armored car design based on the Ford-A 4x2 automobile which he developed in collaboration with engineers at the Izhorskiy plant.

The new vehicle, designated D-8 (Dyrenkov-8) was intended as a service replacement for the BA-27, though it was a lighter class of vehicle, smaller, without tank gun armament but with comparable armor protection. The BA-27 had served with the Red Army as a wheeled tank when there was a need for armored cars to fulfill such a role in the formative years of the Soviet automobile industry. By 1931, light tanks were becoming available in number and the D-8 was therefore introduced as a purpose-designed reconnaissance vehicle with reduced machine-gun armament which was adequate for reconnaissance purposes.

Dyrenkov did not want to install a turret on the D-8, arguing that the added weight involved in mounting a turret could be better used for additional armor, so the armament was placed within the hull of the vehicle. Firing ports in the hull gave the vehicle a potential 360° arc of fire, though space to move weapons within the hull was restricted. On the original prototype D-8, there were up to four machine gun ball mounts: one on either side, one at the hull rear and one in front and to the right of the driver; however, this was impractical for a two man crew and the armament firing ports were reduced on production models of the D-8. The crew consisted of a driver and a busy commander/gunner who operated the vehicle machine gun(s).

D-8 armored car crossing a river. This retouched photo shows the ball-mounted DT machine gun front armament with its armored cover. (Tank Museum, Bovington, UK)

D-8s on airborne maneuvers at Kiev Military District in 1934. This grainy photo is taken from a Soviet film clip, which shows D-8s being unloaded from a TB-3 bomber during an airborne landing. Two D-8s were transported facing each other under the aircraft fuselage.

The D-8 underwent Red Army acceptance trials in late 1931 concurrently with the similar D-12. During these field trials the D-8 was armed with a single 7.62mm machine gun located in the front right of the fighting compartment. Marshal Klimenti Voroshilov witnessed the trials, and at his suggestion a second machine gun was reintroduced, located at the rear of the vehicle, on the right side. After successful completion of evaluation trials, both the D-8 and the D-12 were accepted for service in the Red Army.

The D-8 was the first Russian series-produced armored car of the 1930s. It was built in small numbers at the Izhorskiy Plant between 1931 and 1932 and served with the Red Army in the early 1930s. In 1932, some D-8s in service with the Russian Army underwent a rebuild program which included the mounting of a small turret armed with a 7.62mm DT machine gun. A small number of D-8s were so modified, the vehicle being the basis for the D-8s replacement, the FAI. The D-8 was an

SPECIFICATIONS D-8

Design bureau: Moscow Auto Zavod (KIM)
Crew: 2
Manufacturing plant: Izhorsk
Service date: 1931 Series produced
Combat weight: 2,000kg**

Dimensions: (m)
Length: 3.540
Width: 1.705
Height: 1.680
Wheelbase: 2.63
Track: 1.42
Ground clearance: 0.224

Armor: (mm)
Hull front: 7
Hull rear: 6
Hull sides: 7
Hull floor: 3

Armament:
Main armament: 2x7.62mm DT/4,158*
Secondary armament: None
Firing height: NA
Elevation/depression: NA

Automotive:
Type: Ford-A
Capacity: 3,285 cm^3
Cylinders: 4

Power output: 40hp (29.4kW)) @ 2,200rpm
Fuel type/capacity: Petrol/40 liters
Transmission: 3F 1R
Steering: Rack & pinion
Tires: 5.50-19
Brakes: Mechanical, drums on all wheels
Radio: No

Performance:
Maximum road speed (km/h): 85
Maximum terrain speed (km/h): 30
Road range (km): 225
Terrain range (km): 120-180
Power/weight ratio: 25.3hp (18.9kW)/tonne
Ground pressure: NA
Gradient: 15°
Trench: 0.3m
Fording: 0.5m

Notes:
*   The D-8 was normally armed with two 7.62mm DT machine guns with a claimed 4,158 rounds of ammunition stowed on board. This number of rounds would seem excessive for the size of the vehicle and though normally 2,079 rounds were carried per weapon, a stowage compromise was undoubtedly made.
** The vehicle weight was approximately 1,580kg, with full combat weight including fuel and ammunition being approximately 2,000 kg.

D-8 armored car three-way view.
Artwork: Mikhail Petrovsky
(originally reproduced in *Tekhnika Molodozhi*)

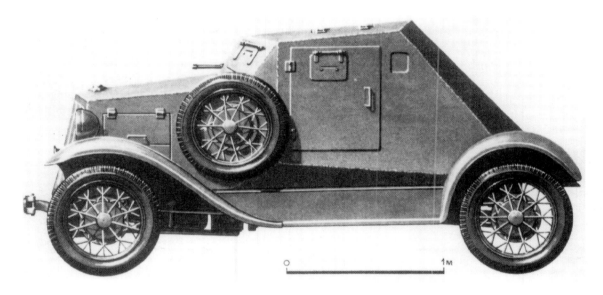

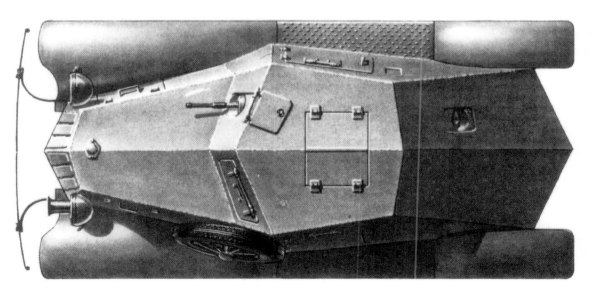

overall successful design but was underpowered and had negligible cross-country performance. Conventional tire chains were used in snow and on bad roads.

In 1934, D-8s were among the first Russian armored cars to be used with airborne forces with D-8s participating in airborne maneuvers in Ukraine during that year. The D-8s were air-transported and landed by TB-3 heavy bombers, each carrying two D-8s mounted in series on a special subframe under the aircraft fuselage. Soviet newsreels of the time show the vehicles being dismounted from the bombers after landing with apparent ease.

No D-8s appear to have remained in service at the time of the outbreak of war with Germany in June, 1941.

Description

The D-8 was built on the Ford-A chassis produced at the KIM plant in Moscow with the armored body manufactured at the Izhorskiy plant, where final assembly was also undertaken. The chassis was strengthened for mounting the additional weight of the armored body, though the vehicle retained the original lightweight spoked wheels of the GAZ-A.

The D-8 had a front-mounted engine with a rear fighting compartment which accommodated the driver and commander. The vehicle commander sat alongside the driver, but as he also operated the two DT machine guns he was rarely found in his seat.

The hull of the D-8 was built from 7mm heat treated steel plates, the armor being sufficient to protect the crew from small arms fire and shrapnel. Access to the vehicle was by two side doors, while the vehicle commander had a two-piece hatch centrally mounted in the fighting compartment roof.

The vehicle was armed with two 7.62mm DT machine guns, one ball-mounted at the front right of the vehicle and the other ball-mounted at the rear on the right side. 2,079 rounds of ammunition were stowed within the vehicle for each weapon, of which 756 were armor piercing rounds.

The D-8 was powered by a four cylinder Ford-A engine developing 40hp (30kW), which gave the vehicle excellent performance on roads, though off-road capability was very limited.

As with the BA-27, the D-8 had to overcome the traditional problem of engine cooling in combat with the intake louvers shut. Dyrenkov designed an armored cowl under the front engine compartment such that with the armored louvers shut, air was drawn into the engine compartment through the cowl. This became a feature on many later Russian armored cars, particularly the BA heavy series.

Prototype D-12 at the Izhorskiy plant. The prototype D-12 has side mounted ball mounts for the DT machine guns. These were deleted on production vehicles as the crew was seriously overworked. Note the AAMG ring mount on the roof.

D-12 Light Armored Car

The D-12 (Dyrenkov-12) light armored car was developed by N.I. Dyrenkov based on his standard D-8 design, but with a modified fighting compartment with an open roof, on which was mounted a 7.62mm PM-1910 (Maxim) water-cooled or DT air-cooled anti-aircraft machine gun.

The original prototype D-12 was armed with one 7.62mm DT machine gun mounted in the front right of the fighting compartment and a 7.62mm DT or 7.62mm PM-1910 machine gun on a ring mount located on the vehicle roof. In addition, the prototype was provided with ball mounts for DT machine guns in each side of the fighting compartment, so that the front or rear DT machine guns could be moved to these positions as required. These side mounts were deleted in series production D-12s, as the armament was excessive for a two-man crew.

Based on the Ford-A light vehicle chassis then being introduced into the Soviet motor industry for mass production at KIM in Moscow and GAZ in Nizhny Novgorod, the D-12 was 280kg heavier than the D-8 but was similar in overall performance.

The D-12 was intended for infantry support and

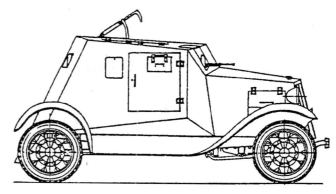

D-12 side view drawing.

occasional anti-aircraft roles. The final prototypes were field trialed alongside the D-8 and were also accepted for service in the Red Army. A small series of D-12 armored cars were subsequently built at the KIM plant in Moscow during 1932 concurrently with the D-8. The vehicle served with the Red Army during the early 1930s and was frequently seen on Red Square during November 7th military parades. Some D-12s remained in service with the RKKA in the Soviet far east after the outbreak of war in 1941, with a few surviving to take part in the victory parade in Mongolia in 1945.

SPECIFICATIONS D-12

Design bureau: Moscow Auto Zavod (KIM)
Crew: 2
Manufacturing plant: Izhorskiy
Service date: 1931 Small series produced
Combat weight: 2,280 kg

Dimensions: (m)
Length: 3.540
Width: 1.705
Height: 2.520 (including AA mount)
Wheelbase: 2.63
Track: 1.42
Ground clearance: 0.224

Armor: (mm)
Hull front: 7
Hull sides: 7
Hull roof: 6
Hull floor: 3

Armament:
Main armament: 1x7.62mm PM-1910/2,090*
Secondary armament: 1/2x7.62mm DT/2,079
Firing height: NA
Elevation/depression: NA

Automotive:
Type: Ford-A
Capacity: 3285cm³
Cylinders: 4
Power output: 40hp (29.4kW) @ 2,200rpm
Fuel type/capacity: Petrol/40 liters
Transmission: 3F 1R
Steering: Rack & pinion
Tires: 5.50-19
Brakes: Mechanical, drums on all wheels
Radio: No

Performance:
Maximum road speed (km/h): 85
Maximum terrain speed (km/h): NA
Road range (km): 225
Terrain range (km): 120-180
Power/weight ratio: 17.5 hp (13.0kW)/tonne
Ground pressure: NA
Gradient: 15°
Trench: 0.3m
Fording: 0.5m

Note:
* As with the D-8, the armament on the D-12 could be a combination of weapons as described.

ABOVE: D-12 prototype at Izhorskiy. Another view of the D-12 showing front, side, and anti-aircraft armament. (Maxim Kolomiets)

RIGHT: D-12 standard production model. The prototype's side-mounted DT machine guns were deleted on the production model D-8. (Tank Museum, Bovington, UK. Ref: 3202/C4)

This remarkable photograph shows two D-12 armored cars during the victory parade in Mongolia in September 1945. The vehicle on the right has the standard anti-aircraft machine gun ring mount of the D-12, while the vehicle on the left has a large single-piece roof hatch. Both vehicles are fitted with later roadwheels as used on the BA-64 series. Behind the D-12s can be seen a mix of FAIs, BA-20Ms, and BA-10s, all of which survived the war intact.

FAI Light Armored Car

The FAI or FA-I (Ford-A - Izhorskiy) light armored car was designed by the FAI OKB and developed to prototype stage in 1931, based on the GAZ-A chassis and mechanicals. The FAI's principal improvement in comparison with the D-8 was the addition of a cylindrical turret mounting a 7.62mm DT machine gun, which provided a true 360° arc of fire, giving the vehicle better combat capability than its predecessor. The addition of a turret did not affect the overall combat weight of the vehicle, which at 1,990kg compared favorably with the D-8, though the vehicle height was increased to 2.24m. As the four cylinder Ford-A engine used in the FAI was the same as that used in the D-8, the FAI's weight was essentially unchanged from its predecessor. The FAI had similar performance to the earlier D-8.

The FAI was successfully field trialed and accepted for service in the Red Army. It entered production at the Izhorskiy plant in Leningrad during 1932, replacing both the D-8 and D-12. The original model FAI on the GAZ-A chassis was series produced from 1932 to 1936, during which 676 were produced. None were provided with

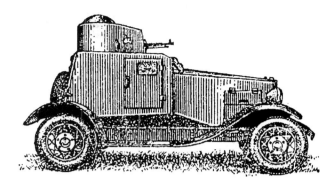

FAI armored car.

radio and extensive use was made of flag communications. The FAI was the standard light armored car in Russian Army service until the introduction of the BA-20 series in 1936. It saw foreign service during the Spanish Civil War, was used in considerable numbers during the Khalkhin Gol campaign against Japan, served with Russian forces during the invasion of Poland in 1939, served in the Baltic Republics and served during the Russo-Finnish War in 1940. By 1941 and the outbreak of war with Germany, few were left in service with the

---

SPECIFICATIONS FAI

Design bureau: FAI bureau
Crew: Two-Commander/gunner and driver
Manufacturing plant: Izhorskiy
Service date: 1932 series produced
Combat weight: 1,990 kg

Dimensions: (m)
Length: 3.75
Width: 1.68
Height: 2.24
Wheelbase: 2.63
Track: 1.42
Ground clearance: 0.224

Armor: (mm)
Hull front: 6
Hull sides: 6
Hull rear: 4
Hull roof: 5
Hull floor: 3
Turret front: 6
Turret sides: 6

Armament:
Main armament: 7.62mm DT/1,323
Secondary armament: None

Firing height: NA
Elevation/depression: NA

Automotive:
Type: Ford-A (GAZ-A)
Capacity: 3,285cm³
Cylinders: 4
Power output: 42hp (31kW) @ 2,200rpm
Fuel type/capacity: Petrol/40 liters
Transmission: 3F 1R
Steering: Rack & pinion
Tires: 5.50-19
Brakes: Mechanical, drums on all wheels
Radio: No

Performance:
Maximum road speed (km/h): 80
Maximum terrain speed (km/h): 30
Road range (km): 200
Terrain range (km): 170
Power/weight ratio: 21hp (15.7kW)/tonne
Ground pressure: 2.3kg/cm²
Gradient: 15°
Trench: 0.4m
Side slope: 12°
Fording: 0.3m

FAIs on maneuvers, Kiev Military District, summer 1935. The FAIs are accompanied by GAZ-As and five AK-1 radio vehicles based on the GAZ-4. The aircraft are R-5 light bombers.

FAIs assemble at the Kiev Military District manuevers, 1934. There are several types of markings evident in this photo. Some FAIs have white turret bands with broken red lines beneath, some additionally have red stars, and some have no marking bands at all. FAI crews made extensive use of flag communication. Also in the photo are BA-Is and a 203mm B-4 tracked howitzer.

FAI standard production model.
(Tank Museum, Bovington, UK. Ref: 522/E3)

FAIs at the Kiev Military District Maneuvers, 1934 or 1935. This rear view shows the standard stowage pattern including fender boxes, rear-mounted spare wheel, and an axe on the vehicle rear.

FAIs on Red Square, Moscow.

Left: FAIs on parade, Red Square, 1st May 1937. Note the tactical number painted on the frontal armor of the FAI to the right in the photograph. (Photographer: Kinelovskiy, photo credit Russian State Cine and Photo Archives)

Right: FAIs on parade during the 1st May Parade, 1936, Kiev. (Russian State Cine and Photo Archives)

FAIs on parade, Red Square, 1st May 1937. On close inspection, all FAIs in this photograph have tactical numbers displayed on the radiator armor. (Kinelovskiy, photo credit R.S.C.P.A.)

Red Army and all were quickly destroyed in combat.

During its production life, there were several experimental attempts to up-armor the FAI, but the vehicle was at the limit of development on the GAZ-A chassis. The GAZ-A chassis was overloaded by forty-five percent when mounting the FAI armored body in combat order (which was a normal Soviet practice also accepted for cargo overloading on military vehicles). However, the new GAZ-M1 chassis became available in 1934-35, which allowed designers at Izhorskiy to modify the body for mating to the new, more powerful vehicle chassis with its 50hp (36.8kW) engine. The FAI was produced on this new chassis from 1938 under the designation FAI-M. Design work also turned at this time to the development of light armored cars on new 6x4 chassis for better weight distribution; examples including the GAZ-TK, LB-23 and BA-21.

FAIs on parade in Kiev during the 1st May parade, 1936. May is particularly warm in Kiev and these vehicles have all apertures open for cooling of both the engine and the vehicle crew.

Description

The FAI had a crew of two, consisting of the driver and commander/gunner who operated the turret-mounted 7.62mm DT machine gun.

The vehicle layout was conventional, with the engine at the front and the fighting compartment behind, surmounted by a small turret. Due to the relatively low fighting compartment roof, the driver and commander had armored domes in the roof above their stations. The vehicle retained the spoked wheels of the original GAZ-A.

The 40hp [29.8kW, some sources state 42hp (31kW)] GAZ engine gave the FAI reasonable performance, with an impressive road speed of 80km/hour but a road range limited to 200km.

The main drawback with the FAI was its thin armor, though the 6mm armor plate was adequate protection from small arms fire. The narrow track tires limited the vehicle's all-terrain performance.

FAI-ZhD

The only series-produced variant of the FAI was the FAI-ZhD (Zheleznaya Doroga or "steel road/rail road") rail scout, built in small numbers in 1933.

FAI-ZhD rail scout vehicle.

The FAI-ZhD rail scout variant was a very successful design. Generally referred to as the FAI-ZhD Bronedrezina, the vehicle could achieve 85km/hour on rails and a moderate 24km/hour in reverse; a major disadvantage for a railbound vehicle. On roads the vehicle could travel at speeds up to 40km/hour, half that of the standard FAI, due mainly to the additional weight of the stowed ZhD wheel rims.

The rail wheels on the FAI-ZhD were actually flanged

FAI-Zhd Rail Scout armored car. The FAI-ZhD rail scout version of the FAI was produced in small numbers. The ZhD rail wheels on the FAI-ZhD were actually steel bands which were fitted over the standard road wheels. Note the mounting point for the ZhD wheels on the hull side. (M. Baryatinsky)

An FAI-M of the 5th Army passes a KV-1 M-1940, Battle of Moscow, December 1941.

ФАИ ж. д.

Легкий бронеавтомобиль ФАИ с железнодорожным ходом 1933 г. Ижорский з-д

1	Полный вес в тн		19			по шоссе	40
		длина в мм	3690	8	Средняя ско-	по проселку	30
2	Габариты автомобиля	ширина в мм	1730		рость в км	по целине	—
		высота в мм	2240	9	Среднее удель-	без подрессорения	2,40
		база в мм	3200		ное давление кг/см²	с погружением на 100%	—
		ширина хода в мм	1690	10	Запас хода	по шоссе	200
		клиренс в мм	224		в км	по проселку	170
		пушек одна кал в мм	—			по целине	—
3	Вооружение и спецоборудование	пулеметов ДТ	1	11	Марка двигателя		ГАЗ-АА
		зенитная установка	—	12	Макс. мощность при n-оборотах		40/2200
		огнеметов	—	13	Удельный вес двигателя		3,93
		фотприборов	—	14	Удельная мощность автомобиля		81
4	Боекомплект	снарядов в шт.	—	15	Сорт горючего		2 сорт
		патронов в шт.	40мм 2520	16	Емкость горючего в литрах	бензина	40
5	Толщина брони	лобовая в мм	6			масла	4,72
		бортовая в мм	6			воды	11,5
		башенная в мм	6	17	Расположение ведущих колес		задн.
		крыша и дно в мм	5-3	18	Число ведущих осей КХ		1
6	Максимальные преодолеваемые препятствия	под'ем в °	16	19	Приборы связи	радиоустановка	—
		боковой крен в °	12			переговорное устройство	—
		глубина брода в мм	300	20	Приборы наблюдения и прицеливания	триплексов	—
		ширина рва в мм	—			перископов	—
		радиус поворота в мм	3200			телескопов	—
7	Максимальная скорость на шоссе км/ч		80 км/ч	21	Экипаж		2

FAI-ZhD datasheet. This original datasheet is typical of the documentation that accompanied a vehicle from the factory for GABTU evaluation trials.

steel rings which were slipped over the standard wheels when required. The vehicle was driven onto railway lines and then a standard tank jack was used to lift first the front and then the rear of the vehicle while the bands were attached over the main road wheels. The disadvantage of this process was that it took the crew a minimum of thirty minutes to complete the task.

The later BA-20 system, in which the main road wheels were replaced with new flanged ZhD wheels, also took time to prepare. It was not until nearly ten years after the FAI-ZhD's introduction that experiments were made with the later BA-64 using smaller diameter ZhD wheels which were permanently attached to the vehicle and could be simply lifted clear of the rails when not required.

When not in use, the FAI-ZhD's wheels were stowed on either side of the vehicle, mounted on stub axles ahead of the vehicle doors.

The FAI-ZhD rail variant carried more ammunition than the standard variant (2,520 rounds of 7.62mm) and had a combat weight of 1,900kg. Length was 3.69m and overall width 1.73m with ZhD wheels fitted.

FAI-M Light Armored Car

In 1936, the Vyksinsky plant began series production of the new BA-20 armored car, based on the newly available GAZ-M1 chassis. The BA-20 was produced in large numbers and quickly replaced the obsolete FAI produced at Izhorskiy as the standard armored car in Russian Army service. The Vyksinskiy plant thereby became the primary manufacturer of light armored cars in the late 1930's, while the Izhorskiy plant continued to concentrate for the most part on the production of heavy armored cars.

Concurrently with the concentration of light armored car production at the Vyksinskiy plant, the Izhorskiy plant produced a final batch of modernized FAI armored cars, designated FAI-M. These vehicles used FAI bodies provided from factory storage mounted on the same GAZ-M1 chassis as the BA-20 series. The resulting FAI-M was built by the Izhorskiy plant concurrently with BA-20 production at Vyksinskiy. Russian sources indicate that the FAI-M was introduced in 1938, concurrently with the modernization of the BA-20 series at Vyksinskiy. It is not clear if FAI-M production started earlier (the GAZ-M1 chassis having been available in 1936), or if not, why the FAI bodies were in storage and available for mounting on the GAZ-M1 chassis as late as 1938.

The FAI-M had an updated engine, improved fuel capacity, and extended vehicle range, but the combat characteristics of the vehicle were otherwise similar to the FAI which it replaced in production. The FAI-M was, in 1938, still not fitted with a radio as standard.

In comparison with the original FAI, the FAI-M was produced in very small numbers; only seventy-six FAI-Ms being built in total. The FAI-M served with Russian forces during the invasion of Poland, during the battles for the Baltic Republics in 1938-39, throughout the 1940 "Winter War" with Finland, and in the opening stages of the 1941-45 war with Germany. All FAI-Ms still in service in 1941 were quickly abandoned or destroyed in combat.

Description

The primary feature of the FAI-M which distinguishes it from the BA-20 is the distinctive FAI hull, which was considerably shorter than the new GAZ-M1 chassis on which it was mounted. This resulted in the rear axle being in line with the rear of the armored body, giving the vehicle a particularly disproportionate appearance. The chamfered lower hull of the original FAI hull required an additional armored plate riveted in place to modify the design for attachment to the GAZ-M1 chassis. The slight

SPECIFICATIONS FAI-M

Design bureau: FAI OKB
Crew: 2
Manufacturing plant: Izhorskiy
Service date: 1938
Combat weight: 2,300kg*

Dimensions: (m)
Length: 4.310
Width: 1.750
Height: 2.240
Wheelbase: 2.845
Track width: 1.44
Ground clearance: 0.235

Armor: (mm)
Hull front: 6
Hull sides: 6
Hull rear: 4
Hull roof: 5
Hull floor: 3
Turret front: 6
Turret sides: 6

Armament:
Main armament: 7.62mm DT/1,323
Secondary armament: None
Firing height: NA

Elevation/depression: NA

Automotive:
Type: GAZ-M1
Cylinders: 4
Capacity: 3,285cm^3
Power output: 50hp (37kW) @ 2,800rpm
Fuel type/capacity: Petrol/60 liter
Transmission: 3F 1R
Steering: Rack & pinion
Tires: 5.50-19
Brakes: Mechanical, drums on all wheels
Radio: No

Performance:
Maximum road speed (km/h): 90
Maximum terrain speed (km/h): NA
Road range (km): 350
Terrain range (km): 270
Power/weight ratio: 25hp (18.7kW)/tonne
Ground pressure: 2.5kg/cm^2
Gradient: 15-16°
Trench: 0.4m
Fording: 0.5m

Note:
* Vehicle weight without ammunition and crew was approximately 2,000 kg.

A side view of the FAI-M preserved at the Central Armed Forces Museum, Moscow. This vehicle was privately restored by enthusiast Anton Shalitov and temporarily displayed at the museum in the autumn of 1996. Note the short hull relative to the GAZ-M1 chassis and the stamped steel wheels.

FAI-M. An unusual photo demonstrating the FAI-M and its parent vehicle, the GAZ-M1 "Emka". Note the distinctive arrangement of the vehicle rear, with the rear axle mounted behind the armored body. This photo is typical of misleading Soviet era illustrations as the body has none of the features of the FAI (such as distinctive head covers). The domed turret hatch common to the FAI and BA-20 is also omitted. (Tank Museum, Bovington, UK. Ref: 3202/C3)

Rear view of the FAI-M at the Central Armed Forces Museum, Moscow.

The FAI-M does not have the chamfered lower hull armor of the FAI and the rear wheels project beyond the armored body.

FAI-M turret with 7.62mm DT armament.

FAI-M hull configuration. The armored engine louvers and large external hinges are evident in this view. Compare the overall vehicle finish with the BA-20.

FAI-M radiator armor.

This is the restored FAI-M which was, for a short time, displayed at the Central Armed Forces Museum in Moscow. The vehicle was restored by the "Ekipazah" military history group which has recovered and restored several wartime Russian tanks in addition to the FAI-M. (Andrey Aksenov)

slope to the front section of the fighting compartment roof and the two roof domes were both retained from the FAI.

The FAI-M was powered by the new GAZ-M1 engine which developed 50hp (37kW). Solid stamped steel disc wheels from the GAZ-M1 were used on the FAI-M, replacing the wire wheels of the earlier FAI. The FAI-M was provided with type GK (Gubchataya Kamera) tires made of sponge rubber, which allowed the vehicle to travel with tires damaged by shrapnel or small-arms fire.

The quality of welding and general workmanship was particularly good on the FAI-M, which was produced in an era when quality workmanship was not eroded by later wartime requirements for quantity rather than quality.

GAZ-TK Light Armored Car

In the mid 1930s the D-8, D-12, and FAI were the standard light armored cars employed by the Red Army for reconnaissance and liaison roles. By 1935, however, the light GAZ-A 4x2 chassis on which these vehicles were based was becoming seriously overloaded, which led to these armored cars invariably bogging down when travelling off-road. Design work was underway at the GAZ and Vyksinsky plants at this time to produce a new light armored car on the GAZ-M1 chassis, which later became the BA-20, but the problem of weight distribution on a light 4x2 chassis was seen by design engineers at NATI and the vehicle manufacturing plants as an ongoing problem. Several design bureaus therefore developed 6x4 chassis in an attempt to increase mobility and these chassis were in several instances also used as the basis for new armored car designs. The GAZ-TK 6x4 vehicle was one such vehicle. Developed at the GAZ OKB, the GAZ-TK (Tryoshka Kurchevskogo — "three axle by Kurchevskiy") was essentially a lengthened GAZ-A with two rear-drive axles and a cargo area which was intended as a weapon's platform. The GAZ-TK was built in small numbers and trialed in specialized tank destroyer roles, mounting the DRK-4 and other recoilless anti-tank guns developed by the engineer Kurchevskiy.

On the GAZ-TK chassis, the Kolomna plant (Zavod №38), near Ryazan in the Moscow region, developed and built an armored car version of the vehicle, also given the identical designation GAZ-TK. Developed to prototype stage in 1935, the GAZ-TK armored car used an elongated and modified FAI hull and turret and retained the same armament configuration as the FAI. The elongated hull provided additional fighting compartment space and allowed the fitting of a heavy 71-TK-1 radio trans-

---

SPECIFICATIONS GAZ-TK

Design bureau: Kolomenskiy (Zavod №38)
Crew: 3
Manufacturing plant: Kolomenskiy (Zavod №38)
Service date: Prototype - 1935
Combat weight: 2,620kg

Dimensions: (m)
Length: 4.60
Width: 1.73
Height: 2.21
Wheelbase: 3.20
Track width: 1.42
Ground clearance: 0.225

Armor: (mm)
Hull front: 6
Hull sides: 6
Turret front: 6
Turret sides: 6

Armament:
Main armament: 1x7.62mm DT/1,764
Secondary armament: None

Firing height: NA
Elevation/depression: NA

Automotive:
Type: GAZ-A
Capacity: 3,285cm^3
Cylinders: 4
Power output: 40hp (30kW) @ 2,200rpm
Fuel type/capacity: Petrol/78 liters
Transmission: 3F 1R
Steering: Rack & pinion
Tires: 5.50-19
Brakes: Mechanical, drums on all wheels
Radio: 71-TK-1

Performance:
Maximum road speed (km/h): 63
Maximum terrain speed (km/h): NA
Road range (km): 188-230
Terrain range (km): NA
Power/weight ratio: 15.3hp (11.4kW)/tonne
Ground pressure: NA
Gradient: 22°
Trench: 0.5m
Fording: 0.5m

GAZ-TK with a 76.2mm recoilless rifle. The original GAZ-TK was a 6x4 all-terrain vehicle capable of mounting recoilless anti-tank weapons such as the one shown here. The chassis was used for the identically named GAZ-TK armored car.

mitter/receiver in the hull rear, for which a frame aerial was mounted around the hull.

With an armor basis of 6mm, the GAZ-TK had a combat weight of 2,620kg which was not excessive for the vehicle's 40hp (30kW) GAZ engine, giving the vehicle a good 15.3hp (11.4kW)/tonne power/weight ratio. A road speed of 63km/hour was achieved during trials.

The GAZ-TK retained the single spoked wheels of the GAZ-A, with field trials showing that the 6x4 concept provided better traction and cross-country performance than the FAI even though the thin section tires were retained. The spare wheels were mounted on stub axles on the engine compartment sides and were free-rotating to allow for obstacle clearance. A third spare tire was mounted at the rear of the vehicle.

The GAZ-TK armored car was a reliable vehicle, but the availability of the new GAZ-AAA 6x4 chassis meant that the lightweight GAZ-TK chassis, which was still not ideal for mounting an armored car body, could be replaced with V.A. Grachev's heavier GAZ-AAA design. The GAZ-TK armored car did not, therefore, enter series production. It did not offer any major armament or armor advantages over the smaller BA series based on the GAZ-M1 then entering production, while the GAZ-AAA chassis was already being employed on the heavy BA series of armored cars. The mobility advantage of a lightweight 6x4 armored car was to resurface as a concept two years later, however, with the development of the BA-21.

BA-20 Light Armored Car

Throughout the 1930s, light armored cars such as the D-8, D-12, and FAI used conventional vehicle chassis modified to accept the additional weight of an armored body. By 1935, the FAI design was at the limits of its development on the GAZ-A 4x2 light vehicle chassis, its light construction and limited power output precluding any additional weight being mounted on the frame. Further development awaited the availability of a new chassis, which duly arrived in the form of the GAZ-M1 "Emka" 4x2 light car, developed at GAZ by A.A. Lipgart and A.M. Kriger. The GAZ-M1 entered series production in 1934-35. In anticipation of the availability of this

GAZ-TK armored car. The GAZ-TK was an experimental armored car based on the 6x4 GAZ-TK chassis. The vehicle had a lengthened hull and radio with a frame antenna. The spare wheels were free spinning on their mounting hubs to aid mobility. The GAZ-TK was not series produced.

SPECIFICATIONS BA-20

Design bureau: Vyksinskiy OKB
Crew: 2 (3) Commander, driver, (radio operator)
Manufacturing plant: Vyksinskiy zavod
Service date: 1936-41
Combat weight: 2,340kg

Dimensions: (m)
Length: 4.10
Width: 1.80
Height: 2.30
Wheelbase: 2.845
Track width: 1.44
Ground clearance: 0.235-0.240

Armor: (mm)
Hull front: 6
Hull sides: 6
Hull rear: 4
Turret front: 6
Turret sides: NA

Armament:
Main armament: 7.62mm DT/1,386 rounds
Secondary armament: 15 x F-1 grenades

Firing height: NA
Elevation/depression: +23°/-2°

Automotive:
Type: GAZ-M1
Capacity: 3,285cm^3
Cylinders: 4
Power output: 50hp (36.8kW) @ 2,800rpm
Fuel type/capacity: Petrol/70 liters
Transmission: 3F 1R
Steering: Rack & pinion
Tires: 7.00 - 16 GK combat tires
Brakes: Mechanical, drums on all wheels
Electrical system: NA
Radio: 71-TK-1 + TPU-2

Performance:
Maximum road speed (km/h): 90
Maximum terrain speed (km/h): NA
Road range (km): 350
Terrain range (km): 270
Power/weight ratio: 21.4hp (16.0kW)/tonne
Ground pressure: 2.7kg/cm^2
Gradient: 15°
Trench: 0.35-0.40m
Fording: 0.5m

new, more powerful chassis, design work began in 1934 at Vyksinskiy and GAZ on a new light armored car which upon completion of field trials in late 1935 was accepted for service in the Russian Army as the BA-20 armored car.

The GAZ-M1 was series produced at GAZ from 1936 with the chassis being shipped to Vyksa where assembly of the BA-20 was undertaken using armored bodies produced by both the Vyksa and Izhorskiy plants. The GAZ-M1 chassis was powered by a GAZ-M1 engine developing 50hp which, when mated to the armored body, gave the BA-20 armored car a very high 21.4hp (16.0 kW)/tonne power/weight ratio. The additional weight capacity allowed for the mounting of a radio as standard, which had been one of the problems with earlier armored cars, as early radio transmitters were extremely bulky and heavy to the extent that they could not easily be mounted in a smaller, less powerful armored vehicle. By the mid-1930s it was apparent that radios were essential for modern combat conditions and provision for their installation was given more consideration, particularly on reconnaissance vehicles.

The BA-20 served in the Red Army from 1936 and became the most numerous (and popular) armored car in the Red Army in the late 1930s, proving to be particu-

larly robust and reliable in service. It saw combat in the battles of the Khalkhin Gol against Japan in 1939, the invasion of Poland, the Russo-Finnish war, in the Baltic Republics, and in the opening stages of the 1941-45 "Great Patriotic War," at which time large numbers of BA-20s were concentrated in the Baltic Republics and Western Ukraine. As with many armored cars, significant numbers of BA-20s were also stationed in the Russian Far East when war with Germany broke out, and were gradually returned to the Western Front during the period from June 1941 to early 1942. Captured vehicles were used in small numbers by the German and Finnish armies; Finland designating captured BA-20s as the Ps 5. BA-20s captured by the German Army were put into service as the Panzerspahwagen BA-202 (r).

In total, 2,056 BA-20 armored cars were produced, including a small number of the BA-20ZhD rail scout conversion variant. The BA-20 was modernized as the BA-20M in 1938. As with the BA-20, the BA-20M saw service in large numbers early in World War II.

Description

The BA-20 armored car chassis was developed on the basis of the GAZ-M1 at GAZ in Nizhny Novgorod

BA-20 prototype. This photograph shows a prototype BA-20 still fitted with chromed headlights, wheel hub caps and indicators as used on the GAZ-M1 on which the BA-20 was based. M. Baryatinsky.

A BA-20 and BA-10M enter Borovsk, Kaluga Oblast, January 1942. The original BA-20 is recognized by its small turret with vertical sides. The whitewash camouflage on this vehicle has been heavily weathered since application. Viewed together and allowing for perspective, it is apparent that the BA-10M heavy armored car is not significantly larger than the light BA-20 vehicle.

BA-20s on Red Square, Moscow. Three of these BA-20s are fitted with radio and have the distinctive frame aerial mounted around the hull. Note that the vehicles are driving with the armored radiator covers open, suggesting expected overheating problems. A Komintern artillery tractor can be seen in the background ready to assist in vehicle recovery.

BA-20 reconnaissance patrol parked in a forest. This is a good comparison shot. The vehicle in the foreground is a BA-20M with the later conical turret, while the vehicle in the background is the earlier BA-20, with a smaller cylindrical turret. Both are fitted with the later whip-type radio antenna. (Sergei Ogorodnikov)

while the BA-20 body was developed at the Vyksinskiy plant where the armored bodies were built and final assembly of the BA-20 was undertaken.

All models of the BA-20 and BA-20M were built on the GAZ-M1 chassis. The GAZ-M1 engine developed 50-52hp (39kW) which gave the vehicle a maximum speed of 90km/hour on good roads. The original GAZ-M1 chassis was redesigned to accept the heavier armored body of the BA-20, modifications including an updated differential, rear axle, and springs.

The BA-20 mounted a 7.62mm DT machine gun in a cylindrical turret which was provided with three vision blocks; one either side and one at the rear. The original cylindrical turret was replaced with a larger conical turret on the BA-20M.

The BA-20 had a crew of two, namely driver and the vehicle commander who also acted as the vehicle gunner. In addition, a radio operator was carried on command vehicles. Normal entry and exit from the vehicle was by means of the doors in either side of the vehicle fighting compartment. The BA-20 also had, for the first time on a Russian armored car, an escape hatch in the fighting compartment floor located between the chassis legs. Described as a desant hatch, its primary purpose was evacuation from a damaged vehicle under fire as with tank escape hatches, rather than for egress of desant troops as the hatch's name would suggest, which would not have been practical given the vehicle's ground clearance.

The BA-20 body on its GAZ-M1 chassis had an overall more balanced appearance than the FAI-M to which it

BA-20 on maneuvers, 1935. Note the large headlamps, also used on the ZiS-5 truck.

BA-20 ZhD Rail Scout Armored Car. This is a rare photograph of an early production model BA-20 fitted with ZhD rail wheels. (M. Baryatinsky)

was otherwise generally similar in layout.

Though using a modernized chassis and up-rated powerplant, the BA-20s performance was similar to the FAI. The engine and mechanical upgrades along with larger section tires gave the BA-20 better off-road performance, particularly in soft ground where earlier vehicles like the FAI were prone to bog down easily. In developing the BA-20, the designers paid much attention to battlefield survivability; the vehicle being fitted with GK bulletproof tires as standard. The BA-20 was overall very reliable in service and popular with its crews.

BA-20ZhD

The BA-20ZhD rail drezine was produced in small numbers in 1935, BA-20ZhD being the designation given to the standard BA-20 when adapted for rail scout duties by having the ability to change the standard wheels out for flanged steel rail wheels. The wheels were replacements for the road wheels rather than additional slip-over bands as on the earlier FAI-ZhD. The rail version of the BA-20 had a combat weight of 2,780kg and could achieve 80km/hour on rails with a rail range of 540km. Due to its rail reconnaissance role, a radio was fitted as standard and a full vehicle crew of three was carried; the third crewman being the radio operator. The BA-20ZhD saw extensive service in the opening weeks of the war.

When not in use, the ZhD rail wheels were stowed with one on either side of the vehicle in front of the doors and two at the vehicle rear.

BA-20 Command Vehicle (BA-20U)

Early BA-20 command vehicles used a frame antenna located round the upper hull. Some later BA-20s were fitted with a dashpot-mounted antenna. Most later model (BA-20M) command vehicles used a whip antenna.

BA-20 Monocoque Body

A single prototype BA-20 with a monocoque body was built in 1939. The intention was to strengthen the vehicle by integrating the separate chassis components into the armored hull of the vehicle, so providing a more rigid load bearing construction which could accept heavier armor weight. The design did not progress beyond prototype stage.

BA-20M Light Armored Car

The original BA-20 was modernized at the Vyksa plant in 1938, with a new, wider conical turret and the 71-TK-1 radio set as fitted on some BA-20s replaced with a new model 71-TK-3 radio set which was installed as standard on all BA-20Ms. With the addition of the radio operator, the BA-20M had a standard crew of three. Other detail changes included the provision of a larger fuel tank giving the vehicle increased operational range.

The first BA-20Ms produced retained the frame antenna mounted around the hull roof which was used on the original BA-20 commander's vehicles fitted with radio. This frame antenna was later deleted and replaced with the standard whip antenna dashpot mounted on the left side of the fighting compartment superstructure or occassionally on the engine deck.

The enlarged ninety liter fuel tank increased the vehicle's operating range to 450km on roads, though due to the higher combat weight of the BA-20M (up from 2,300kg to 2,520kg) the vehicle's road speed was reduced. It was, however, considered that fast road speed was not an essential requirement for a reconnaissance vehicle and reasonable speed with good range was a better design compromise.

The BA-20M continued to be manufactured at Vyksa after the outbreak of war in June 1941, with the factory finally ending production in the early months of 1942. In 1938, 301 BA-20/20Ms were produced, 335 in 1939 (including forty-three ZhD versions) and 439 BA-20Ms were built between 1941-45. In total 2,013 BA-20Ms of all variants were manufactured.

BA-20Ms were used in the invasion of Poland and the Baltic Republics, during the Finnish Winter War and

BA-20Ms in the Transcaucuses Military District, 1939 or 1940.

SPECIFICATIONS BA-20M

Design bureau: Vyksinskiy OKB
Crew: 3
Manufacturing plant: Vyksinskiy zavod
Service date: 1936-1942
Combat weight: 2,520 kg

Dimensions: (m)
Length: 4.310
Width: 1.75
Height: 2.13
Wheelbase: 2.845
Track width: 1.44
Ground clearance: 0.235-0.240m

Armor: (mm)
Hull front: 6
Hull sides: 6
Turret front: 6
Turret sides: 6
Hull rear: 4
Hull floor/roof: 3

Armament:
Main armament: 7.62mm DT/1,386

Secondary armament: 15 x F-1 grenades
Firing height: NA
Elevation/depression: NA

Automotive:
Type: GAZ-M1
Capacity: 3,285cm^3
Cylinders: 4
Power output: 50hp (36.8kW) @ 2,800rpm
Fuel type/capacity: Petrol/90 liters
Transmission: 3F 1R
Steering: Rack & pinion
Tires: 7.00 - 16 GK tires in combat
Brakes: Mechanical, drums on all wheels
Radio: 71-TK-3 / TPU-2 laryngaphone

Performance:
Maximum road speed (km/h): 60-70
Maximum terrain speed (km/h): NA
Road range (km): 450
Terrain range (km): 335
Power/weight ratio: 20hp (14.9kW)/tonne
Ground pressure: 2.9kg/cm^2
Gradient: 15°
Trench: 0.35m
Fording: 0.5m

BA-20M, Stalingrad region, October 1942. This vehicle, №15-02, is commanded by Senior Sergeant M.K. Azorov. The radio antenna mount is clearly seen on the hull side. The wheel rims are much darker than the rest of the vehicle, being painted either a darker green or more likely original black.

Upper left, middle left, and below: Three views of the BA-20M preserved at the Parola Tank Museum, Finland. This BA-20M is also fitted with the early type frame antenna around the hull.

Above and left: Two posed "action" views of another BA-20M in winter camouflage, crew poised for combat. The photo on bottom/left of page 28 is the same vehicle as shown here. All photos during the "Battle for Moscow."

BA-20M command vehicle. The vehicle pictured is a BA-20M fitted with the frame antenna more commonly seen on the earlier BA-20. The photo shows Russian and German soldiers together, after the successful invasion of Poland.

BA-20M command vehicle. A good rear view of a BA-20M with an early frame radio antenna, also taken in Poland during the era of Russian-German military cooperation in the late 1930s.

BA-20M at the Great Patriotic War Memorial Park, Kiev, Ukraine. This BA-20M preserved in Kiev has been less than sympathetically restored, but represents one of only two known preserved BA-20s in the world, the other being a BA-20M located at the Parola Tank Musuem in Finland. The vehicle in Kiev is labelled as a BA-24 for unknown reasons.

Turret view of the same BA-20M.

Above: BA-20M on a forest road, November 1941. (D. Chernov, Russian State Cine and Photo Archives)

Below: BA-20M during battle for Moscow, December 1941. Note the hand-painted winter camouflage on this vehicle. The other vehicle is a ZiS-30 self-propelled gun on the Komsomolyets light artillery tractor chassis.

Below: BA-20M's on parade, Moscow, 7th November 1940. The leading row of BA-20Ms are early commander's variants with the distinctive hull mounted frame aerial. A row of T-28 tanks sit in the background. (Prekhner)

Above: BA-20M column moving through a forest, December 1941. (A. Garanin, Russian State Cine and Photo Archives)

BA-20M at the Parola Tank Museum, Finland.

BA-10M and BA-20M at the Parola Tank Museum, Finland. When viewed in close proximity, it is apparent that the BA-10M on its GAZ-AAA chassis was not greatly larger than the BA-20 series based on the GAZ-M1.

during the initial months of the war against Germany. The Finns captured eighteen BA-20/20Ms and put them into service, the BA-20M being known in Finnish Army service as the Ps 6.

It was recognized by the late 1930s that the armor on the BA-20 and light armored cars in general was unacceptable, even for reconnaissance roles, so an up-armoring program was initiated for the BA-20 series to provide the crew with better protection from small caliber armor-piercing rounds and shrapnel. The design weight of such proposals proved prohibitive, however, and so the move was made towards experimental 6x4 designs, such as the BA-21 on the GAZ-21 chassis which was produced in prototype form.

Wheel changeout on the BA-20MZhD. Though a poor reproduction, this photograph does show the method of jacking up the rear of the vehicle for changing the road wheels to ZhD rail wheels and vice-versa.

BA-20MZhD

A small number of BA-20Ms were manufactured as ZhD variants, provided with flanged ZhD rail wheels. The rail variant of the BA-20M was built in larger numbers than the ZhD variant of the original BA-20, to which performance was similar.

BA-20M ZhD drezine rail scout vehicle, July 1942. Many Russian armored cars, particularly BA-20s and BA-10s, were stationed in the Russian Far East when war with Germany began in July 1941. These vehicles arrived on the "western front" well after most of their contemporaries had been destroyed, hence photographs of vehicles such as this still in service in July 1942. Note the road wheel stowage pattern.

A German column passes a burned out BA-20M ZhD. Note the rail wheel stowed on the rear of the vehicle and the rail tow link. (Tank Museum, Bovington, UK. Ref: 276/D2)

BA-20M ZhD, winter 1943-1944. Two flanged rail wheels are stored behind the hull, the other two being located on either side of the engine compartment.

German forces inspect a captured BA-20M ZhD. (Tank Museum, Bovington, UK)

BA-20M ZhD moving towards the Finnish border, Leningrad Front, winter 1943-1944.

A rare photograph of the LB-23 during field trails being recovered after stalling in a shallow river.

LB-23 Light Armored Car

By 1938, light vehicle chassis were at the limits of their design potential with the increasing armament and armor requirements being demanded by the Red Army. The mid 1930s generation of light armored cars such as the FAI were not well suited to cross-country travel due to their 4x2 chassis and narrow section tires and attempts to increase the armor on these vehicles had only exacerbated their inherent mobility problem. The GAZ-TK 6x4 armored car had been developed in 1935 in an attempt to overcome recognized mobility difficulties with 4x2 armored cars and in 1939 engineers at Vyksinskiy and GAZ returned to the problems once again. Two new armored car types were considered by the Vyksinskiy and GAZ design bureaus, designated LB-23 and BA-21 respectively. These vehicles both utilized newly available GAZ 6x4 chassis which could better accomodate the increasing armor requirements of new armored car designs.

In late 1939 the Vyksinskiy plant produced an experimental version of the BA-20 on the new GAZ-22 light 6x4 truck chassis. The new armored car was originally developed under the designation BA-23 but this was quickly changed to LB-23 ("Legkiy Broneavtomobil" or light armored car). The initials were also coincidentally those of Lavrentyi Beria, head of the NKVD, the feared secret police. The ambiguous designation was no doubt partly in his honor but also likely a case of political expediency at a time when Stalin's purges had led to the execution of countless individuals in the military and senior design posts alike, with many others working while

LB-23. A rare photograph of the LB-23 prototype. Though similar in overall appearance to the BA-21, the LB-23 can be distinguished by the large machine gun ball mount mantlets on the turret and the hull machine gun positions.

SPECIFICATIONS LB-23

Design bureau: Vyksinskiy zavod
Crew: 3
Manufacturing plant: Vyksinskiy zavod
Service date: 1939
Combat weight: 3,500kg

Dimensions: (m)
Length: 4.226
Width: 1.778
Height: 2.268
Wheelbase: NA
Track width: NA
Ground clearance: 0.185m

Armor: (mm)
Hull front: 11
Hull sides: NA
Turret front: 9
Turret sides: NA

Armament:
Main armament: 2x7.62mm DT/1,890
Secondary armament: None

Firing height: NA
Elevation/depression: NA

Automotive:
Type: GAZ-11 prototype
Cylinders: 6
Power output: 72hp (54kW)
Fuel type/capacity: Petrol/66 liters
Transmission: 4F 1R
Steering: Rack and pinion
Tires: 6.50-20
Brakes: Mechanical
Radio: 71-TK-1

Performance:
Maximum road speed (km/h): 72
Maximum terrain speed (km/h): NA
Road range (km): 200-238
Terrain range (km): NA
Power/weight ratio: 20.6hp (15.4kW)/tonne
Ground pressure: 2.2kg/cm^2
Gradient: NA
Trench: NA
Fording: 0.5m

under arrest in prison design bureaus.

A single prototype LB-23 was manufactured. The armament, armor, and overall specifications of the vehicle were similar to the GAZ-developed BA-20, but the vehicle was powered by a prototype six-cylinder engine based on a U.S. Dodge design which produced 72hp (54kW) and was later developed into the series production GAZ-11 engine used on the GAZ-63 and other post-war Soviet Army vehicles. The new engine provided a considerable performance advantage in comparison with the otherwise similar BA-20 and BA-20M; the LB-23 being marginally faster on roads and with significantly increased torque for all-terrain operation.

The LB-23 had a small turret with a 7.62mm DT machine gun, with a second DT machine ball-mounted in the hull front alongside the driver, operated by the commander who sat next to the driver, rather than in the turret as required on previous light armored cars.

The crew of the LB-23 was increased to three with the addition of a radio operator who could also relieve the commander as turret or hull gunner, leaving him free to command the vehicle and operate the remaining DT machine gun.

The hull was generally similar to the BA-21 but with better sloped armor and larger crew access doors. The hull and turret were of welded armor throughout.

A 71-TK-1 radio was fitted as standard and was pro-

vided with a whip antenna.

The LB-23 project was curtailed when the GAZ-22 chassis on which it was based did not enter series production. This fate also overcame the concurrent GAZ-21-based BA-21 design and neither vehicle entered service with the Red Army.

The LB-23 was one of the last 6x4 armored car designs to be considered for service with the Red Army; the next generation of light armored cars being based on 4x4 all-wheel drive chassis.

The LB-23 (BA-23) armored car. The LB-23 is generally very similar in appearance to the BA-21 design developed at GAZ.

BA-21 Light Armored Car

In the summer of 1937, design work began at the GAZ OKB in Gorkiy on a new 6x4 light truck based on the GAZ-M1, designated the GAZ-21. The truck was developed over an eighteen month period by a team headed by I.G. Storozhko as chief project designer and under the ultimate direction of V.A. Grachev as chief engineer. The new GAZ-21 truck was a considerable improvement over previous GAZ designs, having better power and tractive effort than the GAZ-AAA, improved range, a 950kg load capacity and a new four-speed gearbox which greatly increased the GAZ-21's power range in comparison with the GAZ-AAA. The vehicle also had much reduced ground pressure compared with the smaller GAZ-AA 4x2 truck with resultant better all-terrain capability.

The GAZ-21 underwent an extensive eighteen month field testing program, during which time the new chassis was also considered as the basis for a new armored car with better overall performance than the contemporary 4x2 BA-20. This possibility was investigated by engineers at the GAZ OKB from early 1939 in collaboration with engineers at the Vysinskiy plant where the BA-20 based armored body was modified for mounting on the new, longer chassis. The new armored car design, using the GAZ-21 chassis and GAZ-M1 components, was later given the designation Brone Avtomobil-21 or BA-21.

The BA-21's new GAZ-21 6x4 chassis provided the armored car with similar performance to the BA-20 even allowing for the greater combat weight of the new vehicle, which was primarily due to the enlarged hull with increased armor applied over its frontal aspects. The BA-21 had an armor basis of 10-11mm and a greater slope to the hull armor than the BA-20, which provided better ballistic protection than afforded to the BA-20, while being not inferior to the contemporary BA-6 heavy armored car. As with the LB-23, the BA-21 was provided with an additional hull machine gun alongside the driver and fitted with radio as standard, necessitating the addition of a third crew member.

The BA-21 was lighter and faster than the BA-6 heavy armored car to which the BA-21 was comparable in all aspects except armament. With a top speed of 53km/hour, it was still relatively slow for a reconnaissance vehicle, however, particularily in comparison with the BA-20 and LB-23. The maximum road speed (which was mainly due to poor gear ratios on the new four-speed gearbox) was, however, considered acceptable for the intended role of the vehicle.

The prototype BA-21 armored car was field trialed late in 1939 and was moderately successful, however,

---

SPECIFICATIONS BA-21

Design bureau: GAZ OKB
Crew: 3
Manufacturing plant: GAZ/Vyksinsky
Service date: 1939 (Prototype)
Combat weight: 3,240kg

Dimensions: (m)
Length: 4.220
Width: 1.778
Height: 2.263
Wheelbase: 3.36
Track width: 1.44
Ground clearance: 0.195

Armor: (mm)
Hull front: 10-11
Hull sides: 11
Turret front: 10
Turret sides: 10

Armament:
Main armament: 2x7.62mm DT/1,890
Secondary armament: None
Firing height: NA

Elevation/depression: +23° / -13°

Automotive:
Type: GAZ-M1
Capacity: 3,285cm^3
Cylinders: 4
Power output: 50hp (37kW) @ 2,800rpm
Fuel type/capacity: Petrol/100 liters
Transmission: 4F 1R
Steering: Rack and pinion
Tires: 7.00-16
Brakes: Mechanical, drums on all wheels
Radio: 71-TK-1

Performance:
Maximum road speed (km/h): 53
Maximum terrain speed (km/h): NA
Road range (km): 400
Terrain range (km): 340
Power/weight ratio: 15.4hp (11.5kW)/tonne
Ground pressure: 1.8kg/cm^2
Gradient: 20-22°
Trench: NA
Fording: 0.8m

BA-21. This photograph of the BA-21 during evaluation trials shows the vehicle fitted with a front bumber, missing from the example in the NIIBT museum at Kubinka today.

BA-21. The BA-21 prototype preserved today at the NIIBT museum, Kubinka.

BA-21 armored car prototype. This BA-21 is preserved at the NIIBT Tank Museum, Kubinka, near Moscow. Note the hull length in comparison with the standard BA-20 and the offset dashpot mount for the radio antenna.

BA-21. Though resembling simply an extended BA-20 on a 6x4 chassis, the BA-21 has a new hull which is longer, wider, and with better armor slope than the BA-20.

BA-21 overhead view. Note the slope of the rear armor.

development of the GAZ-21 truck on which it was based was curtailed in favor of the GAZ-11 and GAZ-61 light vehicles, and designers at the Vyksinskiy Plant were therefore forced to abandon further development of the BA-21 armored car on the GAZ-21 truck chassis.

A single example of the BA-21 remains intact today, preserved in the NIIBT Tank Museum at Kubinka near Moscow. There are small detail differences between the trials prototype and the vehicle now in the NIIBT tank museum at Kubinka, including the side lights, bumpers, and radiator cap.

Description

The BA-21 superficially resembles a BA-20 on a 6x4 chassis, but the hull is actually wider, longer, and has more steeply angled sides. The vehicle had a crew of three, consisting of commander/turret gunner, hull gunner, and driver. All three crew gained access to the vehicle through the two side doors.

The vehicle was armed with two 7.62mm DT machine guns, one turret-mounted and the other in the front hull superstructure to the right of the driver which was operated by the radio operator.

The new chassis and 6x4 configuration allowed an increase in vehicle armor protection with no loss of overall performance. The BA-21 had a combat weight of 3,240kg, not much less than the BA-6 heavy armored car, but still had better tractability than the earlier light BA-20. The use of six single tires was not, however, ideal for cross country performance. The BA-21 was powered by the 50hp (38.8kvT) GAZ-M1 engine. Mounted on new, bulletproof GK tires, the BA-21 had an improved ground pressure of 1.8kg/cm^2 unladen and 2.7kg /cm^2 with full crew and ammunition load, which compared well with the BA-20.

The BA-21 was fitted with a 71-TK-1 radio as standard. The third crew member acted as both vehicle radio operator and hull machine gunner as required.

LB-62 Light Armored Car

The primary restriction of all Russian armored car designs in the 1930s was that these vehicles were for the most part roadbound due to their limited 4x2 chassis. This was recognized by GABTU, the main armor directorate, and in 1940 a state competition was announced for the development of a new generation of all-wheel drive armored cars with the ability to operate on open terrain.

LB-62 prototypes during evaluation trials. Originally, a single LB-62 prototype was documented as having been built, however as this photograph shows, at least two were field trialled. The vehicles have different tires fitted. Neither vehicle is fitted with armament.

In response to this challenge, the 4x4 LB-62 was developed at Zavod N°38 near Moscow in 1940 which had previously manufactured the T-37 and T-38 amphibious light tanks. The LB-62 was developed in competition with the LB-NATI which was developed in parallel by the NATI Institute and produced by the Vyksinskiy Plant.

At least two LB-62 prototypes were produced and field trialed, based on the new GAZ-62 4x4 truck chassis. The LB-62 was particularly heavy for a "light" armored car with a combat weight of 5,150kg. To compensate for the vehicle weight, the LB-62 was powered by a six-cylinder GAZ-202 engine originally developed for the GAZ built T-40 amphibious light tank which gave the vehicle a high 16.5hp (12.3kW)/tonne power/weight ratio with resultant good overall performance. The LB-62 had a road speed of 70km/hour and range up to 500km, while the 4x4 chassis provided the off road performance which the vehicle's predecessors had lacked.

Unfortunately, development work was interrupted by the outbreak of war which occurred as field trials were being completed. The LB-62 project was consequently abandoned, but many of the general design principles incorporated in the LB-62 were used in 1942 for the development of the BA-64.

Description

The LB-62 resembled the German SdKfz 221/222 series which was known to Russian military intelligence at the time of the LB-62's development, while the highly faceted hull was very similar in appearance to the later BA-64, though longer and wider. The front of the vehicle has a distinctive horizontal slatted radiator grille with headlamps mounted either side at the very front of the vehicle. Storage boxes were mounted over the rear wheel guards.

As with the BA-NATI, the turret and armament were taken directly from the T-40 light tank. The 12.7mm DShK heavy machine gun used as main armament on the LB-62 was becoming a standard light AFV weapon at the time and gave excellent firepower for a light reconnaissance vehicle. A 7.62mm DT machine gun was mounted co-axially with the main armament while a further 7.62mm DT machine gun was ball-mounted in the front of the fighting compartment to the right of the driver.

The LB-62 had an armor basis of 10mm, with 13mm on the hull front, which actually exceeded the armor on contemporary Russian "heavy" armored cars.

SPECIFICATIONS LB-62

Design bureau: Zavod N°38
Crew: 3
Manufacturing plant: Zavod N°38
Service date: Trials prototype (1940)
Combat weight: 5,150kg

Dimensions: (m)
Length: 4.43
Width: 2.00
Height: 2.24
Wheelbase: 3.30
Track width: 1.60
Ground clearance: 0.26

Armor: (mm)
Hull front: 13
Hull sides: NA
Turret front: 10
Turret sides: NA

Armament:
Main armament: 1X12.7mm DShK/500 rounds
Secondary armament: 2x7.62DT/3,150 rounds
Firing height: NA

Elevation/depression: NA

Automotive:
Type: GAZ-202
Cylinders: 6 in-line
Capacity: 3,485cm³
Power output: 85hp (63kW) @ 3,600rpm
Fuel type/capacity: Petrol /150 liters
Transmission: 4F 1R
Steering: NA
Tires: 9.75 -18 (all terrain tread)
Brakes: Mechanical
Radio: 71-TK-1

Performance:
Maximum road speed (km/h): 70
Maximum terrain speed (km/h): NA
Road range (km): 500
Terrain range (km): 360
Power/weight ratio: 16.5hp (12.3kW)/tonne
Ground pressure: NA
Gradient: NA
Trench: NA
Fording: NA

LB-62 armored car. The LB-62 was developed at the Vyksinskiy plant in 1940. It used the new GAZ-62 4x4 chassis and had a highly faceted hull and a T-40 tank turret. Though not series produced, elements of the design, including the highly faceted hull, were used on the later BA-64 series.

The LB-62 was based on the GAZ-62 chassis of which sixty were built in 1940, though series production did not ensue until 1946 in much modified form as the GAZ-63 4x4 light truck. The same chassis was also used in the late war years as the basis for the KSP-76 self-propelled gun. The tires used on the LB-62 were of the heavy all-terrain tread type later used on the KSP-76 and GAZ-63. A spare wheel was carried on the hull rear.

The LB-62's powerplant was the six-cylinder GAZ-202 engine developing 85hp (63kW). This was the same engine as used in the T-40/T-60/70 series of light tanks.

A 71-TK-1 radio was fitted as standard and was provided with a whip dashpot-mounted antenna to the left of the turret.

BA-NATI (LB-NATI) Light Armored Car

The NATI Institute, primarily known for Russian transport vehicle designs, developed the 4x4 BA-NATI armored car in 1940 as a result of a state requirement to provide a new light armored car with increased armament and armor while also improving all-terrain

performance, which had always been the achilles heel of Russian armored car designs in the 1930s.

The BA-NATI was also known as the LB-NATI or Legkiy Broneavtomobil-NATI (light armored car-NATI), perhaps for similar reasons to the LB-23's nomenclature. It was developed over a period of several months in early 1940, using the existing ladder type chassis from the GAZ-MM 4x2 truck. After completion of the conceptual studies, the BA-NATI production drawings were transferred to the Vyksinskiy plant for manufacture of the prototype vehicles, which were produced competitively with the LB-62 design from Zavod N°38 near Moscow.

The BA-NATI was, like the LB-62, considerably better armed than previous light armored cars, using the turret and armament from the T-40 amphious light tank. With its 12.7mm DShK heavy machine gun main armament, the BA-NATI's offensive capability was not inferior to earlier 37mm tank guns, particularly in anti-tank performance. A 7.62mm DT machine gun was co-axially mounted with the main armament and a second DT machine gun was ball-mounted in the front superstructure.

The BA-NATI actually had better armor protection

SPECIFICATIONS BA-NATI

Design bureau: NATI
Crew: 3
Manufacturing plant: Vyksinskiy zavod
Service date: 1940 (prototype)
Combat weight: 4,580kg

Dimensions: (m)
Length: 4.387
Width: 2.125
Height: 2.213
Wheelbase: 3.34
Track width: 1.40
Ground clearance: 0.190

Armor: (mm)
Hull front: 10
Hull sides: NA
Turret front: 10
Turret sides: NA

Armament:
Main armament: 12.7mm DShK/400
Secondary armament: 2x7.62mm DT/2,205

Firing height: NA
Elevation/depression: NA

Automotive:
Type: GAZ-61 (Dodge)
Cylinders: 6
Power output: 76hp (57kW)
Fuel type/capacity: Petrol/129 liters
Transmission: 4F 1R
Steering: Rack & pinion
Tires: 6.50-20
Brakes: Mechanical
Radio: 71-TK-1

Performance:
Maximum road speed (km/h): 57
Maximum terrain speed (km/h): NA
Road range (km): 228
Terrain range (km): 102
Power/weight ratio: 16.6hp (12.4kW)/tonne
Ground pressure: 3.49kg/cm^2
Gradient: NA
Trench: NA
Fording: NA

than the contemporary BA-10 heavy armored car. Though classified as a light armored car due to its 12.7mm armament, the LB-NATI had a combat weight of 4,580kg, which was only 500kg less than the combat weight of the BA-10. To compensate for the vehicle's weight, the BA-NATI was powered by a new six-cylinder GAZ-61 engine based on an original U.S. Dodge design and producing 76hp (57kW) with considerable torque compared to earlier GAZ powerplants. The resulting high power/weight ratio combined with the 4x4 configuration and the use of new all-terrain tires gave the vehicle good off-road performance compared with its predecessors, despite the vehicle's overall weight.

The BA-NATI's 57km/hour road speed was adequate for a scout vehicle, however, it had high fuel consumption and consequent poor range for the amount of fuel carried. The BA-NATI was considered less successful than the LB-62 as it had thinner frontal armor and was slower than the LB-62. It was, however, a considerable improvement over the earlier BA-20 series, but ultimately neither the BA-NATI or the rival LB-62 entered series production.

The LB-62 and BA-NATI were the first Russian all-wheel drive armored cars. Although not series produced, the experience gained in their development was of importance in the development of the later BA-64,

introduced two years after the BA-NATI project was abandoned.

BA-64 Light Armored Car

With the outbreak of war in June 1941 and the rapid advance of German forces eastward, Russian factories located in Western Russia were faced with the threat of being overrun within weeks, and the massive evacuation of Russian factories eastward to safety behind the Ural mountains began. In addition to the famous tank plant evacuations from Kirov in Leningrad and KhPZ in Kharkhov, literally hundreds of smaller fabrication and component plants were evacuated eastward. The GAZ plant was almost singularly lucky in this respect, being one of the few major plants located pre-war in a location already well to the east of Moscow, such that unlike much of Russian industry it was not in immediate danger of being overrun. Its contribution to the war effort would therefore be critical in the initial months of the war, while dislocated Russian military production in the rest of the country struggled to relocate and reorganize east of the Urals at a time when losses of AFVs and equipment at the front were simply colossal.

Immediately on war's outbreak, V.A. Grachev (then chief designer at GAZ) and his engineering team consid-

Two original BA-24-125 prototypes during evaluation trials. These prototype BA-64s (BA-64-125s) have the distinctive wire mesh grenade screens which were later removed as being cumbersome and potentially dangerous for the crew. Note the lack of pistol ports in the hull.

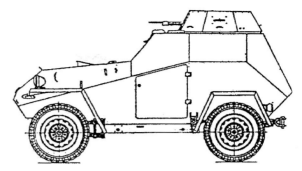

BA-64 (BA-64-125) drawing.

ered how to reorganize for military production, utilizing as far as possible existing components. The GAZ plant increased its light tank production, which had been a small part of its pre-war manufacturing capacity, and continued to produce militarized versions of its GAZ-AA and GAZ-AAA trucks. Potential remained, however, to make use of the existing GAZ-64 light vehicle, and Grachev's

design team set about developing an armored reconnaissance vehicle based on the available GAZ-64 chassis. The GAZ-64 was an ideal basis for an armored car design, as it had a short wheelbase, good ground clearance, and used rugged and proven mechanical components that were already in series production.

Design work on the all-new armored car began on 17th July 1941 under the direction of Yu.N. Sorchkin, with development under the immediate supervision of G.M. Vasserman as senior constructor and design of the

SPECIFICATIONS BA-64 (BA-64-125)

Design bureau: GAZ OKB
Crew: 2
Manufacturing plant: GAZ zavod
Service date: 1942, series produced
Combat weight: 2,360kg

Dimensions: (m)
Length: 3.67
Width: 1.52
Height: 1.875
Wheelbase: 2.10
Track width: 1.278m (f) 1.245m (r)
Ground clearance: 0.210-0.245

Armor: (mm)
Hull front: 12
Hull sides: 12
Hull rear: 6-11
Hull roof: 6
Hull floor: 4
Driver's glacis: 15
Turret front: 12
Turret sides: 6-10

Armament:
Main armament: 7.62mm DT/1,260
Secondary armament: 6 x F-1 grenades

Firing height: NA
Elevation/depression: NA
Traverse: 360° (hand operated)

Automotive:
Type:GAZ-64 (GAZ-MM)
Cylinders: 4 (98.4mm bore/107.9mm stroke)
Power output: 50hp (37kW) @ 2,800rpm
Fuel type/capacity: Petrol/90 litres
Fuel consumption (road): 12.3 - 20liters/100km
Transmission: 4F 1R
Steering: Rack & pinion
Tires: 7.00 - 16 or 6.15 - 16
Brakes: Mechanical
Radio: RB or 12-RP
Electrical system: 6v

Performance:
Maximum road speed (km/h): 80
Maximum terrain speed (km/h): NA
Road range (km): 500-560
Terrain range (km): 450
Power/weight ratio: 21.2hp (15.8kW)/tonne
Ground pressure: NA
Gradient: 30°
Side slope: 18°
Trench: 0.45m

BA-64-125 prototype. The original prototype BA-64-125s had very distinctive radiator armor compared with all later models. Note also the early grenade screens on the turret roof which were subsequently removed.

armored hull under the responsibility of F.A. Lependin, aided by V.T. Komarevskiy. In developing an armored car for series production at GAZ, the group was guided by N.A. Astrov's considerable experience in light tank design and production. The BA-64 series was to be assembled at GAZ from mechanical components produced within the plant and armored hulls and turrets produced by Vyksa, a complete reverse of pre-war assembly logistics, where GAZ had provided the chassis and mechanical components to the Vyksa and Izhorsk plants and the armored hulls were then produced and final assembly undertaken. During development, the new armored car was given the factory designation Izdeliye 64-125 (manufacture object/item 64-125).

The Izdeliye 64-125 was originally intended to be based on the BA-20 armored hull, shortened and modified to fit the GAZ-64 chassis, however, on 23rd August 1941 V.A. Grachev and other GAZ engineers were shown

a captured German SdKfz 221 medium armored car at the NIIBT Polygon at Kubinka near Moscow. The vehicle had been recovered intact and was of sufficient interest that early the following month it was sent to the GAZ plant for more detailed examination by Grachev and his team. Several features of the SdKfz 221 impressed the group, particularly the highly faceted armor configuration, though the BA-62 (LB-62) developed to prototype stage at Vyksa (the Vyksinsky plant) two years previously also had a similar configuration. The hull shape of both the LB-62 and the SdKfz 221 was infinitely superior to the dated BA-20, which was the standard Red Army armored car of the period and therefore an entirely new hull was developed incorporating such highly faceted armor.

Development of the Izdeliye 64-125 was very quick. The first all-welded bodies were completed at the Vyksinskiy plant by the end of November 1941 and

BA-64 in Krivoi Rog, Ukraine, 1943. The winter camouflage on this original BA-64 is well-worn. The desant infantry give a good perspective as to the diminutive size of the BA-64.

The same BA-64 as above, from the rear. Several boxes are tied to the rear of the vehicle, above the spare wheel mounting bracket. The vehicle is following a KV-1S or KV-85 heavy tank.

shipped to GAZ where they were assembled for field trials of the new vehicle, still at this time designated Izdeliye-64-125 or GAZ-64-125. Field trials began on 9th January 1942.

At least three original prototypes were built on armored hulls produced by the Vyksinskiy plant (Zavod N°177). These were originally fitted with open turrets with wire mesh grenade screens. However, it was discovered during evaluation trials that in the confines of the small BA-64 fighting compartment, the commander frequently hit his head on the screens during cross country travel. It was also considered that with the expedient use at the time of "Molotov cocktail" gasoline bombs by Russian troops at the front, the screens would be a major hindrance to exiting the vehicle should the roles be reversed. The screens were therefore removed. The early prototypes also featured simple slatted armored radiator air intake louvers in the frontal armor which extended above and below the vehicle glacis, whereas on later prototypes and production models the modified full width armored intake louvers were located below the glacis only. These early vehicles had no firing ports in the hull sides.

On 10th January 1942 Klimenti E. Voroshilov witnessed the first prototype undergoing trials. The turret with its DT machine gun mount was completed on 23rd January and trials continued with the complete vehicle, which received the Army designation BA-64-125 on 17th February 1942. In Russian Army service the suffix was

dropped and the vehicle simply known as the BA-64. After military trials were complete, on 3rd March the vehicle was also demonstrated to V.M. Molotov and members of the Political Bureau of the CPSU outside the Kremlin (along with a T-70 light tank from the GAZ plant), after which it was finally accepted for service with the Red Army on 14th March 1942 with series production begun immediately thereafter.

The first series production BA-64 (chassis N°69321) was completed on 24th April 1942. By 31st April, fifty were completed, with production steadily rising such that in the first six months of 1943, 1,415 BA-64s were produced, of which 636 were fitted with radio.

By the end of the summer the BA-64 had seen action on the Bryansk and Voronezh fronts and later in the year served in the Stalingrad region. While series production of the BA-64 was underway, further development trials were conducted to determine and eliminate defects in the original design, with a further three prototype BA-64s being extensively trialed in the Gorkiy region between 13-31st May, covering some 1,400km on roads, 400km on unmade roads and 150km cross-country during which the BA-64 performed remarkably well. After production had begun, a specialized driver training school (N°46) was also set up specifically to train BA-64 crews.

The BA-64 series is significant in being the only new armored car to be series produced during the years of the war It had better armor, speed, range, and all-terrain

BA-64s in convoy, south west of Voroshilovgrad, August 1943. These early BA-64s do not feature vision/pistol ports and are fitted with the standard GAZ-M1 road tires, which gave better speed and fuel economy on long route marches.

BA-64s, Don Front, 1942. These early model BA-64s in whitewash camouflage do not have the pistol ports of the later BA-64B.

An early BA-64, 1st Czech Corps.

A BA-64 passing a cavalry patrol, 3rd Ukrainian Front, 1944.

A BA-64 in Germany, 1945. Note the small driving light mounted between the main driving light and the horn.

This photograph is typical of the misidentification of BA-64 models. The base vehicle in the inset is a GAZ-64, on which the original BA-64 armored car was based. The BA-64 featured is, however, a BA-64B, as identified by the wide wheel track and pistol/vision ports.

BA-64s, Belarussian front, February 1944. These early BA-64s are fitted with GAZ-M1 road tires. Note the severe weathering of the white camouflage whitewash.

capability than its predecessors, but with the same 7.62mm DT machine gun armament as the BA-20 series the vehicle was not in the same class as the 45mm tank gun-armed BA-6 or BA-10. The BA-64 was, however, very suited to the reconnaissance role for which it was primarily designed. It was also frequently used to tow

traversing open ground and damaged road surfaces. The BA-64s track (1.278m front and 1.240m rear, the wider front track being due to the steering mechanism) was, however, considered too narrow and was widened on the later BA-64B production model based on the GAZ-67B. The original BA-64 could negotiate 30° slopes, 18° side

BA-64 in Chernovtsy, southwest Ukraine, November 1944. This original BA-64 (BA-64-125) is painted in white winter camouflage which has been badly weathered. Note the lack of vision/pistol ports, typical of the early BA-64.

anti-tank guns and light artillery pieces.

The BA-64 continued in production with few modifications until replaced on the assembly lines by the later BA-64B model from 1st September 1943. In total 3,901 of the original BA-64 were produced before the vehicle was replaced by the later BA-64B. Factory records indicate that the number of original BA-64s produced was 3,903.

In April 1942, Grachev was officially recognized by the state for his role in the development of the BA-64.

Description

The BA-64 represented a major advance in terms of mobility when compared with the BA-20 series, which was the standard light armored car in Red Army service at the time of the BA-64s introduction. Its good power-to-weight ratio and placing of the wheels at the extreme corners of the vehicle, with a resultant low center of gravity, gave the vehicle excellent agility and stability when

slopes, and ford streams to a depth of 0.9m. According to Russian sources, the vehicle could cross plowed fields, sand, and front line roads with ease.

The GAZ-64 field car chassis required significant modification to accept the BA-64 hull. Alterations included relocation of the cooling, fuel, and electrical systems while the rear suspension was strengthened to accomodate the additional weight of the armored body.

The BA-64s open turret was asymmetrical with the 7.62mm Degtyarev (DT) machine gun armament offset to the right. The armament was pintle-mounted to the fighting compartment floor and not an integral part of the turret. Traverse was manually operated. The BA-64s 7.62mm DT machine gun had an effective fighting range of 80-1,000m against ground targets and a claimed and perhaps slightly optimistic 5,000m in the anti-aircraft role. Personal crew weapons and F-1 hand grenades were also carried within the vehicle.

The all-welded hull of the BA-64 was developed under the supervision of G.M. Vasserman by engineers

BA-64s in the Stalingrad area, February 1943. This column of BA-64s is interesting in that the first and fifth vehicles are in standard green , the others being in winter camouflage scheme. The lead vehicle is missing its wheel guards and is fitted with GAZ-M1 road tires, typically fitted during long route marches. (Z. Zenin)

BA-64s in convoy. The retouching on this photograph makes exact model identification difficult, though the wheelbase is that of the BA-64B

BA-64s on the march, south west of Voroshilovgrad, July 1943. These vehicles are fitted with standard tread road wheels as used for prolonged road marches.

U.N. Sorochkin, B.T. Komarevskiy, and V.F. Samoylov. To provide maximum ballistic protection on such a small vehicle most armor plates were angled at approximately 30°. The resulting hull shape consequently provided the BA-64 with better armor protection than pre-war Russian heavy armored cars and contemporary German vehicles despite the BA-64s significantly smaller size and weight. The armored hulls for the BA-64 were initially manufactured from stamped and welded 6, 9, 12, and 15mm armor plate at Zavod N°177 (the Vyksinsky plant) at Vyksa which had both produced the armor for and assembled several armored cars during the late 1930s, but as series production numbers increased, hulls were also produced at the Novo-Kuznovo Auto Body Plant and at GAZ, which produced its own hulls for several prototype variants.

The diminutive size of the BA-64 caused several design compromises to be made during development of the vehicle. In particular, the crew sat in tandem, with the commander/gunner seated above and behind the driver/mechanic. The driver sat centrally in a very restricted space. He was provided with a "triplex" vision device (for the first time on a Soviet armored car), as used on the T-60 light tank. Two further triplex vision devices were provided in the turret sides.

The BA-64 was powered by a four-cylinder GAZ-MM engine developing 50hp (37kW). The engine was a particularly reliable unit which operated well on low octane fuel and low grade oil with little maintenance, an essential characteristic considering Russian wartime conditions. The vehicle had an excellent road range of 500km. To enhance the BA-64s all-terrain performance and survivability in battle, the vehicle was provided with bullet proof GK tires. While very effective in battle conditions, these tires reduced the maximum road speed of the vehicle to 40km/hour. For this reason standard tires from the GAZ-M1 (Emka) with civilian tread were used in rear

areas and long route marches and this type of tire is frequently observed fitted in photographs. A spare wheel was mounted at the rear of the vehicle.

The BA-64 underwent several small changes during its production life and is sometimes difficult to identify from the later BA-64B model. The BA-64 can usually be distinguished from the later BA-64B by its distinctly narrower wheelbase, though this is not always perceptible in photographs. Most BA-64s have no driver's side vision/pistol ports (though these were added to later production vehicles) and the early vehicles lack the engine air intake on top of the engine compartment and driver's air intake on the hull roof above the visor. The turret viewing devices on the original model BA-64 also had small rainguards which were deleted on the later BA-64B.

Tool stowage on the BA-64 changed as production continued. Later BA-64s and all BA-64Bs were fitted with a cylindrical sheet metal exhaust guard, which was introduced in January 1943.

Most BA-64s were equipped with an RB or 12-RP radio set as standard.

BA-64D (DShK)

During 1942, in response to an understood lack of adequate armament on the standard BA-64B, work was carried out at GAZ on the design of a modified BA-64 armed with a 12.7mm DShK M-1940 heavy machine gun in an enlarged turret. The drawings for this uparmed model, designated BA-64D (BA-64 Degtyarev), were completed in October 1942, however, production of a single prototype was held back until March 1943. The new vehicle hull was identical to the standard production model BA-64, however, the enlarged turret required

The 12.7mm DShK heavy machine gun mounted in the BA-64. Despite the use of an enlarged turret for the BA-64D, the weapon was still very difficult to operate from within the turret confines.

BA-64D (12.7mm DShK). The original BA-64D, developed in March 1943, mounted a 12.7mm DShK M-1940 heavy machine gun on the early BA-64 chassis with an enlarged turret and modified hull superstructure. Note the high angle of fire possible with this installation.

armored fillets and splash guards to be mounted on the hull roofline.

In April 1943, the new BA-64D arrived at the Kubinka Polygon in the Moscow region for acceptance trials for service with the Red Army. Though the vehicle was found to be generally very capable and offered significant firepower advantages over the standard BA-64's 7.62mm DT machine gun armament, severe difficulties were found with operating the bulky 12.7mm DShK heavy machine gun within the confines of the turret and providing adequate ammunition stowage for the weapon. Work therefore continued to modify the vehicle with a new variant being prepared at GAZ, based on the modified BA-64B chassis.

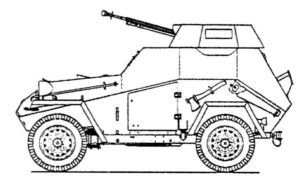

BA-64 DshK. The BA-64 DShK mounted a 12.7mm DShK heavy machine gun in an enlarged turret. This early model is based on the early BA-64. (Nikolai Polikarpov)

BA-64 ZhD Rail Versions

Several specialized variants of the BA-64 were developed under V.A.Grachev's direction. Two such variants were the BA-64 ZhD rail scout vehicles competitively developed to prototype stage by the Gorkiy and Vyksinskiy plants at the end of 1942 and designated re-

spectively BA-64G (Gorkovskiy) and BA-64V (Vyksinskiy).

The BA-64V Vyksinskiy variant of the BA-64 ZhD was the earlier and more conventional variant. It was developed to trials prototype stage in July 1942 on the original BA-64 chassis. The BA-64V was similar in concept to the BA-20ZhD, with the main wheels being replaced with flanged ZhD wheels as required, which

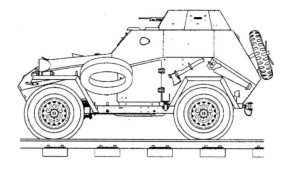

BA-64ZhD rail scout. The Vyksinskiy plant variant of the BA-64ZhD mounted steel flanged wheels over the standard tires. Converting to the rail wheels was time consuming. (Nikolai Polikarpov)

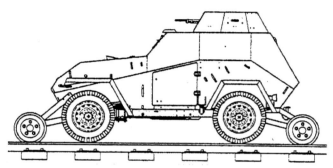

BA-64ZhD rail scout, GAZ variant. The Gorkiy Zavod variant of the BA-64ZhD used outriggers in front and behind the vehicle road wheels. These wheels were manually lifted clear when not required. (Nikolai Polikarpov)

The Vyksinskiy-produced BA-64ZhD, based on the original BA-64.

remained a time-consuming exercise. The BA-64V, with its combat weight of 2,000 kg. was capable of 85km/hour in a forward   direction, but was limited to 13km/hour in reverse, which compared badly with the BA-20ZhD. The BA-20ZhD was capable of double this speed when travelling backwards, important in the rail scout role.

The BA-20ZhD version developed by the GAZ plant in Gorkiy was initially conceived in June 1942. This was slightly before the Vyksinskiy variant, but due to other priorities at GAZ, development was slow such that the prototypes did not appear until November 1942, mounted on the new wide wheelbase chassis, later to be used on the BA-64B, but with an early model hull available at GAZ.

The BA-64V and BA-64G were competitively trialed in December 1942, but neither was accepted for series production. The BA-64ZhD Gorkiy variant is described later in the BA-64B section.

BA-64 with 14.5mm PTRS Anti-Tank Rifle

In November 1942, a prototype anti-tank version of the BA-64 was developed at the GAZ plant, armed with the 14.5mm PTRD anti-tank rifle on a specialized tubular frame mount. The prototype with its 14.5mm PTRD armament was completed at the end of March 1942, however, a single shot anti-tank rifle on a mobile platform was considered impractical and the PTRD was subsequently replaced by the more versatile PTRS. A trials batch may have been built and used in combat.

The 14.5mm PTRS (developed by S.G. Simonov) and the PTRD (developed by V.A. Degtyarev) were both also field mounted on the BA-64. To facilitate operation of the weapon from within the confines of the fighting compartment the turret was usually removed. The single-shot PTRD had better range (1,500m) but a slow rate of fire (8-10rpm) while the PTRS with a reduced range of 1,000m had a better rate of fire (15rpm). The PTRS and PTRD anti-tank rifles were identical in anti-tank performance, both weapons firing the 14.5mm B-32 armor piercing round with a muzzle velocity of 1,012m/s. This gave the vehicle a reasonable anti-tank capability against light tanks and armored vehicles.

Both weapons were heavy and cumbersome within the confines of the BA-64 hull and were used as an expediency measure only.

LEFT: The original GAZ-produced BA-64ZhD, based on the new GAZ-67 chassis, which a few were available in November 1942 but with the hull from the earlier BA-64. GAZ used available bodies for prototypes and modified them within the plant such that a combination of new chassis and old hull is not unusual.

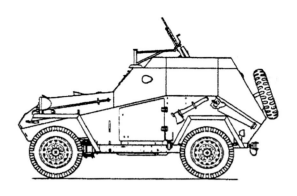

BA-64E APC. (Nikolai Polikarpov)

BA-64Sh (BA-64E) Command Vehicle

A staff and command version of the BA-64 was developed to prototype stage in September 1942. The vehicle, designated BA-64Sh (Shtabnoi or "command") and also known by its experimental designation BA-64E (which gives no clue as to its purpose), had an extended hull roofline which resembled a low turret and was armed with a 7.62mm DT machine gun pintle-mounted ahead of the raised superstructure. The open vehicle was fitted with three seats and was intended as a staff or command vehicle. As configured, the BA-64Sh was too small to accommodate a radio. The BA-64Sh was one of the first Soviet attempts at a custom designed command vehicle. The original BA-64-based vehicle did not progress past trials stage, though a new command/APC model, also known under the experimental designation BA-64E and intended as a command vehicle, was later developed on the BA-64B chassis. Field trial reports on the later BA-64 based vehicle describe it as BA-64Sh, a command vehicle, though both earlier and later variants could have served multiple roles.

BA-64-Z Half-Track

In January 1942, work began at GAZ on a half-track variant of the BA-64 under the designation Izdeliye 175 (manufacture object/item 175). As with other experimental variants of the BA-64, the armored hull for the Izdeliye 175 was produced at GAZ.

The vehicle was developed under the direction of S.S.

BA-64KA(E) APC. The original BA-64E was developed on the early BA-64 chassis in 1943 to investigate the possibility of using the BA-64 series for command vehicle and APC roles. This is the late BA-64KA(BA-64E) desant version based on the BA-64B. (RAC Tank Museum, Bovington, UK. Ref: 3204/E1)

```
┌─────────────────────────────────┐
│  Specifications  BA-64Z          │
│                                  │
│  Weight: 2980kg    Height: 2.02m │
│  Base: 2.425m      Length: 4.56m │
│  Width: 2.28m                    │
└─────────────────────────────────┘
```

Stroev, using a proven track system which had been patented by S.S. Nezhdanovsky as early as August 1925. The tracks and running gear were procured from the GAZ-60 half-track truck and mounted on an open frame arrangement. The new track system was designated GAZ-SKh. The first prototype BA-64 mounted on the GAZ-SKh track system was completed on 15th September 1942 and was designated BA-64-Z (Zimniy or "winter"). The track system replaced the conventional rear axle while steering was affected by way of skis mounted on the front axle. Due to its intended winter role, the BA-64-Z had no fenders mounted on the front or rear of the vehicle.

The vehicle was extensively tested over the winter of 1942-43, with an endurance trial conducted between 30th January and 10th February 1943, traditionally the coldest months of the Russian winter. During this trial

BA-64Z (Zimniy) half-track armored car. The BA-64Z (Zimniy or "winter") was an experimental half-track version of the BA-64 series, fitted with tracks at the rear and skis at the front for steering. It was too slow to be considered for series production.

the BA-64Z was tested over 280km of made roads, 70km of snow roads and 120km in deep snow by test drivers L.N. Sokolov and V.M. Kitaev, all at temperatures exceeding an average of minus 20°C.

The BA-64Z's low ground pressure of $0.12kg/cm^2$ — $0.17kg/cm^2$ in combat order gave the vehicle generally acceptable maneuverability in snow. The vehicle could negotiate an 18° slope and had good ground clearance. It proved extremely slow during trials, however, managing only 7.6km/hour on snow, 16km/hour on ice roads, and had a maximum attainable speed of 28km/hour.

Fuel consumption also proved excessive such that operating range was very limited. Consequently, although the vehicle was generally of interest as a winter reconnaissance vehicle, it was not as effective as existing winter reconnaissance/raider vehicles such as the NKL-26 aerosan. It was not therefore considered for series production.

Despite the BA-64Z being rejected for service with the Russian Army in February 1943, development work on the principle continued intermittently at the GAZ plant. In the winter of 1943-44, V.A. Grachev worked with N.A. Astrov and S.S. Stroev on the development of a BA-64Z

BA-64Z. Another example of how Soviet-era photo retouching distorted images. Compare the track assembly with photographs of the actual vehicle during evaluation trials.

BA-64Z. (Nikolai Polikarpov)

Rear view of the BA-64Z during evaluation trials.

variant mounted on four tracks with steering affected on the front track pair. The project was not realized but it would be a fair assumption that the vehicle would not have been any faster or more fuel-efficient than the original BA-64Z. Some development work was also undertaken at GAZ into specialized ski-mounted trailer systems for use with the BA-64Z armored car.

BA-64-126 Armored Car

At the beginning of 1942, work began at GAZ on a project for the development of a semi-armored car based on the GAZ-64. The vehicle was envisaged for use as a long range reconnaissance and staff vehicle and was to have a crew of three, namely driver plus two. The vehicle was to be semi-armored but with no armament beyond the crew's PPSh machine guns and grenades. No radio was to be fitted.

The vehicle did not progress beyond concept stage, and the index "126" was used at the beginning of 1943 for the development of the SU-76M self-propelled gun (GAZ-15-126).

BA-64 converted as a staff vehicle, 1945. The origins of this interesting vehicle are unknown, but presumably it was salvaged after combat damage and utilized as an officer transport after field rework. The windshield has been taken from a German Schwimmwagen.

BA-64 Staff Vehicle

Probably the most unusual BA-64 which served with the Red Army was photographed in the town of Bogashan in Romania in 1944 being used as an officer transport. This unusual vehicle had the upper bodywork removed and the windscreen from a German Schwimmwagen added. Presumably the vehicle was a one-off converted from a battle damaged vehicle.

BA-64B Light Armored Car

In the summer of 1942, work began at GAZ on an improved version of the GAZ-64 light vehicle, which had several mechanical improvements and a wider wheel track. The replacement model was designated GAZ-67. Consequently, the BA-64 was modified to accomodate the new chassis and several other design changes were also incorporated in the new BA-64 model, which received the designation BA-64B. As with the original BA-64, the new BA-64B was also developed by senior designer V.A. Grachev with modification and development under the direct control of A.A. Lipgart. The new BA-64B, on its new GAZ-67 chassis, was field trialed under the designation GAZ-64-125B or BA-64-125B. The trials were successful and were followed by full factory tests which commenced on 24th November 1942. The new vehicle was given its first major trials at the GABTU proving grounds at Kubinka near Moscowover the week of 2-8 march 1943, covering 400km. The BA-64B finally entered series production on 1st September 1943, with chassis number 7336 being the first vehicle produced.

The BA-64B was based on the new GAZ-67B chassis with its wider 1.446m track. This seemingly minor design change was a major improvement for the high BA-64, which had been known for instability on slopes due to its narrow track; the wider track increasing side slope angle to 25°. Other major automotive improvements included the provision of a new K-23 carburetor which gave better performance on low-grade fuel.

Some of the first BA-64Bs produced on the GAZ-67B chassis were mated to the early production Vyksinskiy BA-64 armored hull, without vision ports. However, a modified hull had begun to be produced at Vyksinskiy simultaneously with the replacement of the GAZ-64 by the GAZ-67 series in production at GAZ. The later armored hulls supplied by Vyksinskiy and assembled at GAZ were provided with pistol ports, which were fitted on all hulls supplied to GAZ from early 1943. The firing ports introduced on the front faceted hull plates were the primary distinguishing feature of the BA-64B, though the last of the GAZ-64-based BA-64s also had this feature due to production changeover at both plants. The mix of hulls may have been due to the stockpiling at GAZ of hulls delivered by Vykska. Many BA-64 vehicles were also significantly reworked in the field.

All small details such as lights were taken from the GAZ-67B, though some BA-64s were fitted with headlights taken from the ZiS-5. A 12RP radio station was mounted in some vehicles.

The BA-64B became the definitive model of the BA-64 series. It was produced from September 1943 until 1946 and saw extensive use with the Russian Army in

Europe, Hungary, Austria, Romania, and Germany. The BA-64 took part in the victory parades in Berlin and Moscow.

The Polish Army had eighty-one BA-64Bs in service, which were ex-Russian Army vehicles delivered to Poland after repair by Remontzavod N°2 (Repair Factory N°2) in Moscow. Of the eighty-one issued to the Polish Army, sixty remained in service in 1944 with fifty-three surviving until the end of the war. Czechoslovakia also had ten BA-64 series armored cars in service.

The BA-64B was a particularly reliable vehicle, achieving an average 6,000-7,000km of combat service between capital repairs or major breakdowns. Further polygon reliability tests conducted in 1944 achieved a figure of 15,000km without major repair or rebuild being required.

From the start of BA-64B series production on 1st September 1943 to 31st December 1943, 405 BA-64Bs were produced, 214 of which were fitted with radio. In 1944, production was increased again to 250 vehicles a month, with 2,950 BA-64Bs produced in that year, of which 1,404 were fitted with radio. By comparison, a total of 1,824 BA-64 and BA-64Bs had been produced in 1943, due to several German bombing raids on the GAZ plant in Gorkiy during that year. From January 1945 to the end of April 1945, another 868 vehicles were produced (420 being fitted with radio) with 1,742 BA-64Bs being completed to the end of the year.

During the wartime period, 8,174 BA-64 and BA-64Bs were manufactured (3,390 being fitted with radio) of which 3,314 remained in service in 1945, mainly the BA-64B model. Production was severely reduced after May 1945, and by 1946 the Russian Army no longer had a need for such large numbers of BA-64s, the last batch of sixty-two BA-64Bs being produced slowly during 1946.

When production ceased in 1946, a total of 9,110 BA-64s of all types had been manufactured during the period 1942-46, of which 5,209 were of the later BA-64B model and 3,901 of the earlier BA-64. GAZ

SPECIFICATIONS BA-64B

Design bureau: GAZ OKB
Crew: 2
Manufacturing plant: GAZ/Vyksinskiy zavod
Service date: 1943-46 Series production
Combat weight: 2,425kg
Towed load: 2,060kg

Dimensions: (m)
Length: 3.67
Width: 1.69
Height: 1.85
Wheelbase: NA
Track width: 1.446 (front & rear)
Ground clearance: 0.235

Armor: (mm)
Hull front: 12
Hull sides: 12
Hull rear: 6-11
Hull roof: 6
Hull floor: 4
Driver's glacis: 15
Turret front: 12
Turret sides: 6-10

Armament:
Main armament: 7.62mm DT /1,074 (1,260?)
Secondary armament: Personal weapons
Firing height: NA

Elevation/depression: NA
Traverse: 360° (hand operated)

Automotive:
Type: GAZ-MM
Capacity: 3,285cm^3
Cylinders: 4
Power output: 54hp (40.3kW) @ 2,800rpm
Fuel type/capacity: Petrol/90 liters
Fuel consumption (road): 12-20 liters/100km
Transmission: 4F 1R
Steering: Rack & pinion
Tires: 7.00 - 16 (GK combat tires) or 6.15 - 16
Brakes: Mechanical,drums on all wheels
Radio: 12RP
Electrics: 6v

Performance:
Maximum road speed (km/h): 85
Maximum terrain speed (km/h): 22
Road range (km): 560
Terrain range (km): 335-450
Power/weight ratio: 22.3hp (16.6kW)/tonne
Ground pressure: NA
Gradient: 30°
Side slope: 25°
Trench: 0.45m
Fording: 0.9m

BA-64B and its GAZ-67 base vehicle (inset). This BA-64B has no pistol ports in the fighting compartment front. GK combat tires are fitted, which gave good cross country performance but poor fuel economy on roads. (Tank Museum, Bovington, UK. Ref: 3204/E2)

BA-64B, Eastern Prussia, April 1945. This vehicle has the tactical number 249 on the turret and the number 30 within a diamond painted on the engine compartment, denoting a tank unit. This vehicle is fitted with GK combat tires.

BA-64Bs on Red Square, Moscow, 1945 Victory Parade.

BA-64B in Germany, 1945.

A BA-64B crossing a pontoon bridge, Germany 1945. The wider track of the BA-64B is obvious in this photograph.

The same BA-64B as above, viewed from the rear.

Czech Army BA-64Bs in Prague, 1945. The second vehicle has the Czech national flag painted on its glacis. As the stowage and light mountings are transposed from the standard Russian configuration, this photograph would appear to have been transposed when originally printed.

A BA-64B commander receives orders, 1944. Note the markings on the side of this vehicle.

A BA-64B in front of the Brandenburg Gate, Berlin, May 1945.

A detail view of the above BA-64B in Berlin.

BA-64B in liberated Kiev, 1943. This photo gives a good view of the driver's triplex vision device and frontal aspect detail.

BA-64B late production model. (Tank Museum, Bovington, UK. Ref: 3204/E4)

BA-64B captured by U.S. forces in Korea. (Tank Museum, Bovington, UK. Ref: 2961/B3)

These two photos of a BA-64B in liberated Kiev show the driver's Triplex vision device very well.

BA-64B

BA-64Bs at the GAZ Plant. The asymmetrical shape of the turret is evident in this photograph. Note also the detail of the driver's rain guard and splash strips.

GAZ BA-64Bs leaving the assembly line, GAZ, 1945.

BA-64Bs outside the GAZ plant, 1945.

BA-64Bs.

GAZ BA-64Bs in the GAZ yard, 1945. Note the commander's vehicles with radio antenna dashpots on the turret side.

BA-64B preserved at the Central Armed Forces Museum, Moscow.

BA-64B rear view.

BA-64B.

BA-64B rear view. This is an interesting view of the Central Armed Forces Museum BA-64B undergoing restoration in 1996. Note the open inspection plate and the spare wheel mounting bracket.

BA-64B driver's position. This view of the driver's position on the BA-64B shows the cramped crew arrangement within the vehicle. Both doors are open in this photograph.

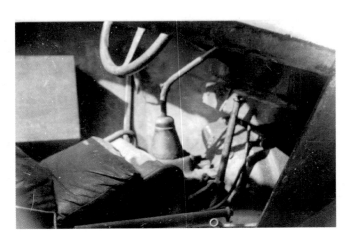

BA-64B after restoration. This BA-64 was restored in 1996 after years of neglect, with many detail fittings being replaced.

BA-64B.

BA-64B. Note the exhaust mounted behind the front wheel guard and the chassis mounting point in front of the rear wheel guard.

BA-64B front view. This photograph clearly shows the assymetrical turret, driver's visor rain guard, and engine air intake on the engine compartment roof.

BA-64B engine compartment. Tow chains or cables were commonly wrapped around the tow hooks.

BA-64B suspension and steering mechanism detail.

Left view of the BA-64B. The highly faceted hull is evident in this view.

BA-64B front armor detail.

BA-64B right view.

BA-64B turret.

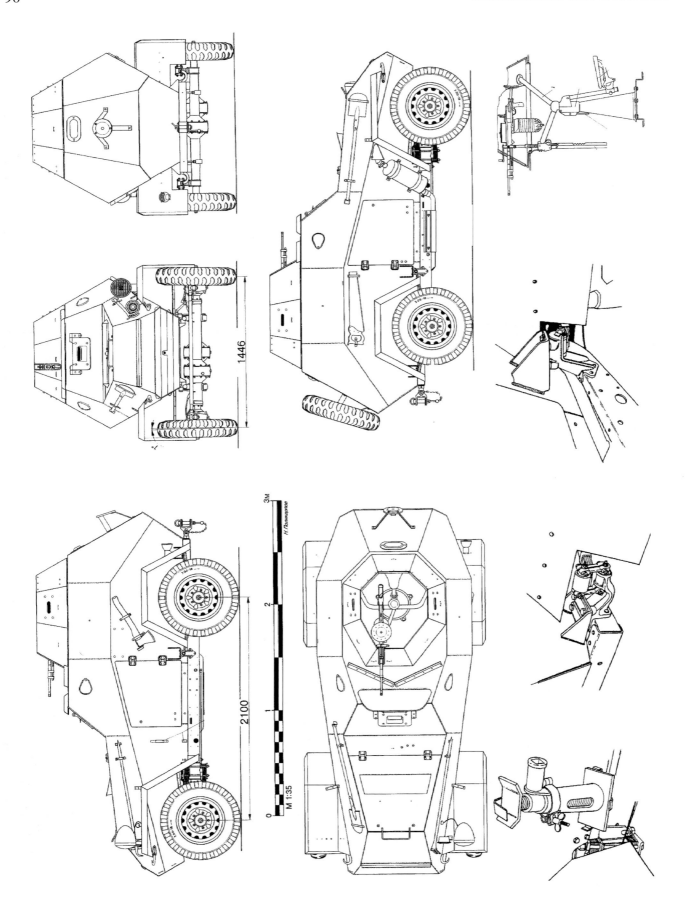

BA-64B drawings in 1:35 scale. (Scrap views not to scale)(Nikolai Polikarpov)

BA-64Bs on Red Square, Moscow, 1st May 1945. The steel towrope was standard stowage even in peacetime.

BA-64s on Red Square, Mosocw, 7th November 1945. The background slogans thank the Army and Navy for protecting the Motherland from the fascists.

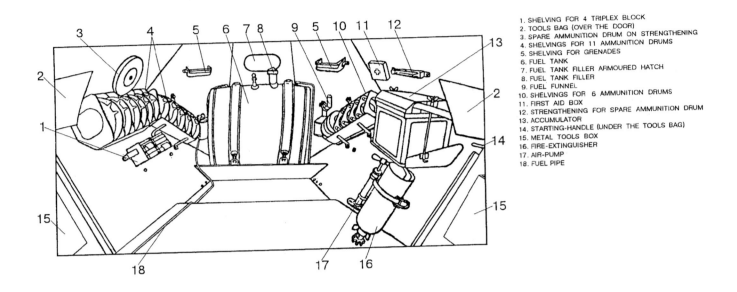

1. SHELVING FOR 4 TRIPLEX BLOCK
2. TOOLS BAG (OVER THE DOOR)
3. SPARE AMMUNITION DRUM ON STRENGTHENING
4. SHELVINGS FOR 11 AMMUNITION DRUMS
5. SHELVING FOR GRENADES
6. FUEL TANK
7. FUEL TANK FILLER ARMOURED HATCH
8. FUEL TANK FILLER
9. FUEL FUNNEL
10. SHELVINGS FOR 6 AMMUNITION DRUMS
11. FIRST AID BOX
12. STRENGTHENING FOR SPARE AMMUNITION DRUM
13. ACCUMULATOR
14. STARTING-HANDLE (UNDER THE TOOLS BAG)
15. METAL TOOLS BOX
16. FIRE-EXTINGUISHER
17. AIR-PUMP
18. FUEL PIPE

BA-64B crew compartment, looking rearward. (Drawing: Nikolai Polikarpov)

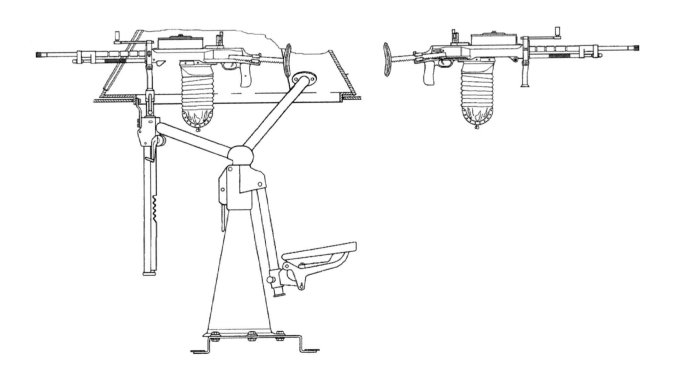

7.62mm DT machine gun mount. (Drawing: Nikolai Polikarpov)

Factory records state 5,160 BA-64Bs were built, which may not include prototypes and evaluation vehicles which were not produced on the main assembly lines.

Spares for the BA-64 series were manufactured until 1953, the last year in which the BA-64 was in operational service with the post-war Soviet Army. The BA-64 series was stockpiled for many years after 1953.

Post-war Poland continued to use its Soviet-supplied BA-64Bs, while the vehicle was also supplied to East Germany (which developed its own SK-1 on the basis of the BA-64B), Bulgaria, Romania, Albania, and China (post 1949). It also saw extensive service with the Korean Army during the 1950-53 Korean War and at least one of these vehicles was captured by U.S. Forces and returned to the United States. Many BA-64s were re-worked by the BTRZ-121 repair plant before export.

Description

The BA-64B was, in principle, almost identical to the earlier BA-64 production model, though certain features distinguish the later production vehicle. The distinct increase in track width is noticeable from some angles, while the provision of pistol ports on the front fighting compartment sides is a feature of nearly all BA-64Bs. These pistol ports were later protected by box section welded strip bent to shape around the pistol ports. Other minor changes included the fitting of an exhaust shield to all BA-64Bs.

BA-64BZhD Rail Versions

V.A. Grachev's design team at the GAZ plant began work on a design for a rail scout version of the BA-64 series in June 1942, however, there were severe delays in development of the vehicle due to other commitments at the plant. The BA-64BZhD was eventually built on the new, widened chassis, later used on the BA-64B, but using an old BA-64 hull. It was built in competition with the Vyksinskiy plant's version, which was based on the earlier BA-64 model.

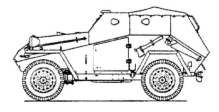

BA-64E armored personnel carrier. (Drawing: Nikolai Polikarpov)

The Gorkovskiy variant of the BA-20ZhD featured four small rail wheels mounted on outriggers, which could be swung upward and out of the way as required, leaving the vehicle free to travel on its standard road wheels. This arrangement, though more complicated than the BA-64 ZhD Vyksinskiy variant, eliminated twenty to thirty minutes of preparation time, a significant improvement over the Vyksinskiy model and other esigns of the 1930s.

By 15th August 1942, production drawings of the BA-64BZhD on the wider wheelbase, which was available in small numbers, were complete and assembly of the first prototype was complete by 8th November 1942. It was then competitively tested against the Vyksinskiy model, with neither variant being considered as having outstanding performance.

At the beginning of January 1943, a modified version of the BA-64BZhD was developed to prototype stage at GAZ and trialed in the region of the plant, while on 21st January 1943 a third variant was also completed. In total during this period, three variants of the GAZ model BA-64BZhD had been completed to prototype stage, none a significant improvement over the earlier Vyksinskiy prototype.

A further attempt to produce a rail scout version of the BA-64B was made by Grachev's design team at GAZ in the spring of 1943, based on the second prototype model developed in January of that year. However, by the summer of 1943 there were few light tanks and armored cars left in front-line service and further development of a rail-scout version of the BA-64B was abandoned at GAZ.

In the summer of 1944, the Moscow Wagon Repair Plant in Voitovich mounted some standard BA-64 or BA-64B armored cars on flanged rail wheels and these saw active service as scout vehicles for armored trains.

BA-64E APC

The original BA-64E (BA-64Sh) command vehicle prototype was developed in September 1942 but did not progress beyond trials stage, though Grachev's design bureau at GAZ retained a strong commitment to developing command and APC versions of the BA-64 series. In the first days of March 1943, a new turretless desant transport version of the BA-64 series was approved by Lipgart, Grachev, and Astrov for development on the new chassis then in development for the BA-64B. This vehicle underwent design modifications and in mid-March 1943 developed into the turretless BA-64E, similar to the earlier model and primarily intended as an APC with a desant crew of six tightly accommodated individuals who entered and exited through a rear door. Three prototypes

BA-64E (BA-64Sh) armored personnel carrier/command vehicle. The BA-64E was a later development of the original concept first used on the original BA-64 chassis. The vehicle is shown here while undergoing evaluation trials. It can be identified by its lack of turret, the four firing ports in the hull, and the rear door. The BA-64E (BA-64Sh) was not accepted for service, though the concept was developed into several similar vehicles with multifunction command/APC roles. (Maxim Kolomiets)

BA-64E (BA-64Sh) armored personnel carrier. The turretless BA-64E had two vision/firing ports in each side of the fighting compartment and a large rear door for desant crew access.

BA-64 KA (BA-64E). An airborne version of the BA-64B was developed to prototype stage, designated BA-64B "desantnai bezbashennai", or "armored personnel carrier without turret". The vehicle featured a turretless hull with the hull roofline extended. It was intended as an airborne APC vehicle and was based on the later BA-64B.

BA-64KA (BA-64E). This vehicle was sent for combat trials with the Third Guards Tank Army in March 1944. The photograph is an extract from the original test summary.

were constructed by the end of the year under the direction of F.A. Lependin. They entered service with the 3rd Guards Tank Army and the 7th Nezhinskiy Mechanized Corps for evaluation in combat conditions, which showed the vehicle to be too small for such a role though it was well suited to use as a command vehicle.

The BA-64E weighed 2,050kg in combat order. A recognition feature of the BA-64B-based version of the BA-64E was the addition of two firing ports in the side of the armored hull, making a total of four vision/pistol ports. The design was abandoned as being too small to be a practical APC and by the end of 1943 a transport variant of the BA-64B was no longer required as other vehicles, including lend-lease M3A1/M3A2s, had adequately fulfilled the role.

GAZ continued with the development of the GAZ-64E APC/command vehicle concept, however, pro-

ducing another three modified prototypes on the BA-64B chassis in September 1944 and a further three in December the same year. These vehicles had modified armor, seating arrangements, and radio equipment installations.

An airborne desant variant of the BA-64E was also developed under the designation BA-64KA. Described as a BA-64B "desantniy bezbashenniya" (turretless desant) during evaluation, this version of the BA-64B did not progress beyond prototype stage either.

BA-64E with 37mm Anti-Tank Gun

In May 1943, an experimental version of the BA-64E was developed mounting a 37mm anti-tank gun. The intention was to mount a 37mm light airborne gun into the BA-64E hull as an air-portable anti-tank system for ground support of airborne landings. The design did not progress beyond prototype stage.

BA-64D (BA-DShK-64B)

In March of 1943, a new prototype BA-64DShK was built on the newly available BA-64B chassis, armed with a 12.7mm DShK heavy machine gun in an enlarged turret. The vehicle, designated BA-DShK-64B, was designed as a reconnaissance vehicle capable of destroying German light tanks and half-tracks. The vehicle had a combat weight of 2,425 kg. Its 12.7mm armament had a range of 3,500m and had been the standard armament of the earlier BA-62 and BA-9 armored cars and the T-40 light tank, though the bulky 34kg weapon was extremely restricted even in an enlarged turret. The BA-64D did not enter series production, though further development was undertaken into mounting a 25mm automatic cannon into the BA-64D chassis. This project did not progress beyond the drawing board.

BASh-64B Command Vehicle

A variant of the turretless BA-64E was developed in 1944, fitted with a 12-RTM radio station and intended as a command vehicle. This variant is sometimes called the BASh-64 (Sh: Shtabnoiy or "command").

BA-64B with 7.62mm SG-43 Machine Gun

In March 1944 an unsuccessful attempt was made to mount the new 7.62mm Goryunov SG-43 in a standard BA-64B. The BA-64B prototype, armed with its 7.62mm

BA-64B with 14.5mm PTRD anti-tank rifle. This turretless BA-64B pictured in Stalino (now Donetsk) in late 1943 is another field modification of the BA-64 series. The vehicle has lost its front wheel guards, which was common for BA-64s. (E. Evzerikhin)

BA-64D. Early artist's impression of the BA-64D based on the later BA-64B. (Tank Museum, Bovington, UK. Ref: 3204/F5)

SG-43 armament was tested at the Kubinka polygon in April 1944. The 13.8kg SG-43 had adequate accuracy and a range of 2,000m, but the turret was found to be too small for the new armament. The vehicle was not recommended for production.

7.62mm SG-43 installation in the BA-64B. The principal reason for the failure of the 7.62mm SG-43 armed BA-64B is apparent here. The SG-43 could not be operated effectively from within the confines of the turret.

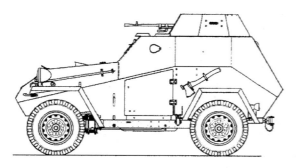

BA-64B with 7.62mm SG-43 installation drawing. (Nikolai Polikarpov)

BA-69

A monocoque-bodied version of the BA-64 was developed in the spring of 1944, using the same principle as used on the earlier pre-war prototype BA-20 monocoque design. As with the BA-20, the principle was to integrate the strength of the chassis into the armored body, the reduced weight thereby allowing additional armor to be added with no loss in performance. The prototype vehicle was based on the GAZ-69, the planned replacement for the GAZ-67B, on which development work began at GAZ in May 1943. Concurrently with development of the monocoque GAZ-69, work began on 30th May 1944 on the new monocoque armored car based on the GAZ-69 chassis. The new armored car was designated BA-69 and work progressed as far as developing a wooden model of the vehicle in June 1944 which was completed on 13th July. Although the design was sound in principle, the war was nearing an end, and in the circumstances it was decided not to disrupt series production of the current BA-64B. The BA-69 did not therefore progress beyond model prototype stage and represents the final development in the BA-64 armored car series.

Two pictures above: BA-64B SG-43 prototype. The BA-64B armed with the 7.62mm SG-43 is seen here during evaluation trials. The vehicle was not accepted for service with the Red Army.

3
Medium Armored Cars

BA-27

BA-27M

D-13

BA-I

BA-3

BA-5

BA-6/BA-6M

BA-9

BA-10/BA-10M

BA-11/BA-11D

BA-27

In 1924 Russia began production of the AMO (Avtomobilnoe Moskovskoe Obshestvo-Moscow Automobile Society) F-15 4x2 truck, a Russian modification of an original FIAT design. The development of the AMO F-15 truck and its production debut in 1924 finally provided the Red Army with a mass production chassis on which to build a new armored car, which was latterly produced as the BA-27.

Development of the BA-27 on the F-15 chassis began at AMO in 1926 under the direction of B.D. Strokanov, with the detail design work undertaken by his deputy E.I. Vazhinsky. By the summer of 1926 the initial design was complete and chassis field trials were conducted under the direction of I.I. Vittenburg. These trials showed that the chassis was not sufficiently rigid for the

weight of the armored body and it was considerably upgraded as a result, particularly with regard to off-road capability.

After completion of chassis field trials, the BA-27 chassis plans were given to the Izhorskiy armor plant where the armored hull and turret were manufactured and mated to the prototype. After further successful field trials of the completed BA-27 prototype, the vehicle was formally given the designation BA-27 and accepted for service in the Red Army. It was subsequently produced in small numbers at the Izhorskiy plant at Kolpino, near Leningrad from late 1927 as the BA-27 Model 1927. The vehicle entered general service with the Red Army the same year and in army service was simply known as the BA-27. Fitted with the turret and 37mm main armament of the MS-1 (T-18) tank, the BA-27 had reasonable firepower for the period but with limited anti-tank capabil-

BA-27s parade on Red Square, Moscow, 7th November 1932. Note the extensive use of flat armor plate and the turret with its offset armament, taken from the T-18 light tank. (Tank Museum, Bovington, UK. Ref: 522/E4).

SPECIFICATIONS BA-27

Design bureau: AMO Moscow
Crew: 4 (3)
Manufacturing plant: Izhorskiy zavod
Service date: 1927-31
Combat weight: 4,400kg (4,100kg for Model 1928)

Dimensions: (m)
Length: 4.617
Width: 1.710
Height: 2.520
Wheelbase: 3.070
Track width: NA
Ground clearance: 0.245

Armor: (mm)
Hull front: 8
Hull sides: 5
Turret front: 5
Turret sides: 5
Hull roof: 5
Hull floor: 3

Armament:
Main armament: 37mm Hotchkiss/40 rounds
Secondary armament: 7.62mm DT/2016 rounds
Firing height: NA
Elevation/depression: NA

Automotive:
Type: AMO F-15 (GAZ-AA)
Cylinders: 4
Capacity: 4396cm^3
Power output: 35hp @ 1,400rpm (40hp)*
Fuel type/capacity: Petrol /70 liters
Transmission: 4F 1R
Steering: NA
Tires: 280-135 Solid rubber.
Brakes: Mechanical,drums on all wheels
Radio: No

Performance:
Maximum road speed (km/h): 35 (45)
Maximum terrain speed (km/h): NA
Road range (km): 270-300
Terrain range (km): 150
Power/weight ratio: 8.0 (9.8)hp/tonne**
Ground pressure: 3.2kg/cm^2
Gradient: 15°
Trench: 0.7m
Fording: 0.6m

Notes:
*   The BA-27 M-1927 developed 35hp (26.1kW)
while the BA-27 M-1928 developed 40hp (29.8kW).
** Power/weight ratios for the BA-27 M-1927 and
BA-27 M-1928 are 8.0hp (5.96kW) and 9.8hp (7.31kW)
respectively

ity. The first series production model BA-27, based on the AMO F-15 chassis, had a crew of four, the fourth crewman being located in a rear command post.

As the first BA-27 M-1927s were being produced, work continued on improving the design and in 1928 the BA-27 was modified at Izhorskiy for production on the newly available Ford-AA chassis with a four-cylinder "GAZ" engine developing 40hp (30kW). The new chassis reduced the BA-27s combat weight to 4,100kg. The chassis was subsequently series produced at the Gudok Oktyabrya (October Hooter) plant at Nizhny Novgorod (later and better known as the GAZ plant) as the GAZ-AA and also at the KIM plant in Moscow. The original BA-27 M-1927 crew of four had proved cumbersome for a small armored car so on the new model, the rear command post position was deleted and the crew reduced to three.

After trials of the modified BA-27 in December 1928 it was also accepted for service in the Red Army and entered series production as the BA-27 M-1928, which became the definitive production model of the BA-27.

While the original BA-27 M-1927 was entering limited production, several other prototypes were also evaluated for service with the Red Army. Some early BA-27 M-1927 armored cars were experimentally fitted with a 37mm main gun and a co-axial twin 6.5mm Fedorov machine gun. These variants did not enter series production but a small number were manufactured and entered service with the army.

The BA-27 was significant in being the first series produced Russian "medium" armored car, though it was actually designated as heavy in the Russian classification system. The BA-27 was series manufactured at the Izhorskiy plant from 1927 to 1931. BA-27 armored cars took part in the battles of the Khalkhin Gol against Japan and the incidents on the Chinese Eastern Railroad. When production ceased in 1931, one hundred BA-27s of all production models had been manufactured.

BA-27s on Red Square, Moscow, 7th November 1932. BA-27 "Caucasian Komsomolets" (left), and "Moscow Komsomolets" (right) lead a column of BA-27s. The right column has three production variants, with flat, louvered, and domed radiator armor plates.

BA-27s during the same 7th November 1932 parade. The inscription on the vehicle on the right reads, "In the name of the Tenth Anniversary of the Domestic Transport Worker's Union". This is the "Caucasian Komsomolets" vehicle in the top picture. This vehicle had flat radiator armor in comparison with the BA-27 on the left, which has radiator armor with four intake louvers.

Although rudimentary and somewhat outdated in its own time, the BA-27 was a good basic design not inferior to contemporary armored cars of other nations. It was strategically significant in that it gave Russian forces experience with mechanized formations, special mechanized units being formed which incorporated the BA-27 with MS-1 tanks, the units comprising a battalion of MS-1 tanks and an auto-armored battalion equipped with BA-27s. These became separate Mechanical Brigades in 1929, the beginning of armored formations in the modern sense.

The AMO F-15 chassis was generally suited for its role, being overall reliable in operation and simple to maintain. It had good ground clearance and large diameter wheels, though the narrow section tires caused some difficulties crossing soft ground. The all-terrain performance deficiencies of the BA-27 were recognized during its service life, with most difficulties being related to the vehicle bogging down in soft ground. In an attempt to lessen the vehicle ground pressure, an elongated 6x4 chassis was developed for the vehicle in 1931. The design work resulted in the BA-27M which entered service with the Red Army late the same year.

Early production BA-27. This is an interesting experimental variant of an early BA-27 with a tandem mount 6.5mm Federov machine gun installed in the turret as secondary armament. The vehicle also has unusual horizontal pattern armored radiator vents. (Mikhail Svirin)

Description

The BA-27 was a relatively simple design, with a front-mounted engine, rear fighting compartment, and the turret and armament taken from the MS-1 (T-18) light tank.

The original AMO F-15 chassis was significantly modified for use with the BA-27 armored car. Modifications included strengthened springs, special heavy duty tires and an uprated clutch, while the fuel tank capacity was increased to improve range. Other significant modifications included an electric starter for the BA-27 (the AMO F-15 was started with a hand crank) and standard electric driving lights, which were only later added to the AMO F-15 cargo truck.

The turret and armament of the BA-27 were taken from the MS-1 (T-18) light tank then in production. The six-faceted turret mounted a 37mm Hotchkiss gun in the left front facet with a newly available 7.62mm DT (Degtyarev-Tankovy) machine gun ball-mounted on the right. The gunner was located in a seat which was mounted to the turret wall. The BA-27 had excellent firepower and was classified as "heavy" due to its armament, despite its diminutive size.

The hull and turret used flat sheet armor which was riveted throughout. The hull armor was built from 5-8mm flat steel plate with an angled front superstructure which gave the vehicle good overall protection from small caliber weapons. There were two access doors in the front fighting compartment. The rear deck had a distinctive step which gave the vehicle better rearward vision against close infantry attack and was also used to mount the spare tires, two of which were often carried stacked on top of each other.

Engine cooling was a design problem which plagued the BA-27 as there was a frequent risk of overheating whenever the front armored radiator doors were closed in combat conditions and the airflow consequently restricted. There were at least four variants of front armor plate on the BA-27, developed as engineers attempted to solve the vehicle's ongoing cooling problems. Early model BA-27s had a horizontally slatted grille, followed by flat armor without cooling slots. This was followed by flat armor plate with four air intake doors. The final solution was the fitting of an 60cm eight-bladed fan which drew air through vents in the front armor and forced it through the radiator in a concept still used to the present day. Later production model BA-27s used domed front vent covers which allowed air to be drawn in by the fan at all times and alleviated the necessity to have the armored radiator armor open in combat conditions. An armored scuttle was mounted under the radiator to maximize the airflow past the engine with the front armored

BA-27s on parade, 7th November 1932. Note the distinctive flat radiator armor and the scuttle mounted under the armor to direct air flow past the radiator.

BA-27s and a T-27 tankette on maneuvers. The BA-27 on the right has the later pattern radiator armor with four separate armored vents which could be opened as required.

Crews receive instruction on new BA-27s. The extensive use of flat armor plate is evident in this photograph of a BA-27 prior to armament installation.

BA-27. Though not a particularly clear photograph, the stepped rear armor and the storage pattern for the two spare wheels is evident in this view. (Tank Museum, Bovington, UK. Ref: 3202/C5)

A BA-27 undergoes gun cleaning in the field. This BA-27 is interesting in that it is painted in parade markings, "10th Anniversary of Domestic Transport," but has clearly been used in the field for some time thereafter without repaint to more subtle markings. (Tank Museum, Bovington, UK. Ref: 3202/D3)

BA-27s line up for a parade on Red Square, Moscow. The markings on the BA-27 in the foreground are identical to those in the top photo.

plates closed.

The BA-27 had an adequate combination of firepower and protection but the 4,400kg combat weight and under-rated 35hp (26.1kW) engine of the original BA-27 gave a disappointing power/weight ratio which led to limited vehicle performance, particularly a maximum speed of only 35km/hour and a very limited 150km range. The 4,400kg vehicle mounted on its narrow section tires also led to a high (3.2kg/cm^2) ground pressure which resulted in the vehicle bogging down in soft ground.

Recognizing the design flaws in the original production model BA-27, the modified BA-27 M-1928 version was developed, externally identical to the earlier series but mounted on the Ford-AA chassis which reduced the chassis weight by 300kg, the corresponding vehicle combat being reduced to 4,100kg. The Ford-AA based BA-27 M-1928 was powered by a four-cylinder 40hp (30kW) engine which gave a marginal increase in overall performance in combination with the vehicle's reduced combat weight. The BA-27 Model M-1928 had a road speed of 40km/hour.

An overturned BA-27 in Poland, 1939. This photograph gives a good view of the BA-27 chassis and transmission.

BA-27M Medium Armored Car

The BA-27 4x2 armored car had proven to be a very successful design when introduced into Russian Army service in 1927. The vehicle was well armed, with identical armament to contemporary light tanks, well armored and reliable in service. Its principle drawback was limited off-road mobility, due to a combination of its 4,400kg combat weight and limited 4x2 chassis. The problem was compounded by the narrow section tires used on the BA-27, which gave good overall traction but led to the vehicle bogging down easily when crossing soft ground. The later BA-27 M-1928 production model with its reduced 4,100kg combat weight and uprated powerplant

had improved the BA-27's performance slightly, but it remained a heavy vehicle on a light chassis with consequent limited cross-country performance.

The mobility difficulties of the otherwise successful BA-27 were investigated by engineers at the Remontbaza N°2 (Repair base N°2) tank rebuilding facility and a six-wheeled variant, the BA-27M, was developed using the

BA-27M. This BA-27M is preserved in excellent condition in the NIIBT Museum, Kubinka.

BA-27M front view. Note the four intake cowlings on the frontal armor. This configuration was also used on the last production series of BA-27s.

SPECIFICATIONS BA-27M

Design bureau: Remontbaza Nº2
Crew: 4
Manufacturing plant: Remontbaza Nº2
Service date: 1931
Combat weight: 4,500kg

Dimensions: (m)
Length: 4.83
Width: 1.93
Height: 2.54
Wheelbase: Ford Timken
Track width: Ford Timken
Ground clearance: 0.24

Armor: (mm)
Hull front: 8
Hull sides: 8
Turret front: 8
Turret sides: 8

Armament:
Main armament: 37mm Hotchkiss/40
Secondary armament: 1x7.62mm DT/2,016
Firing height: NA

Elevation/depression: NA

Automotive:
Type: GAZ-AA
Capacity: 3,285cm³
Cylinders: 4
Power output: 40hp (30kW)
Fuel type/capacity: Petrol/150 liters
Transmission: 4F 1R x2
Steering: NA
Tires: Solid rubber
Brakes: NA
Radio: No

Performance:
Maximum road speed (km/h): 48
Maximum terrain speed (km/h): NA
Road range (km): 300 (approximately)
Terrain range (km): 200
Power/weight ratio: 8.9hp (6.7kW)/tonne
Ground pressure: 3.7kg/cm²
Gradient: 20-23°
Trench: NA
Fording: 1.0m

BA-27M. The BA-27M was based on the Ford Timken chassis and was built by Remontbaza Nº 2 (Repair Base Nº 2) from 1931. The 37mm main armament provided excellent firepower when initially introduced. The BA-27M saw active service in the Khalkin Gol battles and the opening stages of the 1941-45 war with Germany.

A BA-27M abandoned at a ferry crossing, 1941. The vehicle has "overall" tracks stowed on the wheel guards. Note the missing wheel and open rear vision visor.

BA-27M at the NIIBT Museum, Kubinka.

BA-27M. This BA-27M has the simpler flat radiator armor without louvers.

BA-27M preserved at the NIIBT museum, Kubinka, Moscow.

BA-27M at the NIIBT museum, Kubinka, Moscow.

original BA-27 armor body and turret mounted on the 6x4 Ford Timken chassis. The BA-27M was developed in an attempt to spread the weight of the armored body and turret and so reduce the vehicle ground pressure. Trials of the prototype BA-27M actually showed a moderate increase in off-road performance but little change in ground pressure. However, the use of a 6x4 chassis allowed removable rubber tracks with steel grousers to be fitted around the rear wheels when required. These tracks, known as "overall" tracks, were introduced on the BA-27M and proved very effective. Being removable, they did not reduce road speed and when not in use they were stowed on the rear wheel guards or across the vehicle rear. These tracks became standard on the later BA heavy armored car series, all of which were mounted on 6x4 chassis.

After successful completion of field trials the BA-27M was accepted for service in the Red Army. Classified at the time as a medium armored car, a small series of BA-27Ms were built at Remontbaza N°2 in 1931 and entered service with the Red Army the same year.

At the time of its introduction the BA-27M was already a dated design, however, and was based on a chassis for which a domestically manufactured replacement (the GAZ-AAA) was already being prepared for series production. It would be required that future Russian heavy armored car designs be mounted on the new chassis and so the BA-27M remained a stopgap to modernize an existing vehicle design and retain it in service until a new vehicle was available. The BA-27M was quickly replaced by the Izhorskiy plant developed BA (BroneAvtomobil - Armored Car) series which was developed concurrently with the BA-27M but, with the exception of the first series production BA-I vehicles, was produced using the new GAZ-AAA chassis, powerplant, and mechanical components.

The BA-27M served in the Far East Military District where in the summer of 1939 it was engaged against the Japanese Army in the battles of the Khalkhin Gol. It remained in service with the Red Army at the outbreak of war with Germany in 1941 but most vehicles were destroyed or abandoned in the opening weeks of the war.

Description

The BA-27M was basically the body and turret from the BA-27 mounted on the chassis of the 6x4 Ford Timken chassis. The crew of the BA-27M was increased to four, reintroducing the rear command post station which was used on the original BA-27 M-1927 but deleted on the

BA-27M rear view. Note the rear vision port and the turret taken from the MS-1 (T-18) light tank.

later BA-27 M-1928 production model.

The BA-27M was powered by a GAZ-AA engine made available in limited numbers before the GAZ-AA truck entered production the following year. The 40hp (30kW) engine gave a power/weight ratio of 8.9hp (6.7kW)/tonne, giving the vehicle a reasonable road speed of 48km/hour.

The BA-27 turret was taken from the concurrent MS-1 (T-18) light tank, with the 37mm Hotchkiss tank gun mounted on the left front turret facet and a ball-mounted 7.62mm machine gun on the right front facet. The turret traverse was manually operated. Forty rounds of 37mm ammunition and 2,016 rounds of 7.62mm ammunition were carried within the vehicle. The BA-27M had an armor basis of 8mm, with riveted sheet armor used on the hull and turret.

D-13 Heavy Armored Car

The D-13 (Dyrenkov-13) was the first 6x4 "heavy" armored car produced in Russia. It was developed in 1931 concurrently with the BA-27M, with both models actually being classified as medium armored cars at the time. The D-13 was developed by a team directed by N.I. Dyrenkov at the KIM (Kommunisticheskiy Internatsional Molodozhi-Young International Commu-

nists) plant in north east Moscow (now part of the AZLK Moskvitch plant) in competition with the BA-I design from GAZ. The Ford Timken 6x4 based chassis was modified and strengthened at KIM, the completed chassis then being transferred to the Izhorsky plant at Kolpino, near Leningrad, where the armored bodies were built and mounted on the KIM supplied chassis. A small series of D-13s was manufactured at Izhorskiy for trials purposes during 1931.

In addition to good armament and an 8mm armor basis the D-13 was designed with considerable attention to overall performance and battlefield survivability. The D-13 introduced several interesting design features including the provision of two drivers positions, located at either end of the vehicle, which gave both good control in either direction and the ability to evacuate a damaged vehicle from combat operations, albeit the D-13 was particularly slow when moving in reverse gear. The tires were of the new GK or Gubchataya Kamera bulletproof design being introduced onto several armored car types during this time, these being filled with a type of sponge rubber which allowed considerable damage to the tires without disabling the vehicle.

The D-13 did not progress beyond trials production stage and details are unavailable as to how the D-13 performed during evaluation for service in the RKKA. A command variant of D-13 was also produced, designated D-13U (Upravleniya-command).

Description

The D-13 armored body and turret were produced at the Izhorskiy plant and mated to a 6x4 Ford Timken chassis modified and supplied by the KIM zavod in Moscow. The D-13 featured a turret of a new design, with the armament taken from the MS-1 light tank. The vehicle was heavily armed compared with its contemporaries, armament consisting of a turret-mounted 37mm Hotchkiss tank gun with one hundred rounds of ammunition, a co-axial 7.62mm DT machine gun and a further 7.62mm DT machine gun in the hull which could be fitted in several available ball mounts, two in each side, one at the hull rear and one to right of the driver. In addition to the hull armament there was a ring mounted 7.62mm DT or PM-1910 Anti-aircraft machine gun (AAMG) on the roof behind the turret. A considerable 5,040 rounds of 7.62mm ammunition was carried within the vehicle.

The D-13 had a crew of three, consisting of commander/gunner, loader/machine gunner, driver. Had the vehicle entered service, the crew would have been hard worked in combat due to the excessive armament carried on the vehicle. The D-13 was not fitted with radio, which considering the armament was probably good news for

SPECIFICATIONS D-13

Design bureau: Moscow Autozavod KIM
Crew: 3
Manufacturing plant: Izhorskiy zavod
Service date: 1931 Small series produced
Combat weight: 4,140kg

Dimensions: (m)
Length: 4.975
Width: 1.960
Height: 2.50
Wheelbase: NA
Track width: NA
Ground clearance: 0.240

Armor: (mm)
Hull front: 8
Hull sides: 8
Turret front: 8
Turret sides: NA

Armament:
Main armament: 37mm Hotchkiss/100
Secondary armament: 3x7.62mmDT/5,040
Firing height: NA

Elevation/depression: NA

Automotive:
Type: GAZ-AA
Capacity: 3,285cm^3
Cylinders: 4
Power output: 40hp (30kW) @ 2,200rpm
Fuel type/capacity: Petrol /40 liters
Transmission: NA
Steering: Rack and pinion
Tires: NA
Brakes: Mechanical drums on all wheels
Radio: No

Performance:
Maximum road speed (km/h): 55
Maximum terrain speed (km/h):NA
Road range (km): 130
Terrain range (km): 95
Power/weight ratio: 9.7hp (7.2kW/tonne
Ground pressure: 2.5kg/cm^2
Gradient: 20°
Trench: NA
Fording: NA

**Dyrenkov's D-13 heavy armored car. The D-13 was built in small numbers at the Izhorskiy plant from 1931.
The vehicle was armed with 37mm main armament and at least two 7.62mm DT machine guns which could be
moved to several ball mounts within the vehicle. Note also the anti-aircraft ring mount on the hull roof.**

Another view of the D-13 armored car.

the overworked crew.

The D-13 was powered by the new Ford-AA/GAZ-AA engine then entering series production at KIM in Moscow and at the GAZ plant in Nizhny Novgorod. The rudimentary but reliable engine developed 40hp (30kW) which gave the vehicle a reasonable road speed of 55km/hour. The D-13 was provided with large section tires which gave good cross-country performance and the spare wheels mounted either side of the vehicle were free-rotating on their stub axles to assist with obstacle clearance. To further aid survivability in combat the D-13 was also fitted with GK bulletproof tires.

BA-I Heavy Armored Car

Field trials with the D-13 conducted in 1932 did not result in its adoption by the Red Army. Consequently, an entirely new series of 5,000kg class armored cars was developed at the Izhorskiy plant in the suburbs of Leningrad which was to become the definitive Russian heavy armored car series of the 1930s. The first model developed by the Izhorskiy team under the direction of A.D. Kuzmin as plant director was based on the chassis of the Ford Timken 6x4 truck and received the designation BA-I or BronieAvtomobil-Izhorskiy (not BA-1 as often described in the West). Subsequent series production model BA designs were numerically designated BA-3 to BA-11.

Small numbers of BA-I armored cars were produced during 1932 for trials purposes. The trials showed that the 37mm main armament of the BA-I had limited anti-tank capability but was adequate for infantry support requirements. The Ford Timken chassis employed on the BA-I was not particularly strong or rigid to support the vehicle weight but was judged to be acceptable as it was available and required only slight modification to accept the BA-I hull. Subsequent Izhorskiy vehicles were based on the new GAZ-AAA chassis which became available in 1933.

Between 1932 and 1934 a small series of BA-I armored cars were built at the Izhorsky Plant in Leningrad, a total of fifty-three BA-Is being supplied to the Russian Army over the two-year period. The BA-I was super-seded in production by the BA-3 in 1934. It remained in service in small numbers when war broke out with Germany in June 1941. Russian records do not show the development of a BA-2 or BA-4 beyond paper design studies.

Description

The BA-I was of conventional configuration, with a front-mounted engine, rear fighting compartment and a small turret mounted to the rear of the fighting compartment roof. The hull was of welded and riveted construction. The three man crew consisted of commander/gunner, loader/hull gunner and driver. Access to the vehicle was by a door in each side of the vehicle and by a small door on the right side of the vehicle rear. The basic hull

SPECIFICATIONS BA-I

Design bureau: Izhorskiy OKB
Crew: 3
Manufacturing plant: Izhorskiy zavod
Service date: 1932 Small series production
Combat weight: 5,000kg

Dimensions: (m)
Length: 4.770
Width: 2.016
Height: 2.350
Wheelbase: As Ford Timken
Track width: As Ford Timken
Ground clearance: 0.254

Armor: (mm)
Hull front: 8
Hull sides: NA
Turret front: 8
Turret sides: NA

Armament:
Main armament: 37mm Hotchkiss / 34
Secondary armament: 2x7.62mmDT / 3,024
Firing height: NA

Elevation/depression: NA

Automotive:
Type: GAZ-AA
Cylinders: 4
Power output: 40hp (29.4kW)
Fuel type/capacity: Petrol/40 liters
Transmission: NA
Steering: Rack & pinion
Tires: NA
Brakes: Mechanical, drums on all wheels
Radio: No

Performance:
Maximum road speed (km/h): 63
Maximum terrain speed (km/h): 48
Road range (km): 300
Terrain range (km): 90
Power/weight ratio: 8.0hp (6.0kW)/tonne
Ground pressure: 2.8kg/cm^2
Gradient: 25°
Trench: NA
Fording: NA

BA-Is parade in Red Square, Moscow, 7th November 1934. The BA-I (BA-Izhorskiy) was the first of the BA heavy armored car series introduced into service with the Red Army in 1932. The BA-Is here are accompanied by Dyrenkov D-8s (right), and SU-12 self-propelled guns (rear and right).

BA-I side view. The turret used on the BA-I was an original design not related to the MS-1 (T-18) light tank turret. The 37mm main armament was mounted on the right of the turret with the DT machine gun on the left, the opposite arrangement to that used on the BA-27 and BA-27M.

BA-Is in formation, Kiev Military District, 1935. Note the rear access door and tow ropes. In the background can be seen FAIs and Kommunar tractors towing 203mm B-4 tracked howitzers.

BA-I on Red Square, Moscow. The BA-I pictured in this old British Army recognition photograph is following a column of Dyrenkov D-8s. (Tank Museum, Bovington, UK. Ref: 276/D5)

BA-Is entering Red Square, Moscow, 1933.

configuration of the BA series changed little throughout the series, but the turret and armament were updated several times. The BA-I was armed with a 37mm Hotchkiss gun and co-axial DT machine gun in the turret, with another 7.62mm DT machine gun located in the front right of the fighting compartment. The BA-I used a new purpose designed turret, similar to the earlier D-13 turret which differentiated it from later vehicles in the series which used the turret from the T-26 M-1933 tank. The turret armor was riveted throughout.

Though well armed, the BA-I was very underpowered. The four-cylinder GAZ-AA engine developed 40hp (30kW) which gave the five-tonne vehicle reasonable road speed, but the poor power/weight ratio of only 8hp (6kW)/

tonne, together with the overloaded chassis, resulted in nominal cross-country performance. "Overall" tracks, first introduced on the BA-27M, were normally used to good effect when traversing soft terrain.

BA-3 Heavy Armored Car

The BA-I design was followed in production at the Izhorskiy plant by the BA-3 which became the first series produced model of the BA series, the BA-2 having not progressed beyond the conceptual design phase. It was manufactured from 1934 until 1935, with approximately 160 BA-3s built before the introduction of the BA-6 in 1935.

The BA-3 was used throughout the 1930s and small numbers which were stationed in the Russian Far East Military District took part in the Khalkin Gol campaign against Japan in the summer of 1939. Some of these vehicles were later returned to the Russian Western Front to take part in action against the German Army in late 1941 and early 1942.

The BA-3 was built on the newly available GAZ-AAA chassis (some Russian Sources state Ford-Timken), with the turret and 45mm M-1932 tank gun armament taken directly from the T-26 M-1933 light tank.

BA-3 prototype during evaluation trials.

SPECIFICATIONS BA-3

Design bureau: Izhorskiy OKB
Crew: 4
Manufacturing plant: Izhorskiy zavod
Service date: 1934
Combat weight: 6,000kg

Dimensions: (m)
Length: 4.77
Width: 2.11
Height: 2.35
Wheelbase: 3.34
Track width: 1.60
Ground clearance: 0.254

Armor: (mm)
Hull front: 8
Hull sides:NA
Turret front: 8
Turret sides: NA

Armament:
Main armament: 45mm M-1932/40
Secondary armament: 2x7.62mm DT/3,276
Firing height: NA

Elevation/depression: NA

Automotive:
Type: GAZ-AA
Capacity: 3,285cm³
Cylinders: 4
Power output: 40hp (29.8kW) @ 2,200rpm
Fuel type/capacity:Petrol/65 liters
Transmission: 4F 1R Two speed transfer case
Steering: Rack & pinion
Tires: 6.50 - 20
Brakes: Mechanical, drums on all wheels
Radio: No

Performance:
Maximum road speed (km/h): 63
Maximum terrain speed (km/h): NA
Road range (km): 260
Terrain range (km): 140
Power/weight ratio: 6.7hp (4.97kW)/tonne
Ground pressure: 3.2kg/cm²
Gradient: 25°
Trench: NA
Fording: 1.0

BA-3s and FAIs in transit, Kiev Military District Maneuvers, 1935. The new turret easily distinguished the BA-3 from the BA-I. This BA-3 has "overall" tracks mounted on wooden blocks on the rear wheel guards. Small detail changes from the BA-I include the use of internal hinges on the vision blocks and a neatened external appearance to the hull.

The turret armor was welded while the 8mm hull armor was of welded and riveted construction.

The four man crew of the BA-3 consisted of commander/gunner, loader,driver, and hull machine gunner who was introduced as a result of field experience with the BAI which showed that a three man crew was inadequate for a vehicle with the same armament as a contemporary light tank. As the BA-3 still lacked a radio the crew of three proved adequate to the tasks required.

The use of the 45mm M-1932 tank gun from the T-26 M-1933 was a significant increase in armament compared with the BA-I and provided good anti-tank capability which the BA-I lacked. Secondary armament consisted of two 7.62mm DT machine guns, one in the turret mounted co-axially with the main armament, the other mounted in the hull alongside the driver. The BA-3 carried forty rounds of 45mm ammunition and 3,276 rounds of 7.62mm ammunition within the vehicle, a considerable improvement compared with the BA-I.

The BA-3 was fitted with the same 40hp (29.4kW) GAZ-AA engine which powered the BA-I which was some 1,000kg lighter than the 6,000kg BA-3. The BA-3 had an excellent road speed of 63km/hour which was considerable for its day but its power/weight ratio was

actually worse than the BA-I due primarily to the addition of the heavy T-26 turret. Pneumatic tires were introduced for the first time on the BA-3 which helped maintain road performance despite the additional vehicle weight.

Description

The BA-3 was similar in layout to the BA-I, the principle distinguishing feature of the BA-3 being the new turret and armament, taken from the T-26 M-1933 light tank. The vehicle was otherwise generally similar to the earlier BA-I. The BA-3 retained the BA-I's rear hull access door.

BA-5 Heavy Armored Car

The BA-5 was developed in the spring of 1935. It was an unusual vehicle in the BA heavy armored car series, utilizing the chassis and mechanicals from a modified ZiS-6, which had been in production at ZiS in Moscow since 1934, rather than the GAZ-AAA chassis on which all other BA heavy armored cars except the origi-

BA-3s pictured in August 1942. The BA-3s pictured here are accompanied by a BA-20M (foreground) and a BA-10 (background). Many armored cars were serving in the Far East Military District when war broke out with Germany in 1941, and arrived late in the western theater of operations. (Photographer: D. Chernov)

BA-5 Heavy armored car prototype. A rare, though poor quality photograph of a BA-5.

Rear view of the BA-5. Note the rear firing machine gun sponson.

SPECIFICATIONS BA-5

Design bureau: Moskovskiy Zavod (ZiS) OKB
Crew: 5
Manufacturing plant: Moskovskiy Zavod (ZiS)
Service date: 1935 (Prototype)
Combat weight: 8,100 kg

Dimensions: (m)
Length: 5.30m
Width: 2.40m
Height: 2.50m (approx)
Wheelbase: 3.81
Track width: 1.675
Ground clearance: 0.265m

Armor: (mm)
Hull front: 4-9
Hull sides: 6
Turret front: 4-9
Turret sides: 4

Armament:
Main armament: 45mm M-1934/114
Secondary armament: 3x7.62mmDT/3,000
Firing height: NA

Elevation/depression: NA

Automotive:
Type: ZiS-5
Capacity: 5,555cm^3
Cylinders: 6
Power output: 73hp (54.5kW) @ 2,400rpm
Fuel type/capacity: Petrol /120 liters
Transmission: 4F 1R
Steering: Rack and pinion
Tires: 34.00 - 7.00
Brakes: Mechanical
Radio: No

Performance:
Maximum road speed (km/h): 50
Maximum terrain speed (km/h): NA
Road range (km): 260
Terrain range (km): NA
Power/weight ratio: 9.0hp (6.72kW)/tonne
Ground pressure: NA
Gradient: 20°
Side slope: 14°
Trench: 0.5m
Fording: 0.65m

nal BA-I had been based. The armored body was developed by the Izhorskiy plant in Kolpino near Leningrad, concurrently with the chassis development at ZiS in Moscow.

The development principle behind the BA-5 was to upgrade the combat capability and endurance of the heavy BA armored car series by providing a multiplicity of armament in a similar manner to contemporary tanks such as the T-28 medium and T-35 heavy.

The BA-5 was armed with the new 45mm M-1934 tank gun and a co-axial 7.62mm DT machine gun in the T-26 M-1933 turret. A second DT machine gun was ball-mounted in the front right side of the fighting compartment, alongside the driver, while a third DT machine gun was ball mounted at the rear of the fighting compartment in a rear sponson which provided a good rear arc of fire. The BA-5 made good use of the additional space available in the fighting compartment, with an impressive 114 45mm rounds and 3,000 rounds of 7.62mm ammunition being carried on board, significantly increasing the vehicle's battlefield endurance in comparison to its predecessors.

The BA-5 featured several interesting design concepts, the most ingenious of which was the adoption of a second driver's station at the rear of the vehicle, as originally introduced on the earlier D-13 armored car, complete with a second steering wheel and accelerator, clutch, and brake pedals. The vehicle could be driven in either direction which gave a considerable increase in combat capability in terms of general mobility and ability to sustain battle damage. The second driver's station also made the BA-5 better suited than its predecessors for use as a rail drezine.

Though an excellent armored car design in terms of firepower, maneuverability, and battlefield endurance, the BA-5's armament and driver arrangement necessitated a crew of five, which was in part to prove the vehicle's downfall. The crew required for operating the BA-5 efficiently was comparable with that required for a medium tank and represented the largest crew ever contemplated for a Russian armored car.

The BA-5 was longer than the BA-3 and BA-6. It had limited cross-country performance and its 9.0hp/tonne power/weight ratio was unimpressive, though similar to other armored cars of the time. The 73hp (54.5kW) six cylinder ZiS-5 engine did, however, give the vehicle a reasonable road speed of 50km/hour.

The BA-5 had a combat weight of 8,100kg and was as such a particularly heavy armored car, weighing 2,000kg more than the BA-3 and 3,000kg or nearly sixty percent more than the BA-6. As such the chassis was considered overloaded for the required weight of vehicle and this was also a major determining factor in the project being terminated.

The BA-5 did not progress beyond field trials which were conducted at the NIIBT Polygon at Kubinka near Moscow, but the design requirement for a 8,000kg class heavy armored car continued to be considered by engineers at ZiS and Izhorskiy, resulting in a second attempt at the concept, the BA-11, which entered limited production in 1939.

BA-6 Heavy Armored Car

The BA-6 armored car was introduced at the Izhorskiy plant in 1935 as the production replacement for the BA-3 after only 160 BA-3s had been manufactured. Though a good overall design, the BA-3 was, at 6,000kg, considered too heavy and the BA-6 was essentially a minor production modernization of the earlier design, nearly 1,000kg lighter and with a strengthened rear suspension and modified transmission. The BA-6 was armed with the same basic armament as the BA-3, consisting of a 45mm M-1932 tank gun and co-axial 7.62mm DT machine gun in the T-26 turret and a secondary 7.62mm DT machine gun in the hull superstructure alongside the driver. The BA-6 had better battle endurance than its predecessor, with sixty rounds of 45mm ammunition for the main armament stowed internally as against forty for the BA-3.

BA-6 rear view.

The BA-6 was built on a shortened GAZ-AAA chassis and was powered by the same GAZ-AA engine as the BA-3, the power output remaining 40hp (29.4kvT). The redesign of the BA-6 allowed for an improvement in armor to 9mm in vulnerable areas while achieving an overall reduction in weight to 5,120kg. The vehicle's improved power/weight ratio resulted in better all-terrain performance, though the cross-country speed was reduced

Rear view of a BA-6. This photo was taken on 9th May 1993 when some of the more historic AFV's in the Kubinka collection were publicly displayed at the Victory Museum at Paklonnaya Gorya Museum in Moscow.

and the use of bulletproof GK tires reduced road speed to 43km/hour and range to 197km.

The most noticeable recognition feature of the BA-6 was the introduction of a scuttle under the radiator which was later also used on the BA-10 series. The scuttle improved air flow to the engine when the intake louvers were shut in combat, preventing engine overheating. Several minor modifications were made to the BA-6 as production continued. The first few vehicles manufactured retained the small rear access door at the right of the fighting compartment rear which was a distinguishing feature of all BA-3s. Most armored hulls for the BA-6 were produced at the Izhorsk plant, though the Vyksa plant may also have manufactured hulls for the BA-6. Without reference to the lack of rear door, the BA-6 is almost indistinguishable externally from the earlier BA-3.

The BA-6 saw extensive combat service, with its

БРОНЕАВТОМОБИЛЬ БА-6

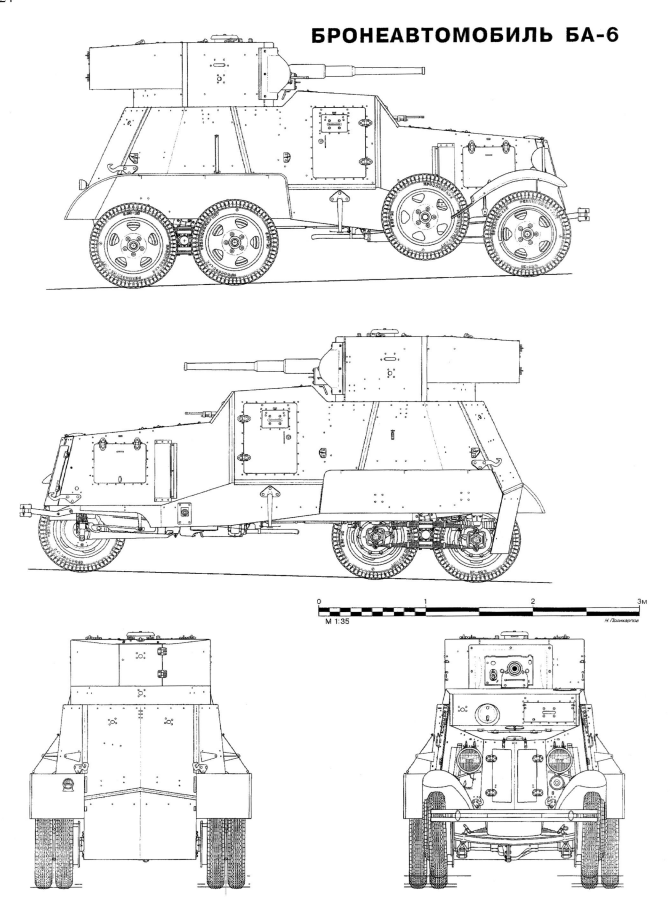

BA-6 drawings in 1:35 scale. (Nikolai Polikarpov)

BA-6 drawing in 1:35 scale.

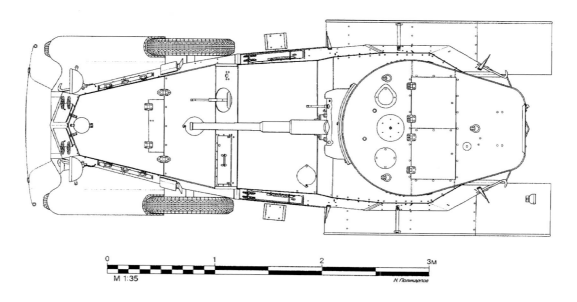

BA-6 during evaluation trials.

The Kubinka Tank Museum's BA-6, Victory Park, Moscow, 1993. On 9th May 1993, the Kubinka Tank Museum near Moscow showed their BA-6 in public, where it remained on display for several months. It is difficult to distinguish later BA-3s from the early BA-6 as there was no distinct model change and some interim model BA-6s retained the rear door which usually distinguishes the BA-3.

BA-6 in its Kubinka storage hangar. The vehicle in the background (Number 402) is a BA-27M, the only known example surviving today.

BA-6 at the Central Armed Forces Museum, Moscow. The vehicle now displayed at the Central Armed Forces Museum is the same vehicle as briefly displayed to the public at the 9th May 1993 victory celebrations in Moscow.

BA-6.

BA-6 at Central Armed Forces Museum, Moscow.

Superstructure and turret details of BA-6.

BA-6 gun and hull details.

From the right rear BA-6.

Hull and turret detail BA-6.

BA-6. The brackets above the two hooks were for securing the "overall" tracks when not in use.

BA-6. Note the leaf spring front suspension inherited from the GAZ-AAA truck chassis on which the BA-6 was built.

BA-6 heavy armored car. This BA-6 is painted in rare pre-war camouflage markings. (Imperial War Museum, London)

BA-6 abandoned in Finland, 1940. The BA-6 replaced the BA-3 in production at the Izhorskiy Zavod in 1935. It was generally similar in appearance to the BA-3 but had many detail changes. (Tank Museum, Bovington, UK. Ref: 3202/F1.)

Front view of the BA-6 (BA-3?) at the NIIBT Museum, Kubinka.

BA-6 (BA-3?) preserved at the Kubinka Tank Museum, Russia. This BA-series vehicle still retains the rear access door which was deleted on the standard production model BA-6. This may be a prototype vehicle used during evaluation trials, or a BA-3 with later modifications. The museum identifies it as a BA-3.

Kubinka's early production BA-6 (BA-3?).

Rear left view, BA-3 or early model BA-6 at Kubinka. The cleats above the wheel guards were used for securing the "overall" tracks.

Right rear view, BA-3 or early model BA-6 at Kubinka. This BA-6 retains the rear door more common to the BA-3. The vehicle may also be a BA-6 prototype based on the BA-3, or a late model BA-3.

BA-6 ZhD.

combat debut being during the Spanish Civil War. It served with Russian forces in the 1939 Khalkin Gol campaign against Japan, in the invasion of Poland, and during the 1939-40 "Winter War" with Finland before serving in the opening stages of the 1941-45 war with Germany. Due to large numbers of BA-6s being stationed in the Far East Military District when Germany invaded Russia in June 1941, these vehicles arrived late into the Western theater of operations, some BA-6s surviving into 1943-44 and longer, while contemporary Russian tanks such as the T-26 light tank were mostly destroyed by early 1942. Many BA-6s were captured by the German Army and pressed into German service as the Panzerspahwagen BA-203 (r).

In addition to service with the Russian Army, the BA-6 was also exported in small numbers (sixty vehicles) to Turkey in the mid-1930s. Spain used the BA-3 and BA-6 designs as the basis for their own Autometralladoro Blindado medio Chevrolet 1937. Some of these Spanish-built vehicles, which were similar to the Russian BA series but were different dimensionally and had a new turret, were used by the German Army in Russia during "Operation Barbarossa" in 1941. A small number of these vehicles, used primarily by German war correspondents, were in turn captured by Russian forces and saw service with the Red Army. A small number of BA-6s also served in China, Mongolia, and Afghanistan.

Most BA-6s were painted standard Russian olive green with unit markings normally located on the turret with bands around the turret roof. A small number were painted in the late 1930s three-color summer camouflage scheme. As with other Russian AFVs, whitewash was applied during winter and this was quickly worn and washed away, leaving BA-6s looking particularly weathered in wartime photographs.

A total of 386 BA-6 armored cars were produced between 1935 and 1939, including a small number of BA-6Ms. The BA-6 series was replaced on the production lines at Izhorskiy by the BA-10 from 1938.

BA-6 ZhD

The only known variant of the BA-6 which served with the Red Army was the BA-6 ZhD rail scout conversion of the BA-6 armored car, fitted with flanged ZhD

SPECIFICATIONS BA-6

Design bureau: Izhorskiy OKB
Crew: 4
Manufacturing plant: Izhorskiy zavod
Service date: 1935 (series production)
Combat weight: 5,120kg

Dimensions: (m)
Length: 4.90
Width: 2.07
Height: 2.36
Wheelbase: 3.34
Track width: 1.60
Ground clearance: 0.240

Armor: (mm)
Hull front: 9
Hull sides: 9
Hull rear: 4-8
Hull floor: 3
Hull roof: 6
Turret front: 8
Turret sides: 8

Armament:
Main armament: 45mm M-1932 / 60
Secondary armament: 2x7.62mm DT/3,276

Firing height: NA
Elevation/depression: +22°/-2° (-5°?)

Automotive:
Type: GAZ-AA
Capacity: 3285cm³
Cylinders: 4
Power output: 40hp (29.4kW) @ 2,200rpm
Fuel type/capacity: Petrol/65 liters
Transmission: 4F 1R x 2
Steering: Rack & pinion
Tires: 6.50 - 20
Brakes: Mechanical
Radio: No

Performance:
Maximum road speed (km/h): 43
Maximum terrain speed (km/h): NA
Road range (km): 200
Terrain range (km): 130
Power/weight ratio: 5.8kW (7.8hp)/tonne
Ground pressure: 3.5kg/cm²
Gradient: 20°
Trench: 0.6m
Fording: 0.8m

BA-6ZhD preparing for rail scout duty, Volkhov Front, August 1942. This interesting photo shows the crew in the process of fitting the steel ZhD rail rims over the standard road wheels. The rims are already fitted to the front wheels, while the rear of the vehicle has been jacked up to mount a complete ZhD wheel on the rear axle.

The BA-6M was almost identical in appearance to the later BA-10, but did not feature the small projection in front of the fighting compartment for the hull machine gun. This machine gun sponson was designed to give the machine gunner more space and was standardized on the later BA-10 series. M. Baryatinsky.

road wheels and built in small numbers in 1935. The BA-6 could attain a reasonable speed of 55km/hour on rails but had a limited rail range of 110-150km. The BA-6ZhD had a combat weight of 5,900kg, due primarily to the steel wheels but also in part due to a larger amount of ammunition being stowed.

To mount the BA-6ZhD system, the front of the vehicle was raised using a tank hydraulic jack mounted under the vehicle hull. The wheels were changed out and the process was then repeated for the rear wheels. The operation of changing the wheels took about thirty minutes to complete.

BA-6M Heavy Armored Car

The BA-6 underwent a modernization program in 1936, resulting in a new production model which was given the designation BA-6M. The BA-6M was powered by the new GAZ-M1 engine in place of the venerable GAZ-AA powerplant used in the preceding model; the new engine producing an additional 10hp (7.5kW) for a total output of 50hp (36.8kW). The overall weight of the vehicle was reduced from 5,120kg to 4,800kg, which combined with the additional power available, signifi-

cantly improving both road speed and all-terrain capability. A new conical all-welded turret was adopted on the BA-6M which subsequently became standard on the later BA-10.

The armor basis on the BA-6M was increased to 10mm, achieved within an overall weight reduction of 300kg. A drawback of using the smaller turret, however, was that the BA-6 only carried only fifty rounds of ammunition, ten rounds less than the BA-6.

A significant tactical improvement was the provision of a 71-TK-1 radio on the BA-6M, the first BA series heavy armored car to be equipped with radio as standard.

The BA-6M was produced in very small numbers; only fifteen to twenty being manufactured in total, as the vehicle evolved into the BA-10, which replaced the BA-6 in production after 1938. The BA-6M is difficult to distinguish from the later BA-10, as the vehicles were externally near identical, the lack of machine gun sponson being the principle distinguishing feature of the BA-6.

As with earlier BA series heavy armored cars, the BA-6M was often fitted with "overall" tracks over the rear wheels for all-terrain travel. These tracks with their rubber block inserts were stowed on the rear wheel guards when not in use.

SPECIFICATIONS BA-6M

Design bureau: Izhorskiy OKB
Crew: 4
Manufacturing plant: Izhorskiy zavod
Service date: 1936, small series produced
Combat weight: 4,800kg

Dimensions: (m)
Length: 4.655
Width: 2.300
Height: 2.150
Wheelbase: 3.34
Track width: 1.60
Ground clearance: 0.235

Armor: (mm)
Hull front: 10
Hull sides: 9-10
Turret front: 10
Turret sides: 10

Armament:
Main armament: 45mm M-1932 / 50
Secondary armament: 2 x 7.62mm DT / 2,520
Firing height: NA

Elevation/depression: NA
Traverse: 360°

Automotive:
Type: GAZ-M1
Capacity: 3,285cm^3
Cylinders: 4
Power output: 50hp (36.8kW) @ 2,200rpm
Fuel type/capacity: Petrol/112 liters
Transmission: 4F 1R x 2
Steering: Rack and pinion
Tires: 6.50-20
Brakes: Mechanical, drums on all wheels
Radio: 71-TK-1

Performance:
Maximum road speed (km/h): 50-52
Maximum terrain speed (km/h): NA
Road range (km): 290
Terrain range (km): 170
Power/weight ratio: 10.4hp (7.6kW)/tonne
Ground pressure: 3.6kg/cm^2
Gradient: 24°
Trench: 0.6m
Fording: 0.8m

No BA-6M is known to have survived intact to the present day.

BA-9 Medium Armored Car

The BA-9 was developed to prototype stage at the Izhorskiy plant in 1937, based on the BA-6M. Armed with a 12.7mm DShK and co-axial 7.62mm DT machine gun mounted in the new conical BA-6M turret, the vehicle was developed as a general purpose scout and infantry support vehicle at a time when heavy armored cars were no longer required to operate as wheeled tanks.

Despite the lighter armament, due to which the BA-9 was actually classified as a medium armored car, the vehicle had similar combat characteristics to some

the vehicle did not enter series production for reasons which are not documented.

BA-10 Heavy Armored Car

By 1938, many in Russia suspected that war with Germany was inevitable, despite political assurances to the contrary and the seemingly good relations with Germany which were soon to be demonstrated with preparations for the joint invasion of Poland by Soviet and German mechanized forces. Realizing the potential threat from Germany, an armored vehicle modernization program began in 1938, and the the BA-10 was one result of this program. The BA-10 was already in development at Izhorskiy at this time, work having begun in 1937, but the program was accelerated due to the changing po-

BA-9. The BA-9 was fitted with the smaller turret employed on the BA-6M but armed with a 12.7mm DShK heavy machine gun as main armament. (RAC Tank Museum, Bovington, UK)

contemporary light tanks. The 12.7mm DShK heavy machine gun had excellent armor penetrating capability at shorter ranges at which the BA-9 might be reasonably be expected to engage enemy targets (two years after the BA-9 was field trialled the weapon was still considered effective as main armament on the T-40 light tank).

The DShK's anti-armor capability was in fact similar to contemporary 37mm tank guns. Armed with the smaller weapon, the BA-9 had far greater ammunition stowage which would have provided considerable battle endurance in comparison with the vehicle's heavier armed counterparts should the vehicle have entered production. The BA-9 was successful during field trials, however,

litical climate. The BA-10 chassis was developed at GAZ by a team headed by V.A. Grachev, assisted by A.A. Lipgart, O.V. Dibov, and others, using a shortened version of the venerable GAZ-AAA chassis. The armored hulls were built at Izhorskiy (with the Vyksa plant also manufacturing a few hulls, according to some sources) with final assembly also being carried out at the Izhorskiy plant. The BA-10 entered series production in 1938 and entered service with the Red Army the same year.

The BA-10 was a minor modification of the existing BA-6M and used the same turret. The BA-10 was to become the definitive model of the BA series, with the original BA-10 design being again modernized in 1939

SPECIFICATIONS BA-9

Design bureau: Izhorskiy OKB
Crew: 4
Manufacturing plant: Izhorskiy zavod
Service date: 1937 (Prototype)
Combat weight: 4,500kg

Dimensions: (m)
Length: 4.635
Width: 2.30
Height: 2.15
Wheelbase: 3.34
Track width: 1.41m (f) 1.42m (r)
Ground clearance: 0.235

Armor: (mm)
Hull front: 8-10
Hull sides: 8
Turret front: 8-10
Turret sides: 8

Armament:
Main armament: 12.7mm DShK/? rounds
Secondary armament: 7.62mm DT
Firing height: NA
Elevation/depression: NA

Traverse: 360°

Automotive:
Type: GAZ-M1
Capacity: 3,285cm³
Cylinders: 4
Power output: 50hp (37kW) @ 2,800rpm
Fuel type/capacity: Petrol/112 liters
Transmission: 4F 1R x 2
Steering: NA
Tires: 6.50-20
Brakes: Mechanical, drums on all wheels
Radio: 71-TK-1

Performance:
Maximum road speed (km/h): 55
Maximum terrain speed (km/h): NA
Road range (km): 180-230
Terrain range (km): 150-170
Power/weight ratio: 11.1hp (8.3kW)/tonne
Ground pressure: 3.1kg/cm²
Gradient: 24°
Trench: 0.6m
Fording: 0.8m

as the BA-10M. The BA-10 was numerically the most significant of the BA heavy armored car series produced at the Izhorskiy zavod; some 1,400 BA-10/BA-10Ms being manufactured over a three-year period.

The BA-10 was used during the battles of the Khalkin-Gol against Japan in the summer of 1939, during the invasion of Poland and Finland and in the opening stages of the 1941-45 "Great Patriotic War." In addition to service with the Red Army, a total of twenty-three BA-10/10M vehicles were taken into Finnish Army service under the designation Ps25, 26, and 27. The German Army made use of captured BA-10s after 1941, though the German designation system did not distinguish between the BA-6, 10, and 10M heavy armored cars, all receiving the German designation Panzerspahwagen BA-203 (r).

Description

The BA-10 was initially armed with the 45mm M-1934 tank gun. On later production vehicles this gun was replaced with the modified 45mm M-1938 which was simpler to manufacture (having less parts) and had improved optical sights.

The BA-10 was built from 1938 on the GAZ-AAA chassis. To accommodate the BA-10 armored car body, the chassis was shortened 20cm in the center and the rear chassis legs were shortened an additional 40cm.

The hull and turret of the BA-10 were all of welded steel construction. The gun mounted in its new conical turret had a traverse of 360°, elevation of +20° and depression of -2°. Ammunition stowage was reduced to forty-three rounds due to the smaller turret and other internal changes. Secondary armament consisted of two 7.62mm DT machine guns, one mounted co-axially with the main armament, the other ball-mounted in the fighting compartment front. Some BA-10s were fitted with an external armored mantlet for the hull machine gun.

The BA-10 had similar overall road and all terrain performance to the BA-10. Like all BA heavy armored cars it was fitted with "overall" tracks when required. These tracks were stowed at the rear of the vehicle when not in use. In addition to the standard drum brakes used on the BA-10, the vehicle was also fitted with a transmission brake.

The fuel tank, which was mounted below the hull rear, was protected by an armor plate which projected below the hull. The BA-10's vulnerable headlights were

BA-10 and BA-10M in Schlisselburg, Leningradskaya Oblast, January 1943. The BA-10 on the right is fitted with "overall" tracks and still retains the original rear toolbox on its mounting bracket. **(V. Tarasevich)**

SPECIFICATIONS BA-10

Design bureau: Izhorskiy OKB
Crew: 4
Manufacturing plant: Izhorskiy zavod
Service date: 1938
Combat weight: 5,140kg

Dimensions: (m)
Length: 4.655
Width: 2.070
Height: 2.210
Wheelbase: 3.00
Track width: 1.41 (f) 1.42 (r)
Ground clearance: 0.23

Armor: (mm)
Hull front: 10 (glacis 10-15)
Hull sides: 10
Hull rear: 6-10
Hull roof: 6
Hull floor: 4
Turret front: 10
Turret sides: 10

Armament:
Main armament: 45mm M-1934-38/49
Secondary armament: 2x7.62mm DT/2,079

Firing height: NA
Elevation/depression: +20°/-2°

Automotive:
Type: GAZ-M1
Capacity: 3,285cm³
Cylinders: 4
Power output: 52hp (38kW) @ 2,800rpm
Fuel type/capacity: Petrol/118 liters
Transmission: 4F 1R
Steering: Rack & pinion
Tires: 6.50 - 20 GK combat tires
Brakes: Drums on all wheels, transmission brake
Radio: 71-TK-1

Performance:
Maximum road speed (km/h): 53
Maximum terrain speed (km/h): NA
Road range (km): 260-300
Terrain range (km): 180-200
Power/weight ratio: 10.1hp (7.5kW)/tonne
Ground pressure: 2.8kg/cm²
Gradient: 24°
Trench: NA
Fording: 0.6m

Russian BA-10s in Poland, 1939. Both vehicles are carrying tracks and additional spare track links on the rear wheel guards. (Tank Museum, Bovington, UK. Ref: 3708/G5)

Russian BA-10s in Poland, 1939. Note the ribbed turret mantlet on the BA-10 in the background. (Tank Museum, Bovington, UK. Ref: 241/C3)

BA-10s in Vyborg, 1944. All vehicles are travelling with their engine covers open, as was common during the summer months.

A BA-10 leads a convoy of BA-6s during the battle of Moscow, November 1941.

ABOVE: BA-10 ZhD and BA-20M ZhD rail scout vehicles. The BA-10 was rarely seen configured as a rail scout vehicle, as here, escorting an armored train.

RIGHT and BELOW: These BA-10 turrets, recovered in Finland and currently held at the Parola Tank Museum workshops, give a good view of the turret roof detail on the BA-10.

BA-10s in Schlisselburg, Leningradskaya Oblast, January 1943. From left to right the vehicles are a BA-10 (all white), a BA-10M (№471, vehicle №2), and another BA-10 (№476, vehicle №1). These vehicles are fitted with "overall" tracks.

BA-10s assemble for a Red Square parade. The left column consists of BA-10s with a column of BA-10Ms on the right. Note the difference in track stowage between the vehicles. The BA-10Ms are fitted with a rear shelf bracket on which the tracks are mounted. These vehicles also show the standard tool box and jack mounting points.

BA-10 commander, Leningrad front, October 1941.

BA-10 ZhD. A rare photograph of the BA-10ZhD. The road wheels on the leading rear axle were not removed during conversion to rail mode.

often fitted with distinctive armored covers in action. A small distinguishing feature of the BA-10 was the replacement of the front towing hooks used on earlier vehicles with small "D" shackles.

A 71-TK-1 radio was fitted as standard on the BA-10 series.

BA-10 ZhD

A small series of BA-10 ZhD vehicles was produced in 1938 for rail scout purposes, utilizing the same principle as the earlier BA-6ZhD.

BA-10M Heavy Armored Car

The BA-10 series underwent a further modernization program in 1939, resulting in an improved model which was designated BA-10M.

The BA-10M was, at 5,360kg, approximately 300kg heavier than the earlier BA-10, with most of the additional weight being given over to additional armor for vulnerable areas. Despite the weight increase, overall vehicle performance was not significantly affected.

A 45mm M-1934/38 tank gun was installed in the turret of the BA-10M. This gun had been introduced on the later BA-10 vehicles, being simpler to produce than the earlier 45mm M-1934, and featured minor optical improvements. Other internal improvements on the BA-10 included the installation of a new 71-TK-3 transmitter/receiver.

The BA-10M was externally very similar to the earlier BA-10 model and the two models are frequently misidentified. The primary distinguishing feature of the BA-10M is the boxes mounted above the rear wheels. Contrary to popular belief, these boxes were not used for track stowage, being physically too small but were in fact reserve fuel tanks. The tracks on the BA-10M were stowed at the rear of the BA-10M on a special support bracket welded on the vehicle rear for the purpose. In action the tracks were sometimes strapped to the top of the rear fuel tanks.

The BA-10M saw action in the Far East against Japan in 1939, during the invasion of Poland, in Finland in 1940, and in the early stages of World War II.

SPECIFICATIONS BA-10M

Design bureau: Izhorskiy OKB
Crew: 4
Manufacturing plant: Izhorskiy zavod
Service date: 1939 series produced
Combat weight: 5,360kg

Dimensions: (m)
Length: 4.65
Width: 2.07
Height: 2.19
Wheelbase: 3.00
Track width: 1.41 (f) 1.42 (r)
Ground clearance: 0.22

Armor: (mm)
Hull front: 10 (Glacis 10-15)
Hull sides: 6
Hull rear: 6
Hull roof: 6
Hull floor: 4
Turret front: 10

Armament:
Main armament: 45mm M-1934-38/49
Secondary armament: 2x7.62mm DT/2,079
Firing height: NA

Elevation/depression: +20°/-2°
Traverse: 360°

Automotive:
Type: GAZ-M1
Capacity: 3,285cm^2
Cylinders: 4
Power output: 52hp (37kW) @ 2,800rpm
Fuel type/capacity: Petrol/118 liters plus a reserve tank (quantity not known)
Transmission: 4F 1R
Steering: Rack & pinion
Tires: 650-20 GK combat tires
Brakes: Drums on all wheels, transmission brake
Radio: 71-TK-1 or 71-TK-3

Performance:
Maximum road speed (km/h): 53-55
Maximum terrain speed (km/h): NA
Road range (km): 300
Terrain range (km): 210
Power/weight ratio: 9.37hp (7.2kW)/tonne
Ground pressure: NA
Gradient: 20°
Trench :0.35m
Fording: 0.6m

BA-10M in "Fighter's Square", Stalingrad, August 1942. The additional fuel tanks above the rear wheels distiniguish the BA-10M from the earlier BA-10. Note also the headlight covers. (Photographer: E. Evzerikhin)

BA-10Ms on patrol. Note the "overall" tracks and tarpaulin stowed at the rear of the vehicle.

BA-10M and T-34 M-1941, 1st Guards Tank Brigade, Western front, January 1942. (Photographer: T. Tarasevich)

A BA-10M and KV-2 M-1940 heavy tank abandoned in June 1941. (Photographer: Roth)

A destroyed BA-10M, summer 1941. The spare track links are stowed on top of the side fuel tanks in this view. Note also the machine gun mantlet. (Jochen Vollert collection)

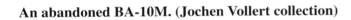

An abandoned BA-10M. (Jochen Vollert collection)

A completely destroyed BA-10M pictured in 1941. (Jochen Vollert collection)

BA-10Ms on the Western front, 1943. (Photographer: Chernov)

BA-10Ms on the Western front, 1943. (Chernov)

BA-10M on a forest track, 1943. Note the prominent fuel tanks on the BA-10M. (Soviet State Cine and Photograph Archives)

BA-10M in Turki, Carpathian region, 1944.

BA-10Ms in Schlisselberg, 13th March 1943. (V. Kinelovsky)

A BA-10M on the streets of Schlisselburg, 20th January 1943. This BA-10M is fitted with "overall" tracks.

BA-10M Number I-36. (Konovalov)

BA-10M. This vehicle has an external mantlet for the 7.62mm machine gun which was fitted to later BA-10Ms.

BA-10M, Western front, winter 1942-43. Note the air identification triangle painted on the turret roof. It is clear from this photo that the tracks were not stored in the side fuel tanks as sometimes referred to in the West. They were physically too large, being strapped on top, as seen here, or at the rear of the vehicle. Note also the external machine gun mantlet.

A BA-10M totally engulfed in flames. The all-too-common fate of Russian armored cars, completely destroyed by internal explosions. Many war-time photographs attest to the BA-10 series in particular being literally blown apart by their exploding 45mm ammunition. (Tank Museum, Bovington, UK. Ref: 2946/A6)

BA-10M in Vyazma, March 1943. Vyazma was the scene of bitter fighting, including an abortive Soviet airborne attempt to recapture the town which claimed the lives of over twenty thousand Russian airborne soldiers. The BA-10M is seen here after the town's final liberation in early 1943.

BA-10Ms on the Leningrad front, winter 1941. These vehicles are freshly painted in winter camouflage. The "overall" tracks and tarpaulins are stowed at the rear of each vehicle. (Photographer: Konov)

BA-10Ms in convoy.

BA-10M at the Parola Tank Museum, Finland. (Esa Muikku.)

BA-10M at the Parola Tank Museum, Finland. (Esa Muikku.)

The BA-10M preserved at Parola was fitted with a Ford V-8 engine to maintain the vehicle in running order. Consequently. the front axle has been moved rearward slightly in comparison with the standard GAZ-AA engined vehicle. (Esa Muikku.)

The BA-10M at Parola Tank Museum in 1999. The BA-10M and BA-20 have recently been moved within the museum building to better protect them from the elements.

Moving to the front, March 1943. The lead vehicle, commanded by Guards major A.I. Kolotiy, is a BA-6, followed by a mixed column including a BA-10M, BA-10, and BA-6. Photo credit: TASS (Photographer: D. Chernov)

Production of the BA-10M continued well after the outbreak of war with Germany, with a total of 331 BA-10M's being built after June 1941.

The BA-10M was particularly numerous, with some 1,400 BA-10/10Ms being produced in total.

BA-10M ZhD

A small number of ZhD rail scout vehicles were produced in the BA-10 series, the system being a modification of the standard BA-10M rather than a purpose built variant. When not in use, the BA-10M ZhD's steel flanged rail wheels were stowed two at the rear of the vehicle and one on each stub axle located on the engine compartment sides. The BA-10M ZhD had a combat weight of 5,800kg due to the weight of the steel wheels and additional ammunition load carried.

BA-11 Heavy Armored Car

In 1935 the Moskovsky Avto Zavod imeni Stalina (ZiS) in Moscow had worked with the Izhorskiy Plant at Kolpino near Leningrad to develop the BA-5 8,000kg class heavy armored car. The BA-5 had many interesting features, including heavy armament (consisting of a 45mm M-1934 tank gun and three 7.62mm DT machine guns), large ammunition complement (114 rounds), and two driver stations, allowing the vehicle to be driven in either direction.

The prototype BA-5 had been field trialled in late 1935 at the NIIBT Polygon at Kubinka, near Moscow,

but was deemed underpowered and complex for an armored car. The BA-5 had required a crew of five, the same as that required by a contemporary medium or heavy tank. It was not therefore recommended for series production.

For the remainder of the decade, the Izhorskiy armor plant continued to work primarily with GAZ in Gorkiy, which provided the chassis and automotive components for the BA heavy armored car series for which the Izhorskiy plant manufactured the armored bodies and turrets and undertook final assembly. However, design work began at the Izhorskiy plant as early as 1936-37 on a new 8,000kg class design on a ZiS chassis, in effect continuing the BA-5 program of 1935. The new heavy armored car was eventually to be known as the BA-11.

Development of a new chassis suitable to mount the BA-11 hull and turret was entrusted to the direction of engineer A.S. Aizenberg at ZiS, who also had responsibility for the final assembly of the vehicle on its ZiS chassis at the Izhorskiy plant. He was aided by a development team including D.V. Salomatin, B.M. Fitterman, and V.N. Smolin. The BA-11 team may have taken some ideas from the Landsverk 181 armored car developed in Sweden in 1933, and the German SdKfz 231 developed in 1936, to both of which the BA-11 bears some resemblance.

A new heavy 6x4 chassis designated ZiS-34 was developed by ZiS for the BA-11, modified from the experimental ZiS-6K chassis. The new ZiS-34 chassis was completed in 1938 and several were delivered to the Izhorskiy plant for mating to the BA-11 hull.

While designers at ZiS worked on the chassis and automotive components, the Izhorskiy plant set up a design team under the direction of A.N. Baranov which worked concurrently on developing the armored hull and turret for the new design. Although superficially resembling a modified BA-10M, the BA-11 was an entirely new design with few links to the GAZ-based BA series. The BA-11 had a new ZiS sourced chassis, engine, and

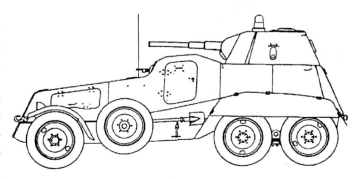

BA-11 heavy armored car.

transmission. The armored hull and turret were also entirely new and the vehicle was considerably larger overall and had better hull armor slope when compared with the BA-6 and BA-10 series.

Main armament used on the BA-11 was the 45mm M-1934 tank gun with a co-axial 7.62mm DT machine gun and a second DT machine gun in the front right side of the fighting compartment. The BA-11 carried a considerable amount of ammunition, the 114 rounds carried on board providing a significant increase in combat endurance compared with its predecessors.

Two prototypes were manufactured in 1938 under Baranov's direction and these were completed at the end of the year. They immediately underwent successful GABTU evaluation trials at the NIIBT Polygon at Kubinka, after which the BA-11 was accepted for service with the Red Army. At the time of its introduction, the BA-11 was one of the most heavily armed and armored cars in the world.

Unfortunately, production of the BA-11 was not given a high priority and between 1940 and the outbreak of war in June 1941. Only sixteen BA-11s were built and delivered to the Red Army. The vehicles were used on the Leningrad Front and most were destroyed in the opening weeks of the conflict.

Side view of a BA-11. The ZIS-6 origin wheels are evident in this view.

Description

The BA-11 was developed on the short wheelbase 6x4 ZiS-34 chassis, derived from the ZiS-6 which had been in production at the Moskovskiy Avto Zavod imeni Stalina (ZiS) from 1934. The ZIS-34 frame was shortened by 350mm from the standard ZiS-6 chassis.

The BA-11 had a highly faceted hull (more so than appears obvious in photographs) on which was mounted a new turret similar but not identical to that fitted on the BA-10M. The hull of the BA-11 was wider and proportionally larger compared with the concurrent BA-10/BA-10M. The welded armor was made of sheets 4, 8, 10, and 13mm in thickness and the hull shape maximized ballistic protection with armor angled away from the vehicle centerline. The frontal armor basis was 13mm (possibly 18mm on the turret front) which compared favorably with most contemporary Russian and German light tanks.

The vehicle was powered by a six-cylinder ZiS-16 petrol engine developing 93-99hp (69-74kW), double that afforded any previous Russian heavy armored car. This power output provided good cross country capability and a high road speed of 64km/hour despite the vehicle's combat weight which exceeded 8,100kg. The higher power output figure for the ZiS-16 engine used in the BA-11 was achieved with the engine fitted with an aluminium cylinder head.

The BA-11 featured several novel concepts in its design. A complex transfer box arrangement in the transmission provided the vehicle with nine forward and six reverse gears with a maximum reverse speed which approached ninety percent of forward speed. Other minor details were a ball-mounted radio antenna which could be swung back along the hull side for safety and feelers mounted on the front wheel arches to allow the driver to judge distances better when maneuvering in confined spaces. These feelers are still mounted on some Russian military vehicles today.

Battlefield survivability was increased by the use of GK combat tires with a unique form of military tread. The ubiquitous "overall" tracks were provided for use in soft ground. The vehicle carried two spare wheels which were mounted forward of the crew doors on free-spinning hubs which also aided trench crossing capability.

BA-11D Heavy Armored Car

Soon after the introduction of the BA-11 in 1939, a group of engineers at ZiS in Moscow, led by P.V. Smetannikov, began work on a new diesel engine; the ZiS-D-7. This new engine developed 96-98hp (72-74kW) @ 2,200rpm and was as such no more powerful than the petrol engined variant. However, the use of diesel fuel gave the vehicle an extended range of 420km with the same 150 liter fuel tank capacity as the petrol BA-11, while also having the advantage of being less likely to ignite if the vehicle was damaged in combat.

In 1940, engineers at ZiS mounted the new six-cylinder ZiS-D-7 diesel engine on a modified ZiS-34D chassis and after evaluation, the chassis was mated with a standard Izhorskiy BA-11 armored body and turret in

BA-11 rear detail view. Note the "overall" track pattern and its stowage. (M. Baryatinsky)

BA-11 during field trials. This BA-11 has an unusual camouflage scheme and is fitted with splash guards on the rear wheels. (M. Baryatinsky)

BA-11 during evaluation trials. The frontal armor pattern, tire treads, and other minor details differ from the other known variant of the BA-11. (M. Baryatinsky)

SPECIFICATIONS BA-11

Design bureau: ZiS OKB
Crew: 4
Manufacturing plant: Izhorskiy
Service date: 1939 series produced
Combat weight: 8,130kg

Dimensions: (m)
Length: 5.295
Width: 2.390
Height: 2.490
Wheelbase: 3.55
Track width: NA
Ground clearance: 0.292

Armor: (mm)
Hull front: 13 (18?)
Hull sides: 10-13
Hull roof: 8
Hull floor: 4
Turret front: 13-18
Turret sides: 13

Armament:
Main armament: 45mm M-1934/114
Secondary armament: 2 x 7.62mm DT/3,087
Firing height: NA

Elevation/depression: NA
Traverse: 360º

Automotive:
Type: ZiS-16
Cylinders: 6
Power output: 93-99hp (69-74kW)
Fuel type/capacity: Petrol/150 liters
Transmission: 9F 6R through transfer box
Steering: Rack & pinion
Tires: 34.00 - 7.00 GK bulletproof tires
Brakes: NA
Radio: 71-TK-1

Performance:
Maximum road speed (km/h): 64
Maximum terrain speed (km/h): NA
Road range (km): 316
Terrain range (km): 178
Power/weight ratio: 12.2hp (9.10kW)/tonne
Ground pressure: 4.25kg/cm²
Gradient: 22º
Side slope: 14º
Trench: 0.5
Fording: 0.65

BA-11 heavy armored car.

early 1940. The resulting armored car was designated, unsurprisingly, BA-11D (diesel).

Fitted with the ZiS-D-7 diesel engine, the BA-11D had a combat weight of 8,650kg, some 500kg heavier than the petrol-engined BA-11. The BA-11D was, as a result, slightly slower than the BA-11, however, the 48km/hour road speed was considered more than adequate for a heavy armored car.

The BA-11D was accepted for series production, but only six were completed in the autumn of 1940. The BA-11D was externally identical to the petrol variant, though radiator armor patterns varied. The BA-11D was significant in being the first Soviet diesel-powered armored car to enter service with the Red Army. All were destroyed on the Leningrad Front in the opening weeks of Operation Barbarossa in 1941.

Improvised Armored Cars

During the siege of Leningrad, a small number of military vehicles were converted within the city for use as mobile artillery. A number of ZiS-5 vehicles had an armored cab and partially armored cargo body added. They were normally armed with 45mm guns although several variations existed. Some of these improvised armored vehicles were fitted with a hull machine gun next to the driver in a mounting similar to that used on the BA-6/10 series of heavy armored cars.

The exact number of these armored vehicles produced is not known, though they were used on the Leningrad Front in small numbers. Conversions may also have been made on other vehicle chassis although the ZiS-5 was the most commonly seen.

SPECIFICATIONS BA-11D

Design bureau: ZiS OKB
Crew: 4
Manufacturing plant: Izhorskiy
Service date: 1940 series produced
Combat weight: 8,650kg

Dimensions: (m)
Length: 5.295
Width: 2.390
Height: 2.490
Wheelbase: NA
Track width: NA
Ground clearance: 0.292

Armor: (mm)
Hull front: 13
Hull sides: 10-13
Hull roof: 8
Hull floor: 4
Turret front: 13-18
Turret sides: 13

Armament:
Main armament: 45mm M-1934/114

Secondary armament: 2x7.62mm DT/3,087

Automotive:
Type: ZiS-D-7
Cylinders: 6
Power output: 96-98hp (72-74kW)
Fuel type/capacity: Diesel/150 liters
Transmission: 9F 6R via transfer box
Steering: Rack & pinion
Tires: 34.00 - 7.00 GK bulletproof tires
Brakes: NA
Radio: 71-TK-3

Performance:
Maximum road speed (km/h): 48
Maximum terrain speed (km/h): NA
Road range (km): 420
Terrain range (km): NA
Power/weight ratio: 11.3hp (8.3kW)/tonne
Ground pressure: 4.50kg/cm^2
Gradient: 22°
Side slope: 14°
Trench: 0.5m
Fording: 0.65m

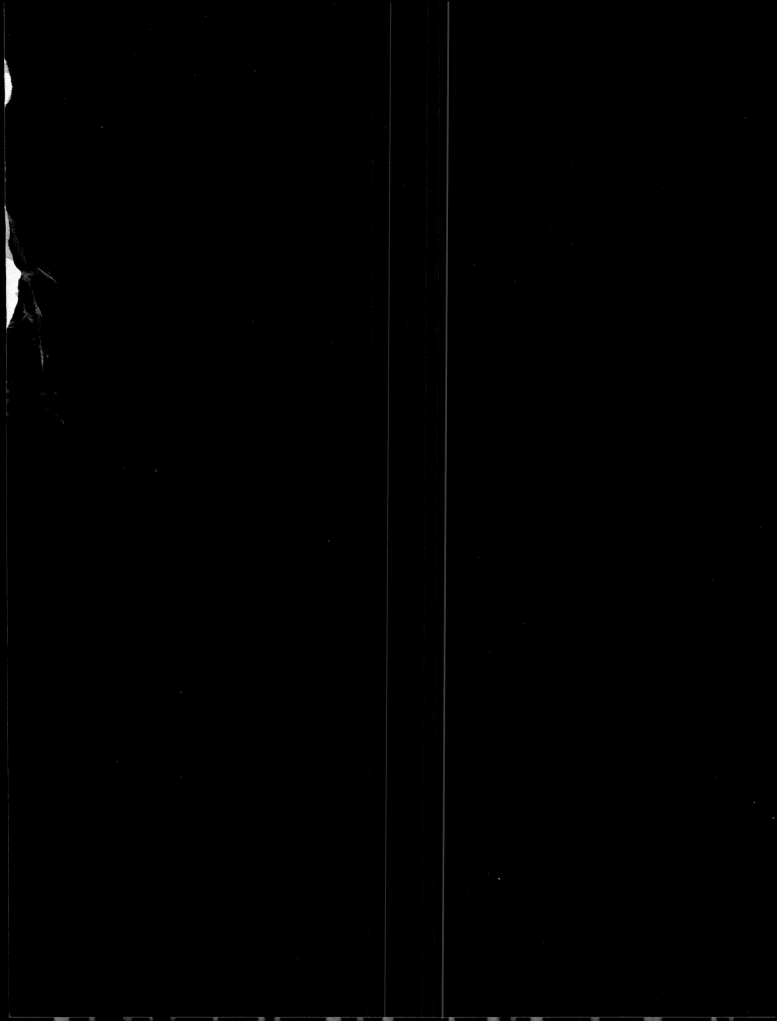

4
Specialized Armored Vehicles 1930-1945

BAD

BAD-2

PB-4

PB-7

B-3 half-track

BA-30 half-track

BA-22 armored ambulance

KSP-76 wheeled SPG

BAD Armored Car

The experimental twin turreted BAD (Brone Avto Drezine) was developed and produced in 1932 at the Bolshevik Plant in Leningrad as an armored car intended for long range reconnaissance roles. The BAD, which was latterly also known as the BAD-1, was built on either an elongated AMO F-15 4x2 chassis or, according to some sources, on the Ford-AA chassis. Both chassis may have been used, as in 1932 the AMO F-15 was being replaced in production by the Ford AA (GAZ-AA) in Moscow and the GAZ-AA was also entering production at the new Gorkiy Avtomobilniy Zavod (GAZ) during 1932.

The BAD had a narrow crew compartment with vertical sides and a wider box section lower half which extended out over the front and rear wheels, providing armored protection for the wheels and tires. The wide lower box sections may have been intended to provide buoyancy for a contemplated amphibious role. The BAD had a very narrow front wheel track, which when coupled with its narrow tires, resulted in limited all-terrain mobility.

The armament arrangement was similar to that of a warship deck, the main turret being mounted on a raised superstructure and armed with a ball mounted 7.62mm DT machine gun, while an identical rear turret with 270º traverse also mounted a 7.62mm DT machine gun. A third DT machine gun was ball-mounted to the right of the driver.

The BAD was built in small numbers for trials purposes but no further production was undertaken. Despite the name, which might suggest that its role might include operation as a rail scout car, the BAD appears according to available Russian sources to have had neither the capability to operate as a rail scout nor was it amphibious.

BAD-2 Amphibious Armored Car

Russia has a large number of small rivers and lakes, particularly on its western borders, and in the 1930s most rural bridges were of wooden construction and not all could carry the weight of an AFV. Consequently, considerable effort was expended in the 1930s towards developing amphibious tanks to overcome these obstacles. Experimental and limited production amphibious versions of T-26 and BT tanks were developed in the early 1930s, these latterly being replaced by purpose designed amphibious tanks such as the T-37, T-38, and T-40 series. This interest in water crossing capability also extended to armored car designs and the BAD-2 (Brone Avto Drezina-2) was the first successful attempt in Russia to develop an amphibious armored car.

Designing an amphibious armored car required much

BAD armored car. The BAD had a twin deck armament arrangement providing good firepower. There is some doubt as to whether the BAD was originally designed to be amphibious or not. (M. Baryatinsky)

**BAD, front view.
(M. Baryatinsky)**

**BAD, rear view.
(M. Baryatinsky)**

BAD, side view. The turrets are of identical design. The wide body, wheel covers, and overall design suggest that the BAD was intended to be an amphibious vehicle. However, available Russian sources do not confirm the vehicle as having had such a capability. (M. Baryatinsky)

The BAD-2 is shown fitted with "overall" tracks on the rear wheels.

This rare photograph shows the BAD-2 ZhD configured as a rail scout vehicle.

more engineering effort than required for an amphibious tank and a team was therefore assembled at the Izhorsky plant in Leningrad in early 1932 to specifically investigate amphibious armored car development, under the direction of senior project engineer N.Ya Obukhov.

Armored cars in the early 1930s had several inherent disadvantages in comparison with tanks when being considered for amphibious vehicle roles. In particular, it proved difficult to manufacture a vehicle with adequate amphibious characteristics while retaining acceptable overall dimensions, as armored cars of the time had a high center of gravity while their chassis, with wheels and wheel arches, were not particularly streamlined in water. Amphibious light tanks also had an advantage over armored cars because in addition to their more flatter boat-like shape and consequent better stability in water, their tracks aided both water propulsion and egress from soft riverbanks.

As a result of their investigations, Obukhov's team developed the twin-turreted BAD-2 during 1932, the boat-shaped vehicle being mounted on the 6x4 Ford Timken chassis rather than the GAZ-AAA which was being introduced at the KIM and GAZ plants at the time.

Development of the BAD-2 was completed at the end of 1932 and small numbers were produced for long-term evaluation trials of both the vehicle and the general concept of using amphibious reconnaissance vehicles in combat.

The vehicle was shown at the 1st May 1933 parade in Leningrad after which it impressed the military representatives present and the general public with a swimming demonstration across the Neva river. The military officials were generally satisfied with the demonstration but requested that the vehicle program be further continued with a view to increasing reliability of the vehicle and providing more powerful main armament.

The BAD-2 gave the Russian Army claim to having adopted the first gun-armed amphibious armored car in the world. BAD-2 vehicles served with the Russian Army from 1932 to 1934. As this was also the period of Russo-German military cooperation, German tank officers stationed at Kazan also had the opportunity to evaluate the vehicle. The BAD-2 was an effective if ungainly armored car and apparently was reasonably successful during its brief trials service with the Red Army, however, series production was not undertaken.

SPECIFICATIONS BAD-2

Design bureau: OKMO (Izhorskiy)
Crew: 4
Manufacturing plant: Izhorskiy
Service date: 1932 Trials only
Combat weight: 4,600kg

Dimensions: (m)
Length: 5.280m
Width: 2.00m (approx)
Height: 2.36m (approx)
Wheelbase: NA
Track width : NA
Ground clearance: 0.24m

Armor: (mm)
Hull front: 6
Hull sides :4
Turret front: 6
Turret sides: NA

Armament:
Main armament: 37mm Hotchkiss/60
Secondary armament: 2 x 7.62mm DT/3,000
Firing height: NA
Elevation/depression: NA

Traverse: 360°

Engine:
Type: GAZ-AA
Cylinders: 4
Power output: 40hp (30kW)
Fuel type/capacity: Petrol
Transmission: Ford Timken
Steering: Rack & pinion
Tires: 6.50 - 20
Brakes: Mechanical
Electrical system: NA
Radio: 71-TK-1

Performance:
Maximum road speed (km/h): 50
Maximum terrain speed (km/h): NA
Road range (km):NA
Terrain range (km): NA
Power/weight ratio: 8.7hp (6.49kW)/tonne
Ground pressure: NA
Gradient: NA
Trench: NA
Fording: Amphibious @ 6km/hour

BAD-2 amphibious armored car. The BAD-2 retained the turret arrangement of the original BAD-1, but the longer wheelbase allowed for a better proportioned boat shaped hull.

Description

The BAD-2 had a boat-shaped hull with a rounded nose surmounted by a twin turret arrangement as earlier used on the BAD, but with a 37mm gun in the main turret and a 7.62mm DT machine gun in the smaller subsidiary turret at the rear. As with the BAD, a further DT machine gun was mounted in the front of the crew compartment to the right of the driver. The hull and turret were of all-welded construction using 6mm armored sheet as a basis. The use of all-welded armor was rare in 1932 but was considered essential for providing a relatively watertight hull. The rear wheels were covered with plates to reduce turbulence in water, while the front wheels, by which the vehicle maneuvered in water (by turning them in the appropriate direction), remained exposed.

The BAD-2 was driven in water by a small propeller which gave the vehicle a water speed of 6km/hour. Bilge pumps were fitted within the vehicle hull and were always required when the vehicle was waterborne as the watertight seals for the wheels and propeller shaft did not function reliably. To increase the vehicle's poor ability to climb riverbanks when exiting rivers, the rear wheels were provided with the same removable "overall" tracks as fitted to the BA series of heavy armored cars. These were stowed at the rear of the vehicle when not in use.

Unusual for an armored car of the period, the BAD-2 was fitted with two smoke dischargers which allowed the vehicle to retreat under a defensive smoke screen. Each discharger was provided with twenty liters of fuel. Another addition advanced for a contemporary vehicle was the installation of a 71-TK-1 radio as standard.

The BAD-2 could also be modified for use as a rail scout. The standard wheels and tires could be replaced with steel flanged rail wheels and when modified the vehicle was referred to as the BAD-2 ZhD. The BAD-2 ZhD could travel at up to 65km/hour on rails.

PB-4 Amphibious Armored Car

During the 1930s the Russian Army made many attempts to develop amphibious light tanks, including the T-37 and T-38 which were series produced in large numbers. This amphibious capability requirement had also been investigated with the BAD-2 in an effort to also provide armored cars with better overall capability in the reconnaissance role.

The Izhorskiy design bureau returned to the amphibious armored car concept in 1935 and using the experience gained during trials of the earlier BAD-2 some three years before a new amphibious armored car design was developed, designated the PB-4 (Plavayushiy Broneavtomobil 4 - Amphibious Armored Car-4). The numbering sequence would suggest that there was a third intermediate design, the BAD-3 or PB-3, but no documented evidence is available on such a vehicle having been developed.

The PB-4 was developed at Izhorskiy based on the

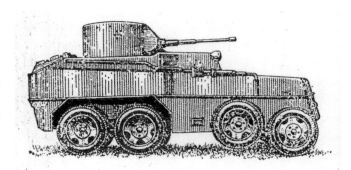

The PB-4 amphibious armored car.

BA-3 heavy armored car. It was produced in small numbers for state evaluation trials which demonstrated the PB-4 to be an effective armored car, however, its engine was underpowered and the vehicle consequently slow on roads, while its amphibious role was limited by poor water speed and maneuverability. It also suffered the same problems as the BAD-2, frequently bogging down when attempting to exit anything but shallow, firm river banks.

The PB-4 was a significant improvement on earlier Russian attempts to develop an amphibious armored car, but during state evaluation trials it was judged overall to be an unreliable vehicle which was heavy and underpowered for its intended role. Series production was not therefore approved and work continued at Izhorsky on developing a better proportioned vehicle which required to be lighter and more maneuverable, resulting in the PB-7 which was completed in early 1937.

A prototype PB-4 remains preserved today, displayed at the NIIBT museum, Kubinka, near Moscow.

Description

The PB-4 was a conventional design, proportionally similar to the BA-3 heavy armored car series on which it was based. The frameless, all-welded hull was built on the Ford Timken or GAZ-AAA 6x4 truck chassis. The vehicle was somewhat ungainly, with high hull sides relative to its narrow width. The PB-4 had an armor basis of 7mm.

The turret and armament used on the PB-4 was originally taken from the T-26 light tank and was identical to the arrangement used on the BA-3 but without the turret bustle. The 45mm M-1932 tank gun had a useful ammunition complement of fifty-two rounds. A co-axial 7.62mm DT machine gun was mounted in the turret with a further 7.62mm DT machine gun was located alongside the driver in the front superstructure. 2,268 rounds of 7.62mm ammunition were carried on board.

The vehicle was powered by a standard GAZ-AA 4 cylinder engine developing 40hp (30kW) which gave reasonable overall performance on land, however, the PB-4 suffered from the same maneuverability problems as its predecessors, particularly when leaving rivers and climbing steep or soft river banks. To overcome this, the standard "overall" tracks used on the BA series were fitted over the rear wheels when needed and stowed at the

---

SPECIFICATIONS PB-4

Design bureau: Izhorskiy OKB
Crew: 4
Manufacturing plant: Izhorskiy zavod
Service date: 1935 (small series)
Combat weight: 5,280kg

Dimensions: (m)
Length: 5.30
Width: 1.98
Height: 2.255
Wheelbase: 3.150
Track width: NA
Ground clearance: 0.254-0.275

Armor: (mm)
Hull front: 7
Hull sides: 7
Hull roof: 5
Hull floor: 4
Turret front: 7
Turret sides: NA

Armament:
Main armament: 45mm M-1932/52 rounds
Secondary armament: 2x7.62mm DT/2,268

Firing height: NA
Elevation/depression: +20° /-2°

Automotive:
Type: GAZ-AA
Cylinders: 4
Power output: 40hp (30kW) @ 2,200 rpm
Fuel type/capacity: Petrol/72 liters
Transmission: 4F 1R x 2
Steering: Rack and pinion
Tires: 6.50 - 20
Brakes: Mechanical drums on all wheels
Radio: Not fitted

Performance:
Maximum road speed (km/h): 50
Maximum terrain speed (km/h): NA
Road range (km): 200
Terrain range (km): 140
Power/weight ratio: 7.57hp (5.65kW)/tonne
Ground pressure: NA
Gradient: 15°
Trench: NA
Fording: Amphibious @ 4-5km/hour

PB-4 amphibious armored car. (Tank Museum, Bovington, UK. Ref: 3201/F5)

PB-4 at NIIBT Tank Museum Kubinka, near Moscow.

PB-4 at the NIIBT Museum, Kubinka. Note the flotation tanks and the exhaust system running up the side of the vehicle.

PB-4, NIIBT Museum Kubinka Note the vertical slab sides of the PB-4, which arevery apparent in this view.

Overhead view of the PB-4 at NIIBT Museum, Kubinka.

PB-4 engine compartment. Note the two-piece driver's hatch, folded forward in this view. The reason for the odd dual stowage arrangement of the spare wheels is not known.

PB-4 turret and upper superstructure.

PB-4 rear superstructure and turret rear.

PB-4 hull rear. The propeller has been removed but the mechanical power take-off (PTO) from the rear transmission is evident here.

PB-4 general view. The PB-4's turret is unique and does not feature the turret bustle of the BA-3 and BA-6 armored cars.

PB-4 at the NIIBT Kubinka Tank Museum, Moscow. The free-rotating spare wheels were used to assist in clearing obstacles. Note the prominent exhaust pipe located well above the vehicle waterline.

PB-4. The PB-4 was fitted with double rear wheels, not single as shown on this museum exhibit.

hull rear when not required. The spare wheels were designed to rotate on their lower hull side mounting axles which aided obstacle clearance.

In water the PB-4 was driven by a small three-bladed propeller giving the vehicle an amphibious speed of 4-5km/hour. A design problem with the PB-4 resulted in the power take-off for the propeller not disengaging the drive wheels in water such that they rotated under power causing considerable turbulence which made the vehicle difficult to maneuver and also decreased speed. Pontoons were added to the PB-4 hull sides to increase buoyancy. Steering in water was rudimentary, achieved by moving the front wheels in the appropriate direction. The engine was provided with a heat exchanger (for which the intake was in the vehicle nose) which used the surrounding water to cool the engine when the vehicle was waterborne. The exhaust was routed up right side of the hull to ensure engine breathability under all circumstances.

Note: *Most Russian sources state that the PB-4 was based on the Ford Timken chassis, though the date of manufacture would suggest the GAZ-AAA chassis as more likely. Ford Timken chassis were, however, used in moderate numbers during the early 1930s on other vehicles, such as the SU-12 SPG.*

PB-7 Amphibious Armored Car

The PB-4 amphibian of 1935 was followed by the PB-7 which was developed at the Izhorskiy plant from January 1937. The PB-7 was essentially a rework of the PB-4 design, with a more rationally proportioned hull and turret arrangement and lighter armament, resulting in a vehicle with better armor and amphibious maneuverability than the earlier PB-4, with armament which was not inferior to contemporary amphibious light tanks.

The PB-7 was a much more modern design than the PB-4, based on the well tried and reliable GAZ-AAA chassis which was delivered to the Izhorskiy plant from GAZ for final assembly of the vehicle at Izhorskiy. The vehicle featured a new upper superstructure with the frontal hull and turret armor increased 1mm over that of the PB-4, the increased armor base of 8mm being achieved while actually decreasing the overall weight by 800kg due to the more compact design of the vehicle.

The new conical turret mounted the 12.7mm ShKAS cannon and a co-axial ball mounted DT machine gun, with a secondary 7.62mm DT machine gun installed to right of driver. As with the concurrent BA-9, the use of a 12.7mm heavy caliber machine gun armament was considered acceptable for the PB-7's intended role as a reconnaissance vehicle, particularly as the armor-piercing capability of the 12.7mm weapon compared favorably with the 37mm tank gun which was still in service on many contemporary Russian tanks. With the replacement of the 45mm tank gun used on the PB-4 with a 12.7mm cannon, the crew of the PB-7 was reduced to three, namely commander, driver, and gunner.

The PB-7 was powered by a GAZ-M1 engine developing 50hp (37kW). This power output combined

PB-7 during evaluation trials. The PB-7 was lighter armed than its predecessors but better proportioned for its amphibious role. The "overall" tracks seen fitted here were essential for traversing riverbanks.

The PB-7 amphibious armored car. This photograph has been subjected to Soviet-era photo-retouching. (Tank Museum, Bovington, UK. Ref: 3201/F2)

SPECIFICATIONS PB-7

Design bureau: Izhorskiy OKB
Crew: 3
Manufacturing plant: Izhorskiy zavod
Service date: 1937 (small series)
Combat weight: 4,500kg

Dimensions: (m)
Length: 5.08
Width: 2.15
Height: 2.073
Wheelbase: 3.34
Track width: 1.60
Ground clearance: 0.24m

Armor: (mm)
Hull front: 8
Hull sides: NA
Turret front: 8
Turret sides: 8

Armament:
Main armament: 12.7mm ShKAS/1,000
Secondary armament: 7.62mm (?)
Firing height: NA

Elevation/depression: NA

Traverse: 360°

Automotive:
Type: GAZ-M1
Cylinders: 4
Power output: 50hp (37kW)
Fuel type/capacity: Petrol/45 liters
Transmission: 4F 1R x 2
Steering: Rack and pinion
Tires: 6.50 - 20
Brakes: NA
Radio: No

Performance:
Maximum road speed (km/h): 50-60
Maximum terrain speed (km/h): NA
Road range (km): 120
Terrain range (km): 87
Power/weight ratio: 11.1hp (8.3kW)/tonne
Ground pressure: NA
Gradient: 20°
Trench: NA
Fording: Amphibious

with the reduced combat weight gave the vehicle a power/weight ratio of 11.1hp (8.3kW)/tonne, a substantial improvement over the 7.57hp (5.65kW)/tonne of the earlier PB-4. The vehicle had a very small fuel tank, however, which severely limited range to 120km, and was not particularly useful for a reconnaissance vehicle. As with the earlier PB-4, the exhaust system was run along the side of the vehicle and then mounted well above the waterline.

A small number of PB-7s were produced and extensively field trialled during 1937. The field trials showed the PB-7 to be more maneuverable than its predecessors, with significantly improved amphibious performance, though still not considered adequate for a reconnaissance vehicle. The vehicle suffered the same difficulties as all-wheeled armored cars in that exiting rivers was problematic even when fitted with "overall" tracks. The tracks were stowed along the upper hull sides when not in use.

As a result of field trials, the PB-7 was considered a major improvement over previous designs, but with the exception of road speed the vehicle offered few advantages over amphibious light tanks such as the T-37 which were available to perform the same role. The PB-7 was produced in small numbers for long-term field evalua-

tion trials with the Red Army but the conclusion of these service trials is not known.

Using the standard Russian classification system of the day, the PB-7 would have been categorized as a "light" armored car, as although it had a combat weight of 4,500kg the vehicle was armed with a turret-mounted 12.7mm ShKAS aircraft cannon.

B-3 Half-Track APC

In 1939 the ZiS plant in Moscow developed the B-3 half-track armored personnel carrier (APC) based on the ZiS-22 6x4 chassis. The B-3 was designed primarily as an APC but was also considered for command and reconnaissance duties. The vehicle had a total crew complement of two plus ten infantry in the open rear of the vehicle.

A single prototype of the B-3 half-track armored vehicle was produced and underwent GABTU evaluation trials at the Kubinka Polygon near Moscow. The vehicle, which shared many components with and generally resembled the BA-11 heavy armored car, was powered by a 73hp (55kW) engine, which gave the B-3

SPECIFICATIONS B-3

Design bureau: ZiS
Crew: 2 + 10
Manufacturing plant: ZiS
Service date: 1939 (Trials prototype)
Combat weight: 7,100kg

Dimensions: (m)
Length: 6.53
Width: 2.35
Height: 2.40
Wheelbase: NA
Track width: NA
Ground clearance: 0.33

Armor: (mm)
Hull front: 15
Hull sides: NA
Turret front: NA
Turret sides: NA

Armament:
Main armament: 1x12.7mm DShK
Secondary armament: None
Firing height: NA

Elevation/depression: NA
Traverse: NA

Automotive:
Type: ZiS-16
Cylinders: 6
Power output: 73hp (55kW)
Fuel type/capacity: Petrol/150 liters
Transmission: NA
Steering: Front wheels
Tires: NA
Brakes: Tracks
Radio: No

Performance:
Maximum road speed (km/h): 40
Maximum terrain speed (km/h): NA
Road range (km): 150
Terrain range (km): NA
Power/weight ratio: 10.3hp (7.7kW)/tonne
Ground pressure: 0.3kg/cm2
Gradient: NA
Trench: NA
Fording: NA

B-3 half-track, first prototype.

B-3 half-track, second prototype.

BA-30 half track armored car. Note the unditching wheels on their outriggers and the frame-type radio antenna.

BA-30 rear view. Note the skis mounted on the track guards

with its combat weight of 7,100kg, a maximum speed of only 40km/hour. The B-3 utilized the track mechanism from the T-40 light tank but with the capability of fitting rubber block inserts to the steel tracks. Armament consisted of a single pintle-mounted 12.7mm DShK machine gun provided for defensive armament.

The prototype B-3 was not enthusiastically received during its GABTU trials; the vehicle receiving criticism in particular for its very slow speed. It was decided, however, to field-trial the vehicle in combat conditions and the vehicle was sent to participate in the winter fighting of 1939-40 with Finland. Its performance during this time is not recorded, however, the vehicle was not accepted for series production.

BA-30 Half-Track Armored Car

In 1937 the NATI institute developed an experimental half-track armored car in an attempt to improve the all-terrain capability of the GAZ-produced light BA series of armored cars.

The experimental vehicle, designated BA-30, was based on the chassis of the NATI-3 half-track transporter, also developed at the NATI institute. The all-welded hull was based on the BA-20 armored car but was not identical. The turret was from the early BA-20 and armed with a 7.62mm DT machine gun.

The NATI-3 track mechanism used on the BA-30 consisted of two large and four small wheels and one return roller. The system was essentially that used on the GAZ-60 half-track truck which was used in small numbers by the Red Army. The steel tracks were fitted with rubber inserts.

With a combat weight of 4,600kg, the BA-30 was a light vehicle for an armored half-track and its excellent power-to-weight ratio gave the vehicle good all-terrain

and gradient crossing capability. Steering was by means of the front road wheels over which skis were fitted for operations in snow. The vehicle was classified as a light armored car, despite its weight class.

A small series of BA-30s were built for evaluation purposes and extensively field trialled during 1937. The design was considered as generally acceptable by the Red Army, but was not accepted for series production as the vehicle was heavy for a light armored car and offered few advantages over contemporary, more heavily armed vehicles such as the BA-6, which could be fitted with "overall" tracks when required to attain similar cross-country performance while maintaining acceptable road speed with them removed. The vehicle's good all-terrain performance was also compromised by its slow road speed.

Although the BA-30 was rejected for series production and service with the Red Army the design was considered worth pursuing and several BA-30s were sent to Finland and took part in the Finnish campaign in 1940. The results of these combat evaluation trials is not known.

SPECIFICATIONS BA-30

Design bureau: NATI
Crew: 3
Manufacturing plant: NATI/Vyksinskiy zavod
Service date: 1937 (trials production)
Combat weight: 4,600kg

Dimensions: (m)
Length: 4.94
Width: 2.40
Height: 2.34
Wheelbase: NA
Track width: NA
Ground clearance: 0.30

Armor: (mm)
Hull front: 6
Hull sides: 4-6
Turret front: 6
Turret sides: NA

Armament:
Main armament: 1x7.62mmDT/1,512
Secondary armament: None
Firing height: NA
Elevation/depression: NA

Traverse: 360°

Automotive:
Type: GAZ-M1
Cylinders: 4
Power output: 50hp (37kW)
Fuel type/capacity: Petrol/115 liters
Transmission: NA
Steering: Front wheels
Tires: 7.00 -16
Brakes: Tracks and drums on front wheels
Electrical system:
Radio: 71-TK-1

Performance:
Maximum road speed (km/h): 37-55
Maximum terrain speed (km/h): NA
Road range (km): 253
Terrain range (km): 163
Power/weight ratio: 10.9hp (8.13kW)/tonne
Ground pressure: 0.2kg/cm^2
Gradient: 32°
Trench: NA
Fording: NA

The BA-30 was fitted with a 71-TK-1 radio as standard, with a frame antenna mounted around the upper hull superstructure.

BA-22 Armored Ambulance

In 1939, an armored ambulance version of the BA-10 armored car was developed to prototype stage at the Izhorskiy plant, based on the standard GAZ-AAA chassis and mounting an armored body designed and constructed at Izhorskiy. Primarily intended as an armored battlefield evacuation vehicle, the BA-22 design was also considered as a potential armored personnel carrier.

The BA-22 had a vehicle crew of two (driver and

BA-30 side view. The track mechanism for the BA-30 was taken from the GAZ-60 half-track. Note the skis for the front wheels stowed above the track guards.

BA-30 track mechanism. The use of tarpaulins over vehicles for security purposes during evaluation was and remains standard Russian practice.

BA-22 armored ambulance.

SPECIFICATIONS BA-22

Design bureau: GAZ OKB/Izhorskiy OKB
Crew: 2 + 10
Manufacturing plant: Izhorskiy
Service date: Prototype - 1939
Combat weight: 5,240kg

Dimensions: (m)
Length: 6.10
Width: 1.98
Height: 2.88
Wheelbase:
Track width:
Ground clearance: 0.24

Armor: (mm)
Hull front: 6
Hull sides: 6

Armament:
Main armament: None
Secondary armament: None
Firing height: NA
Elevation/depression: NA

Automotive:
Type: GAZ-AA
Capacity: 3485cm^3
Cylinders: 4
Power output: 40hp (30kW)
Fuel type/capacity: Petrol /109 liters
Transmission: 4F 1R x 2
Steering: NA
Tires: 6.50 - 20 Rear DT
Brakes: Mechanical
Radio: 71-TK-1

Performance:
Maximum road speed (km/h): 40
Maximum terrain speed (km/h): NA
Road range (km): 250
Terrain range (km): NA
Power/weight ratio: 7.7hp (5.7kW)/tonne
Ground pressure: 3.6kg/cm^2
Gradient: 24°
Trench: NA
Fording: NA

BA-22 armored ambulance. The BA-22 was evaluated for service with the Red Army but did not enter seriesproduction.

medic) and could accommodate a maximum of ten sitting wounded.

The vehicle had a high sided hull, made of all-welded 6mm steel plates. Access to the vehicle was by two crew access doors, one either side of the vehicle and a large door at the rear of the vehicle.

With a maximum road speed of 40km/hour, the 6x4 BA-22 was a slow and not particularly agile vehicle, but this was not considered a prime consideration for the vehicle's intended role.

A small series of BA-22 vehicles were built for evaluation trials and these vehicles may have remained in service in 1941. There is photographic evidence of at least one BA-22 in service during the Battle of Stalingrad. No preserved example remains today.

KSP-76 Self Propelled Gun

Throughout the 1941-45 war, Russian military manufacturing concentrated heavily on the development and production of self-propelled guns, usually intended for close-support tank destroyer roles rather than conventional artillery fire support on the field, for which numerous towed weapons existed. In the summer of 1943 the tracked SU-76 light self-propelled gun entered production. Although an adequately armed design and produced in large numbers, the SU-76 was slow, travelling at less than 40km/hour on roads, a major disadvantage in an offensive role.

In August 1943 V.A. Grachev at the GAZ OKB began work began on a wheeled tank destroyer as an alternative to tracked designs. The requirement was for a lightweight, versatile vehicle with identical firepower to the tracked SU-76 but better range and economy of operation. It was also to be capable of deployment with airborne forces.

Design work on the new vehicle, originally known by the factory index 63-SU, was begun on 19th October 1943 by a group of engineers supervised by I.V. Gavalov and A.A. Lipgart while N.A. Astrov assisted in developing the armament and mechanical layout for the new vehicle. The armored hull, weighing 1,140kg, was developed by Y.N. Sorochkin and A.N. Kirilov. In the last weeks of 1943 a wooden model was completed and the 63-SU was given the new factory designation GAZ-68. After studying the model and associated design drawings, the project was approved by the Senior Armoured Directorate of the Red Army (GABTU) on the 7th of February 1944. By the end of April the armored hull was ready and the first example of the new wheeled self-propelled gun was complete by 4th May 1944. In November 1944 the vehicle was road tested at the Kubinka Polygon west of Moscow where the vehicle

KSP-76 during field evaluation trials. This is the only known photo of the KSP-76 during trials.

SPECIFICATIONS KSP-76

Design bureau: GAZ OKB
Crew: 3
Manufacturing plant: GAZ
Service date:Prototype only. 1944
Combat weight: 5,340kg

Dimensions: (m)
Length: 6.36
Width: 2.11
Height: 1.65
Wheelbase: 3.30
Track width: 1.60
Ground clearance: 0.273

Armor: (mm)
Hull front: 16.5
Hull sides: 7
Hull floor: 4

Armament:
Main armament: 76.2mm ZIS-3/54 rounds
Secondary armament: None
Firing height: 0.7m
Elevation/depression: +15°/-3°

Traverse: 37° total

Automotive:
Type: GAZ-11
Cylinders: 6
Power output: 85hp (63.4kW) @ 3,600rpm
Fuel type/capacity: Petrol/140 liters
Transmission: 4F 1R manual
Steering: Rack & pinion
Tires: 10.00-18 All terrain tread
Brakes: Mechanical main and parking
Radio: 12 RT

Performance:
Maximum road speed (km/h): 63-70
Maximum terrain speed (km/h): NA
Road range (km): 300
Terrain range (km): NA
Power/weight ratio: 15.9hp (11.9kW)/tonne
Ground pressure: NA
Gradient: NA
Trench: 0.6m
Fording: 0.9m

achieved a 60km/hour road speed and a reported 500km range. The 63-SU (GAZ-68) was given the Army designation KSP-76 at the time of these trials in late 1944, but it was by then clear that the war was coming to an end and it was not considered appropriate to disrupt SU-76 production at such a time. The KSP-76 did not therefore enter service with the Russian Army and the project was abandoned with preference being given to small tracked SPG's such as the prototype ASU-76 and the series produced ASU-57 in the post-war years.

Built on the chassis of the GAZ-63 4x4 truck (which was designed during the war but did not enter series production until 1946) the KSP-76 consisted of the ubiquitous 76.2mm M-1942 ZIS-3 dual-purpose gun with its standard double baffle muzzle brake mounted in a forward fighting compartment in an armored open vehicle chassis.

Designated as a wheeled self-propelled gun, the KSP-76 was provided with 16mm frontal armor, making it particularly well protected for a wheeled vehicle,

KSP-76 fighting compartment. The KSP-76 was unusual in that the driver sat on the right side of the vehicle, allowing the gunner and loader to work right-handed.

KSP-76 at the NIIBT Museum, Kubinka.

KSP-76 at NIIBT Museum, Kubinka. Note the standard configuration 76.2mm ZiS-3 gun and barrel travel clamp.

Right rear view, KSP-76. The louvered section on the right is the engine exhaust. The engine air intakes are located on the rear internal wall of the fighting compartment.

Left rear view, KSP-76.

KSP-76 overhead view, looking forward.

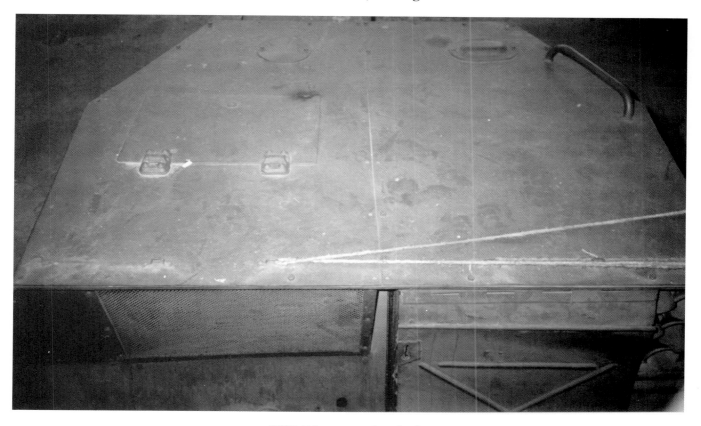

KSP-76 rear engine deck.

reflecting its intended close-support role. The all-welded hull was highly faceted in a similar manner to the BA-64, maximizing deflection of projectiles and shrapnel.

The KSP-76 was significantly more versatile than the tracked SU-76. It had a good road speed of 63-70km/h and a road range of over 300km. Cross country performance was also acceptable, the 4x4 GAZ-63 chassis and cross country tires giving the vehicle good traction on most surfaces.

A single prototype KSP-76 remains today, preserved at the NIIBT Tank Museum at Kubinka near Moscow.

Description

The hull of the KSP-76 was split into three compartments, with the gun mounted at the extreme front of the vehicle, the fighting compartment in the center, and the engine at the rear. The vehicle had a crew of three, consisting of commander/gunner, gunner/loader, and driver who sat to the right of the front fighting compartment in an open seating arrangement. This driving position is almost unique for a Russian AFV and was dictated by the tactical preference to have the loader load the 76.2mm ZIS-3 gun from the left side of the vehicle, using his right hand. The highly faceted armor layout provided the crew adequate protection from small arms fire but the open arrangement gave little protection from overhead shrapnel or the elements.

The 76.2mm M-1942 ZIS-3 dual-purpose gun was fitted in a limited traverse mount (37° total) with 15° elevation and -3° depression. The firing height was only 0.7m, considerably lower than the SU-76M and particularly good for concealment purposes.

The GAZ-63 4x4 chassis provided a highly mobile and stable gun platform. The vehicle was fitted with bulletproof all-terrain tires.

The engine used in the KSP-76 was a tank variant of the 85hp (63.4kW) GAZ-11. The engine and radiator were mounted at the rear of the vehicle, allowing the ordnance to be mounted forward while also decreasing vulnerability of the engine to battle damage. The gearbox was that used with the GAZ-202 engine on the SU-76. The radiator was mounted at the rear of the vehicle and was protected by armored louvers.

The 140 liter fuel tank was located to the left of the engine, with the fifty-four rounds of 76.2mm ammunition located next to the fuel tank, an exceptional arrangement by any standards.

KSP-76 self-propelled gun in the NIIBT Tank Museum at Kubinka.

5
Post-War Armored Cars,
1945-2000

BTR-40

BRDM

BRDM-2

GAZ-3934

GAZ-39344

GAZ-3937

GAZ BP M-97

Lavina/Lavina-M

BTR-40 Armored Scout Vehicle

The first post-war armored car to enter service with the Soviet Army was the BTR-40, introduced into service in 1950 and first publicly displayed on Moscow's Red Square during the 7th November 1951 military parade.

By the end of the war, the highly dangerous tactic of "tank desant" (infantry riding into battle on the rear of tanks) was being slowly superseded by the use of armored personnel carriers (APCs), particularly the M3A1/M3A2 White vehicles. Wartime experience had shown that the

The original BTR-40 prototype. The prototype was very different from the series production vehicle. Note the angled hull and wheel fenders, reminiscent of the BA-64 series. The vehicle was too small internally to be used in an APC role, which was a prime requirement for the design.

Red Army had an urgent post-war requirement for a small scout vehicle and APC. The American lend-lease M3A1 and M3A2 had been widely utilized during the war for reconnaissance, liaison, and personnel carrier roles, and had provided the Red Army with a degree of mechanization, though Russia at this time remained well behind other nations in the development of such vehicles.

The wartime BA-64 armored car was manufactured in its modernized BA-64B version until 1946 and continued in service with the Soviet Army until the mid-1950's. The BA-64B was a good scout vehicle, but its primary drawback was its diminutive size and consequent inability to improve the armament, armor, or increase the vehicle crew utilizing the existing GAZ-67B chassis. A new vehicle was therefore needed in the immediate post-war era and the GAZ-63 4x4 truck chassis was selected as the basis for the first post-war generation of armored cars. The GAZ-63 had been developed as early as 1944 but series production had been delayed until after the war.

To develop armored car models in the post-war era, a new design bureau was set up at the Gorkovskiy Avtomobilniy Zavod (GAZ). The new Dedkov OKB, directed by V.A. Dedkov, started design work on the BTR-

40 at the end of 1947 under the designation "Izdeliye 141". Design responsibility for the Izdeliye 141 was assigned to senior engineer V.K. Rubtsov, who was to become the primary designer of Russian armored cars for the next three decades.

The Izdeliye 141 was developed in response to a military requirement for an APC capable of transporting eight infantry. It was always intended as more than a simple APC, however. The Izdeliye 141 was designed to fulfill two vehicle requirements, one for a general APC and the other for a ground support vehicle with limited air defense capability. Both requirements were addressed with the simultaneous development of two purpose-designed prototype variants; one for scout/APC duties and the other for ground support/air defense.

The prototype 141s were completed at the end of 1947. These prototypes were significantly different from later series production models. They had a chamfered, highly faceted hull with half doors in the lower hull sections and angular sheet steel rear wheel arches; the design bearing some resemblance to the earlier BA-64. The early pre-series 141s were consequently excellent designs from a ballistics perspective, but were very restricted internally on a chassis which was considerably larger than the BA-64.

BTR-40 in standard configuration.

The ground support version of the Izdeliye 141 was designed from the outset as a ground support vehicle with anti-aircraft capability and not purely as an anti-aircraft system. It was built in small numbers for trials evaluation purposes, however, the chamfered sides of the Izdeliye 141 proved too restrictive internally to allow efficient operation of the twin 14.5mm KPV machine guns on their ZPTU-2 mount.

The trials prototypes of both the standard and fire support versions of the Izdeliye 141 were consequently reworked and a new vehicle with a slab-sided fighting

Standard BTR-40 fitted with a pintle-mounted 7.62mm SGMB machine gun.

Rear overhead view of the same BTR-40.

compartment and rear was developed; the definitive series appearing in prototype form in 1949.

State trials of the new, second series prototypes were conducted in 1949 and the vehicle was accepted for service with the Soviet Army under the army designation BTR-40. Series production began in Gorkiy at the end of 1950 under the factory designation "GAZ-40". The BTR-40 was sometimes known colloquially in service as the "Sorokovka", the diminutive form of "40" in Russian. The BTR-40 and BTR-40A fire support vehicle were developed and produced concurrently; the BTR-40A employing the same open AA turret as mounted on the BTR-152A APC.

The Dedkov OKB subsequently received a state prize for the BTR-40 design before moving on to develop the

A BTR-40 commander and M-72 dispatch rider team discuss orders.

BRDM and BRDM-2 armored reconnaissance vehicles.

Designated as a Bronetransporter (armored transporter) by the Soviet Army, the BTR-40 was used in service as an scout car, command vehicle, fire support vehicle and a number of other roles in the absence of more specific vehicle types to perform these duties. The BTR-40 remained basically an interim vehicle, however, designed to replace the U.S.-supplied M3A1/M3A2. It was used both as a scout and armored personnel carrier and was not particularly suited to either role, being large for scouting duties and too small for efficient use as an armored personnel carrier. It was ultimately used by the Soviet Army as a scout, command and communications vehicle, APC, fire support vehicle, artillery prime mover, and general transporter. Being an open vehicle, the BTR-40 crew was vulnerable to indirect fire and this was rectified in later models of the BTR-40. The vehicle was not an ideal scout vehicle either, particularly as it was not amphibious. Design work began in the early 1950s to

replace it with a purpose-designed and more sophisticated scout vehicle, the BRDM, which was based on the BTR-40 chassis and was originally designated BTR-40P (P- Plavayushiy - amphibious).

In total, approximately 8,500 BTR-40s of all variants were manufactured. The BTR-40 was series produced between 1950 and 1960, being supplemented by the BRDM from 1958. The BTR-40 was also widely exported to client nations of the former Soviet Union and many other countries. It has not been in service with the Russian Army for many years.

Driver's position, BTR-40. Note the differences between this picture and the one below. (Steven J. Zaloga)

Driver's position, BTR-40, Budge collection, UK. (Steven J. Zaloga)

BTR-40s on night maneuvers, 1962. These vehicles are fitted with rear facing, pole mounted night driving lights.

BTR-40s on reconnaissance patrol during the 1960s.

SPECIFICATIONS BTR-40 (Series production)

Design bureau: Dedkov OKB
Crew: 2 + 8
Manufacturing plant: GAZ
Service date: 1947 series production
Combat weight: 5,300kg

Dimensions: (m)
Length: 5.00
Width: 1.90 (rear), 2.010 (front)
Height: 1.83 (including tilt)
Height: 1.945 (including weapons)
Hull side: 8-9
Wheelbase: 2.70
Track width: 1.588 (f),1.605 (r)
Ground clearance: 0.276

Armor: (mm)
Hull front: 13-15
Glacis: 11
Hull rear: 7
Hull roof: 6
Hull floor: 4

Armament:
Main armament:1x7.62mm SGMB/1,250
Secondary armament: 8AP, 2AT grenades
Firing height: NA

Elevation/depression: +15°

Automotive:
Type: GAZ-40
Capacity: 3485cm^3
Cylinders: 6
Power output: 78hp (58.2kW) @ 3,400rpm
Fuel type/capacity: Petrol (A-70/B-70)/120 liters
Transmission: 4F 1 R
Steering: Rack and pinion
Tires: 10.00 - 18 (9.75 - 18 on early vehicles)
Brakes: Hydraulic assisted, Drum brakes F + R
Electrical system: 12v
Radio: 10RT-12
Night vision equipment: IR (driver only)

Performance:
Maximum road speed (km/h): 78
Maximum terrain speed (km/h): 20-25
Road range (km): 300-480
Terrain range (km): 240
Power/weight ratio: 14.7hp (11kW)/tonne
Ground pressure: 4.0kg/cm^2
Gradient: 30°
Side slope: 20°
Trench: 0.35m (0.7m with channels)
Fording: 0.9m
Vertical obstacle: 0.47m

BTR-40 front view.

BTR-40s. Note the tarpaulin cover on one of the vehicles and the open double rear doors.

Field decontamination of BTR-40s, 1964.

BTR-40s of the Czech Army cross a PMP bridge, March 1969. (Photographer: Udovitchenko, TASS)

BTR-40 on display in Kiev, Ukraine. This BTR-40 is displayed at the Central Memorial Park of the Great Patriotic War.

BTR-40 on display at the Central Armed Forces Museum, Moscow.

BTR-40 detail view of the upper superstructure.

BTR-40 and BRDM-2.

BTR-40 3/4 rear view.

BTR-40, Military Transport Museum, Ryazan, Russia.

BTR-40, Military Transport Museum, Ryazan, 3/4 rear view.

BTR-40. Polish Armed Forces Museum, Warsaw, Poland.

BTR-40. Close-up of the engine compartment. There are many detail differences between BTR-40s displayed in museums. Compare this photograph with the BTR-40s in Moscow or Kiev.

An original BTR-40 preserved at the NIIBT Museum, Kubinka.

Overhead view of the BTR-40 at Kubinka.

Description

The BTR-40 has a conventional layout, with a front-mounted engine and rear fighting compartment. The driver sits on the left of the vehicle with the vehicle com-

Ammunition stowage, BTR-40. (Steven J. Zaloga)

mander seated to his right. Access to the vehicle is via two side doors and double doors at the rear of the vehicle. The BTR-40 hull is constructed of welded armor throughout.

Rear fighting compartment, BTR-40. (Steven J. Zaloga)

Though designed to hold eight infantry in the rear, the usual complement was four. Typical armament was a single pintle-mounted 7.62mm SGMB machine gun, though an additional weapon could be mounted on each side of the hull as was often the case in foreign service. The crew could use firing ports in the hull sides, through which to fire their personal weapons from within the vehicle.

In developing the BTR-40, the GAZ-63 4x4 truck chassis on which the BTR-40 was mounted was shortened 600mm to suit the all-terrain requirements of the new vehicle. The GAZ-63 truck had entered series pro-

duction in 1946 and had a strong chassis and powerful engine uprated 7.4kW (10hp) from the GAZ-63 for use with an armored car body. The GAZ-40 engine was protected behind the distinctively shaped "pig snout" frontal armor, with the radiator mounted behind the lower front section of the front armor.

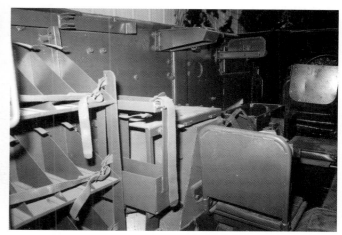

Left side looking forward, BTR-40. (Steven J. Zaloga)

Rear of fighting compartment, BTR-40. (Steven J. Zaloga)

BTR-40A

The BTR-40A fire support vehicle was developed concurrently with the standard series production model BTR-40. As with the pre-series BTR-40A mounted on the early Izdeliye 141 chassis, the series production model BTR-40A was developed as a ground support vehicle with air defense capability.

The series production model BTR-40A fire support vehicle mounted twin 14.5mm KPV machine guns on a ZPTU-2 mount in a similar manner to the earlier pre-series production models. The pre-series prototype model BTR-40A was produced in 1950 and series production

BTR-40A self-propelled air defense system.

BTR-40A self-propelled air defense system.

The original BTR-40A prototype. The original anti-aircraft vehicle was based on the Izdeliye 141 prototype, with its heavily chamfered hull sides. Internally, the   vehicle was too restricted for the 14.5mm KPVT machine gun crew to operate efficiently. The concept was therefore dropped in favor of a modified vehicle.

BTR-40A SPAAG system. The BTR-40A mounted twin 14.5mm KPVT machine guns for ground support and limited anti-aircraft roles.

BTR-40A SPAAG system. This rare overhead photograph shows the 360° turntable mount and ammunition boxes in place.

began in 1951. The 14.5mm KPVT heavy machine guns in the BTR-40A were capable of bringing fire to bear from +90° to -5° with a 360° manual traverse. The weapon system increased the combat weight of the vehicle to 5,600kg, marginally reducing vehicle performance. The height of the vehicle with guns lowered was 2.23m. 1,200 rounds of 14.5mm ammunition was carried on board.

BTR-40V Prototype with CTPRS

The BTR-40V was a prototype built in 1956 in an effort to improve the cross-country capability of the original vehicle. The BTR-40V was fitted with a Central Tire Pressure Regualtion System (CTPRS) with external air lines and other mechanical modifications including a self locking differential. During field trials, the CTPRS system provided a considerable increase in off-road performance, but the external air lines were found to be very prone to snaring on undergrowth. The BTR-40V also

BTR-40As in South East Asia. Although unmarked, these vehicles are likely to be in service with the armies of Vietnam or Laos. Large numbers of BTR-40 and BTR-40A vehicles exported.

BTR-40A SPAAG system, preserved at the NIIBT collection, Kubinka.

BTR-40Bs in convoy.

The BTR-40B at the NIIBT Museum, Kubinka. From most angles, the overhead roof armor of the BTR-40B is almost indiscernable.

The BTR-40V on display in the NIIBT Kubinka armor collection. The BTR-40V was an experimental version of the BTR-40 series built in 1956. Improvements included CTPRS, which improved all-terrain mobility, though the external air lines were vulnerable to snaring on undergrowth Infra-red driving lights were also fitted.

BTR-40B at the Ryazan Military Transport Museum, Ryazan, Russia.

BTR-40B 3/4 rear view.

introduced IR driving lights to the BTR-40 series. The vehicle was developed and field trialled concurrently with the BTR-40B, but was not series produced. An original prototype remains on display at the NIIBT Tank Museum at Kubinka, near Moscow.

BTR-40B

The BTR-40s principle disadvantage was that it remained an open vehicle at a time when Soviet Army doctrine was preparing for operations in an NBC battlefield environment. Additionally, Russian losses of open

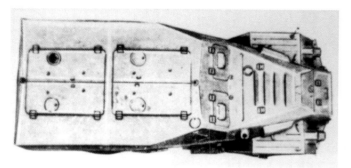

BTR-40B overhead view. This photograph illustrates the roof hatch arrangement used on the BTR-40B.

AFVs were very high during the Hungarian uprising and the need for overhead armor for armored vehicles, particularly in built-up areas and in street fighting, was urgently recognized. A new version with long overdue overhead armor was therefore developed from 1956, and entered limited series production in 1957 as the BTR-40B. The new vehicle was nominally capable of operating in an NBC environment, but offered no NBC overpressure system or other specialist NBC equipment. The BTR-40B was series produced in small numbers from 1958 to 1960, concurrently with the BRDM which eventually superseded it.

The BTR-40B had an almost indiscernible steel roof, resembling the tarpaulin of the early BTR-40 at a distance. Two large two-piece roof hatches were provided, with a firing port in each section. The hatches opened outward towards the vehicle sides. Due to the reduced internal crew space, the vehicle had a reduced crew of six in addition to the driver and commander.

The BTR-40B retained the 8mm armor base of the earlier BTR-40, and with the roof armor still weighed close to 5,300kg, identical to that of the base model BTR-40. Vehicle performance was therefore similar to the earlier vehicle. IR driving lights, first used on the

BTR-40B and BTR-152K. The BTR-40B is nearly identical to the open BTR-40 when fitted with its canvas roof. The angular raised roofline and open hatches are a recognition feature of the BTR-40B.

prototype BTR-40V, were fitted as standard on the BTR-40B. The BTR-40B was armed with a single pintle-mounted 7.62mm machine gun with 1,250 rounds of ammunition carried on board.

Dimensionally, the BTR-40B was similar to the earlier BTR-40 (length 5.00m, width1.90m, height 2.060m).

BTR-40RKh

A number of BTR-40 vehicles were, after a period of service, reworked as RKh chemical reconnaissance vehicles, fitted with twin flag dispensing boxes which were subsequently used in greater numbers on the BRDM and BRDM-2. Many standard BTR-40Bs were also used in the chemical reconnaissance role, with their crews dismounting to manually place yellow warning pennants.

BTR-40 ZhD Variants

In 1969, very late in the BTR-40s service life, small numbers of elderly BTR-40s were converted as rail scout vehicles, using outrigger ZhD wheels similar in concept to those developed at GAZ for the BA-64G ZhD vehicle in 1942. Small numbers of these BTR-40 ZhD vehicles were produced and these were primarily used in border regions of the former USSR. The BTR-40 ZhD retained the 7.62mm SGMB armament of the original roadbound vehicle, and was fitted with a modernized R-113 radio. It took three to five minutes to bring the BTR-40 ZhD

BTR-40B (RKh) on chemical reconnaissance duty, August 1966. The marking pennants are being emplaced by hand. Later systems mounted on the BRDM and BRDM-2 used mechanical pennant dispensers while the crew remained within the vehicle. (Photographer: G. Omelchuk, TASS)

The BTR-40A ZhD SPAAG at the NIIBT Kubnika collection. Note the ancillary rail wheels and rail connection mountings.

into service as a rail scout vehicle.

A small number of BTR-40As with the twin 14.5mm KPV system were also converted as rail scouts in 1969. These vehicles were, not surprisingly, designated BTR-40A ZhD. As late as 1991 these vehicles remained in service with the Russian Army as rail scout vehicles for armored trains in the Ural and Far East regions of Russia.

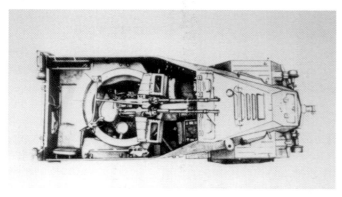

BTR-40A ZhD SPAAG system. A very small number of BTR-40A SPAAG systems were converted as rail scout vehicles, as this interesting overhead view shows.

BTR-40 7.62mm ZPTU-2 SPAAG

An experimental BTR-40 AA vehicle was developed in 1950 concurrently with the BTR-40A. A small series was produced in 1951 for trials purposes, mounting two 7.62mm machine guns on a ZPTU-2 mount. The BTR-40 ZPTU-2 weighed 5,600kg and had a road speed of 75km/hour. The vehicle was not series produced.

BTR-40 9M14 (AT-3) ATGM Vehicle

Though no Russian ATGM version of the BTR-40 is known to have been developed, the East German Army developed an ATGM version of the BTR-40, firing the 9M14 (NATO: AT-3 Sagger) missile. The vehicle was based on a modified BTR-40 with the rear fighting compartment reduced in height. No ATGM version of the BTR-40 is known to have entered service with the Soviet Army.

Below: BTR-40A ZhD, with its twin 14.5mm KPVT system.

BRDM Armored Car

While the BTR-40 performed functional service as a scout and command vehicle in addition to its APC role during the 1950s, a decade passed between the ending of BA-64 production in 1946 and the entry into production of a purpose designed post-war armored car in 1957. The BTR-40 design, which had fulfilled the role of a reconnaissance vehicle during the intervening years, was essentially an armored truck based on a 4x4 chassis. It fulfilled the role of scout vehicle and APC reasonably, but was a compromise design based on an urgent post war requirements to modernize and mechanize the Soviet Army. V.K. Rubtsov and his design team considered the need for a specialized scout vehicle and began work on a new, amphibious vehicle in 1954. The base design requirement was for a 5.6 tonne vehicle with a crew of five, a road speed of over 80km/hour, a road range of 500km, and amphibious capability.

The new design, which was given the factory designation BTR-40P, was based on the BTR-40 with a modified engine, gearbox, transmission, and axles. The BRDM was developed by a team of engineers led by V.A. Dedkov under the overall direction of V.K. Rubtsov. The new vehicle was specifically developed as a scout vehicle for mechanized formations. It was fully amphibious and had a far greater terrain capability than its predecessor. In military service, the vehicle later became known as the BRDM (Bronirovannaya Razvedivatelno Dozornaya Mashina: literally Armored Reconnaissance Duty Machine), reflecting its intended role.

There were several significant design modifications which greatly improved the performance of the BRDM compared with the earlier BTR-40. The primary advantage of the BRDM was its significantly increased mobility on land and the introduction of amphibious capability, a severe drawback associated with the BTR-40. The BRDM was fully amphibious, being powered in water by a single hydrojet system.

The BRDM was provided with a standard driver-controlled CTPRS, which varied the tire pressures between 0.5-3.0kg/cm^2 to suit ground conditions. This system significantly reduced the vehicle ground pressure and aided traction on soft ground. Cross-country mobility was also aided by an additional device introduced with the BRDM as the post-war reintroduction of a concept previously used in some all-terrain vehicles, particularly in Germany. The BRDM was assisted in rough terrain by a set of four small chain-driven wheels fitted with 700 x 250mm aviation tires, adjustable between 4.0 and 4.5kg/cm^2. These

BRDM in parade markings. The standard BRDM with overhead armor (BRDM M-1958) entered service with the Soviet Army in 1958.

BRDMs on parade in Red Square, 1964.

These BRDMs are painted in parade markings with Guards insignia.

BRDM. This exceptional example of the standard production model is located at the Tank Museum, Bovington, England. It was provided by the NIIBT Museum at Kubinka. (Tank Museum, Bovington, UK, 3624/D6)

wheels were lowered by the driver as required, preventing the vehicle from bottoming out and aiding all-terrain travel by providing additional traction. This is particularly important in negotiating river banks, the bane of all amphibious wheeled military vehicles, which had previously employed cumbersome "overall" tracks for this purpose. When not required, these wheels were retracted into nacelles in the hull floor, with the lower half of the wheels remaining visible.

Originally designated by the factory designation GAZ-40P and as the BRDM after entry into Soviet Army service, the designation was only later unofficially altered to BRDM-1 after the introduction of the BRDM-2. The BRDM officially retained the original designation without any suffix, though in practice it was also referred to as the BRDM-1.

V.K. Rubtsov and the Dedkov OKB at GAZ developed the BRDM concurrently with the BTR-60P armored personnel carrier. The BRDM development program began in 1954 and the first prototype was completed in February 1956, with a small number of prototype vehicles field trialled in the Black Sea area that same year. After further GABTU acceptance trials, the BRDM was accepted for Soviet Army service in 1957 and was series produced from 1957 to 1966. It was first seen in service with the Soviet Army and in public in 1959. In total, approximately 10,000 BRDM vehicles of all variants were produced at GAZ between 1958 and 1966, of which approximately 1,500 were exported. The BRDM left

service with the Soviet Army in the late 1970s. In the East German Army the BRDM was designated the SPW-40P. The vehicle was not used by the Hungarian and Czechoslovakian Armies, which used the Hungarian FUG armored car to perform reconnaissance duties.

The primary disadvantages of the BRDM were its light armament and the vulnerability of the front mounted petrol engine. Usually the armament consisted of single 7.62mm SGMB mounted externally, though some vehicles were later re-armed with a 12.7mm DShK and two 7.62mm SGMB on side pintle mounts. This was always a difficult configuration which made the crew extremely vulnerable while operating the weapons.

The BRDM could not easily be modified to mount a turret, as the fighting compartment was at the rear and the fitting of a rear-mounted turret would seriously affect buoyancy. Further development of the base model BRDM was therefore limited and work quickly began on a replacement vehicle, with the first design being undertaken as early as 1961, culminating in the BRDM-2 in 1966.

Description

The BRDM was based on the BTR-40 chassis, which was in turn derived from the GAZ-63 4x4 truck, from which many mechanical parts were utilized. The vehicle featured a distinctive long nose with a front mounted engine and the fighting compartment at the rear. The fighting compartment was fully enclosed on all but the

BRDMs in the desert, 1964. (M. Baryatinsky)

BRDMs fording a river, Northern Caucases, 1964.

Left: BRDM on reconnaissance patrol, June 1966. (Photographer: Peredelskiy)

Below: BRDMs on exercise in the mid-1960s.

BRDM, Polish Armed Forces Museum, Warsaw, Poland.

An abandoned BRDM, (a 9P110 ATGM vehicle), located in the NIIBT reserve collection at Kubinka. This photograph is interesting in that it shows all hatches in the open position.

Rear view of a BRDM abandoned in southern Russia. (Aleksandr Razvodov)

BRDM abandoned in southern Russia. (Aleksandr Razvodov)

BRDM. This BRDM is preserved in the NIIBT collection, Kubinka, Moscow.

Rear view of Kubinka's BRDM.

BRDM right front overhead view.

BRDM left front overhead view.

BRDM left rear view.

BRDM wheels with CTPRS system in the wheel hubs. Note the stowed location of the auxiliary wheels.

Overhead view of Kubinka's BRDM. This vehicle has three mountings for machine guns, but only a single 7.62mm SGMB was normally mounted in Soviet service.

BRDM. This BRDM is preserved at the military museum, Fort IX, in the Sadyba district of Warsaw, Poland.

earliest (M-1957) production vehicles.

The BRDM had a hermetically sealed boat-shaped hull with vertical sides and rear. The vehicle was of all-welded construction, fabricated from 6, 8, and 12mm steel sheets. The driver sat on the front left of the vehicle, with the commander to his right. Both had windshields which were covered by top-hinged hatches with vision blocks for use in a combat environment. There were a further two vision blocks in the front side of the fighting compartment and a firing port on either side of the vehicle. In addition to the commander and driver, a combat crew of two to three were carried in the rear of the vehicle.

BRDM hydrojet system. Note the four-bladed propeller and twin rudder assembly.

Access to the vehicle was by twin roof hatches (in the standard BRDM M-1958) and a small rear hatch which opened either side. There was a firing port in each hatch section. The rear fighting compartment section sloped at 30º.

The BRDM introduced a hydrojet propulsion system similar in principle to that developed for the PT-76 amphibious light tank. Water was drawn in under the vehicle hull and exited under pressure through a single rear hydrojet, which was protected by an armored cover

when not in use. Before entering the water, the wave deflector plate was manually relocated from its stored position under the hull front and locked into place on the vehicle nose and the electric bilge pump system switched on. The BRDM could travel at a constant 9km/hour in water with a water endurance of twelve hours. A small mooring capstan was located on the hull nose.

The main design flaw associated with the BRDM was that the crew access on both early open models and late closed roof models was over the fighting compartment roof, which proved extremely hazardous for the crew under combat conditions. The front placement of the engine was also problematic in terms of vulnerability and vehicle trim in water.

Armament on the BRDM consisted of a 7.62mm SGMB pintle-mounted at the front of the vehicle. A 12.7mm DShK was often mounted on this position with two 7.62mm SGMB's on pintle mounts either side of the vehicle. On some vehicles, the SGMB was replaced by the PKT after capital repair work.

The BRDM was powered by a front mounted GAZ-40P six cylinder in-line 3485cm³ water-cooled petrol engine developing 67kW (90hp), which gave the 5,600kg BRDM a very respectable road speed of 90km/hour and range of 500km.

The BRDM originally mounted an R-113 radio as standard, with a whip antenna on the right side of the hull. The BRDM was also fitted with a TNA-2 land navigation system as standard.

The BRDM was widely used in Soviet Motorized Rifle Divisions (MRDs) and Tank Divisions (TDs). The Tank Division Reconnaissance Battalion had twelve; the Tank Regiment had seven.

BRDM M-1957

The first BRDM vehicles were series-produced in 1957. The first production model was an open design, armed with a single pintle-mounted SGMB machine gun. Very few of the original BRDM M-1957 production model were produced before the vehicle was replaced in production by the definitive M-1958 production model, which had closed roof armor. The BRDM M-1957 had a height of 1.87m. CTPRS was fitted on all BRDMs from the very first vehicles built.

BRDM M-1958

The BRDM M-1958 was the second production model of the series, provided with a fully enclosed body with armored roof. There were two hatches in the roof

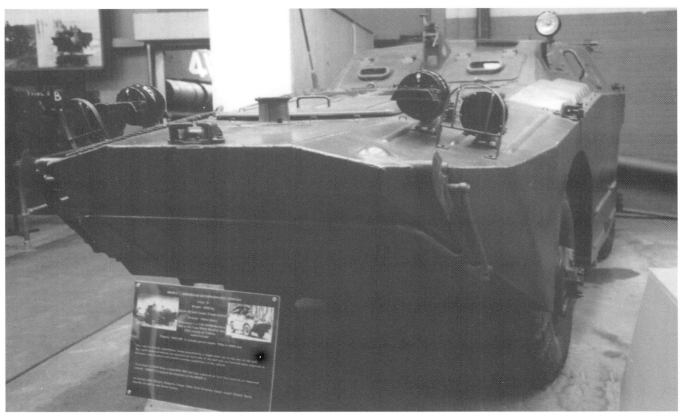

BRDM preserved at the Tank Museum, Bovington, UK. This BRDM, together with a BTR-60PK APC, were provided by the Kubinka Tank Museum in Russia in the late 1980s. In return, Kubinka was provided with a Conqueror heavy tank and two wheeled AFVs.

Interior view of the BRDM located at the Tank Museum, Bovington, UK.

SPECIFICATIONS BRDM (BRDM M-1958)

Design bureau: Dedkov OKB
Crew: 2 + 3
Manufacturing plant: GAZ
Service date: 1958-mid-1970s
Combat weight: 5,600kg

Dimensions: (m)
Length (overall): 5.70
Length (hull): 5.60
Width: 2.17
Height: 2.25 (including SGMB)
Wheelbase: 2.80
Track width: 1.66
Ground clearance: 0.315m (axles)

Armor: (mm)
Hull front: 12
Hull sides: 12
Hull roof: 8
Hull floor: 4

Armament:
Main armament: 1x7.62 SGMB/PKT/1,250
Secondary armament: 2xAK47/AKM
Other armament: 9xF-1 grenades
Firing height: 2.20m
Elevation/depression: -14°/+24.5°

Automotive:
Type: GAZ-40P
Capacity: 3485cm^3
Cylinders: 6 in-line (Bore/Stroke 82mm/110mm)
Power output: 90hp (67kW) @ 3,400rpm
Fuel type/capacity: Petrol B-70, A-72/150 liters
Fuel consumption: 0.3liters/km
Transmission: 4F 1R x2 Single dry plate clutch
Steering: Rack & pinion, Manual
Tires: 12.00-18*   CTRPS 3-0.5kg/cm^2
Brakes: Drums all round, Hydraulic assisted
Electrical system: 12v
Radio: R113 or R-123M

Performance:
Maximum road speed (km/h): 90
Maximum terrain speed (km/h): 50
Road range (km): 500
Terrain range (km): 350-410
Power/weight ratio: 16.1 hp/tonne
Ground pressure: NA
Gradient:30°
Side slope: 20-25°
Trench: 1.20m
Fording: Amphibious @ 9km/h
Vertical obstacle: 0.4m
Snow:0.65m
* Note:The 700 x 250 auxiliary tires had adjustable tire pressure 4.0 - 4.5kg/cm^3

Rear view of the BRDM with hydrojet port open.

and the height was increased from 1.87m to 2.29m (including armamnet). The BRDM M-1958 became the definitive production model of the BRDM series and was manufactured from late 1957 to 1968.

The BRDM M-1958 production model, with its hermetically sealed fighting compartment and simple overpressure system, was equipped to reconnoiter NBC environments. This was a major advancement over the BTR-40 series, as the great majority of those were open vehicles. In service, BRDMs carried a VPKhR-54 portable chemical detection system and a DP-3B roentgenmeter on board.

The BRDM was armed with a pintle-mounted 7.62mm SGMB with a 45° traverse. Some vehicles were fitted with a 12.7mm DShKM at the front and one or two 7.62mm SGMBs, though this configuration was more common in foreign service. BRDMs in Russian service were provided with 1,250 rounds of 7.62mm ammunition in five magazines.

Early production model BRDM vehicles did not have any specialized night vision equipment. FG-125 infrared driving lights and a searchlight were subsequently introduced on new vehicles and retrofitted on older vehicles.

BRDM-U (BRDM-IU) Command Vehicle

Small numbers of BRDM command versions were used by the Soviet Army, designated BRDM-U or BRDM-1U. These were distinguished by the mounting of additional radio antennae on the vehicle, in total four antennae being mounted on the BRDM-U, one on either side of the vehicle and two at the rear.

2P27 (AT-1 Snapper) ATGM Vehicle

The first anti-tank version of the BRDM was developed from 1958 concurrently with the standard reconnaissance model. The ATGM complex was designated 2K16, while the vehicle, designated 2P27, mounted three 3M6 Schmel (Bumblebee) wire guided anti-tank missiles on a retractable launcher in an enclosed rear compartment. The system initially complemented the 2K15 system, which was mounted on an unarmored 2P26 launch vehicle based on the GAZ-69 chassis, though the latter system was eventually replaced by the 2P27. Both systems were intended to supplement conventional anti-tank guns at longer engagement ranges. In the West, the system was better known by its NATO designation "AT-1 Snapper".

The 3M6 Schmel was developed by the KBM missile design bureau in Kolomna from 1958, in cooperation with the Ts NIIAG, NII-125, and NII-6 institutes, and manufactured at the Saratov Mechanical Factory. It was developed for use with the BRDM launch vehicle which was designated 2P27. The complex was designated 2K16, the first Soviet armored car-mounted ATGM, with an effective range of 500-2,500m but a slow missile speed of 105m/s. The armor-defeating potential of the missile warhead was, however, a significant 380mm, which made the system a considerable threat to contemporary main battle tanks.

The Schmel complex was not accepted for service with the Soviet Army until 1960, when the vehicle became available to the Soviet Army. The 2P27 was produced from 1960-63 and served with the Soviet Army into the 1970s. The vehicle is not known to have been exported and is not believed to have seen combat.

BRDM 2P27 ATGM system, 1964. Note the large size of the early 3M6 Schmel missiles. This photograph is a mirror view, printed in reverse, as it was printed in contemporary Soviet press articles. (Photographer: G. Omelchuk, TASS)

BRDM-U command vehicle. Faintly seen in the background is a BTR-40.

BRDM-U command vehicle. This detailed photo gives a good overall view of the superstructure of the BRDM. Note the small details such as the props for the front visors and the antennae locations.

Above: BRDM 2P27 ATGM system. This particular vehicle is on display in the Artillery, Engineering, and Communications Forces Museum in St. Petersburg.

Right: 3M6 "Schmel" (NATO: AT-1 Snapper) missile.

BRDM 2P27 ATGM vehicle in service with the Polish army. Note the lowered belly wheels on this vehicle. (Tank Museum, Bovington, UK. Ref: 3799/E3)

BRDM 2P27 ATGM vehicle. This vehicle is preserved at the military museum, Fort IX Czerniakowski, Sadyba, Warsaw.

Rear view of a 2P27 ATGM vehicle. Note that the cantilever doors on the vehicle run the entire length of the hull rear.

Close up of the 3M6 missiles on their launch rails.

BRDM 9P27 ATGM vehicle. This version of the BRDM is on display at the Memorial Museum of the Great Patriotic War in Kiev, Ukraine.

BRDM 9P27 ATGM vehicle, rear view. The rear superstructure is raised along the entire length of the vehicle rear. Note the rear vision/pistol port.

To launch the system, the "W" barn doors were opened on either side and the missile launcher system, with its three 3M6 missiles, was raised into position. The missiles were joystick controlled, Manual Command Line of Sight (MCLOS) guided, and had an effective range of 2,500m, which took the missiles thirty seconds to cover. The operator required considerable training in order to quickly locate the missile on launch and guide it to its target by use of a trailing wire link. Because of the short amount of time available for target acquisition, the minimum range was about 500m. That was not ideal considering that expected tank engagement ranges in any confrontation in Europe at the time were under 1,000m.

Due to the large size of the 3M6 missiles, the 2P27 also had very limited reload capability within the rear fighting compartment, and having only three missiles on launch rails limited the vehicle's performance.

The 2P27 was normally deployed within an anti-tank battery attached to a Motorized Rifle Regiment (MRR). Each battery had three platoons, each with three 2P27 launch vehicles and a BRDM-U command vehicle.

2P32 (AT-2 Swatter) ATGM Vehicle

The 2P32 began to replace the 2P27 in service from 1962. The 2P32 was armed with four 3M11 Fleyta (Flute) missiles (NATO designation: AT-2 Swatter). Though the 2P32 was intended as a replacement for the 2P27 system, the two vehicles were used concurrently for several years; a reconnaissance platoon often having one 2P27 and two 2P32 vehicles. Anti-tank platoons in MRR anti-tank batteries were also often organized with two 2P32 vehicles and one 2P27 vehicle.

The AT-2 Falanga was developed by the OKB-16 design bureau in Moscow from 1960, under the direction of A.Ye. Nudelman. The new missile was designated Fleyta, the system designation being 2K8 Falanga. There were several variants of the 2P32, mounting modified missiles. The original 2K8 system firing the 3M11 Fleyta (AT-2a Swatter A, as it was known by NATO) had a manual command line-of-sight targeting system with a radio link. Range was 500-3,000m with a claimed armor defeating capability of 510mm armor @ 0° incidence.

Soviet Army BRDM 2P32 ATGM vehicles pictured in 1964. The two 2P32 ATGM vehicles in the foreground (N° 416 and 411) are following a 2P27 ATGM vehicle (N° 393). These vehicles were used concurrently for several years, the 2P32 providing better long range anti-tank capability. (Photographer: G. Omelchuk, TASS)

A BRDM 2P32 in Soviet parade colors.

BRDM 2P32 in parade colors approach Red Square during a November parade. (Tank Museum, Bovington, UK. Ref: 2479/D6)

Rear view of a BRDM 2P32 ATGM vehicle. The 2P32 has three roof doors; two opening sideways and one folding to the rear. There are variations in the design of the door strengthening ribs, as seen when compared to the top photo.

BRDM 2P32 ATGM vehicles on parade in Red Square, 7th November 1964.

BRDM 9P110 ATGM vehicles on Red Square, 7th November 1969. (M. Baryatinsky)

The missile speed remained a slow 150m/s, however, better than the 105m/s of the earlier 3M6 Schmel but still relatively slow and therefore vulnerable to countermeasures.

The 2K8 system was later modified and the 3M11 missile was replaced with the 9M17 Skorpion missile, which had an increased range of 3500m.

As with the earlier 2P27, the 2P32's missile launch mechanism was raised from its under armor storage when required. The launch assembly was retracted under two side-opening barn doors and a drop down rear door section.

2P32 launch vehicles were later modernized to mount the later 9M17P missile, though this modification was done on relatively few vehicles, as at the time the 2P32 was already being replaced in service with the Soviet Army. The 9M17P Falanga-P (NATO designation AT-2 Swatter C) was the final modification of the 9M17 missile used with the original BRDM, used in small numbers from 1972. The system retained the 2K8 designation. The missile had a longer and wider range of 600-4,000m with a flight speed of 170m/s. The weapon had the same armor-piercing capability as the 3M11 (AT-2A) missile.

The later model of the 9M17P missile, designated 9M17M "Falanga M" system, was mounted on the later BRDM-2, the vehicle being designated 9P124.

As with the earlier 2P27 and its 3M6 missiles, a drawback of the 2P32 system was the limited storage capacity for reload missiles, though four spare missiles were located within the armored hull of the vehicle.

Each MRR had nine 2P32 vehicles arranged in a single anti-tank company, consisting of three platoons of three vehicles.

The 2P32 had side-opening doors like the 2P27, but also had a full width door at the rear of the fighting compartment which opened to the rear, distinguishing the vehicle from other ATGM vehicles in the BRDM series.

9P110 (AT-3) ATGM Vehicle

The last ATGM version of the original BRDM was the 9P110 (NATO designation: AT-3 Sagger) mounting six 9M14 Malyutka (meaning "little one") missiles. The vehicle was built in small numbers in 1963, only a year after the 2P32 was introduced. It was the last of the BRDM ATGM vehicles modified from the early BRDM armored car series, as the BRDM-2 was nearing production at the time. It was, however, considered important to rush the 9P110 into service so that the new 9M14 missile system complex could be integrated into the Soviet Army and evaluated, albeit mounted on an obsolescent

BRDM 9P110 ATGM system in service with the East German army.

9P110 ATGM vehicles approach Red Square in a 7th November military parade. Note that the raised superstructure on the 9P110 does not extend to the rear of the vehicle, as on the 2P27 and 2P32. With the launch mechanism lowered and the overhead armor in place, the vehicle is difficult to distinguish at a distance from a standard BRDM reconnaissance vehicle.

BRDM 9P110s leave Red Square after a 7th November parade.

9P110 ATGM vehicle, side view.

9P110 ATGM vehicle, overhead view.

chassis. The 9P110 was first seen in public during the 1965 May Day parade in Red Square.

The 9P110 mounted six 9M14 Malyutka (AT-3 Sagger) missiles on a retractable launch system, the top of which formed the fighting compartment roof. The system used a smaller missile with shorter range than the earlier 2P27/2P32 vehicles, which it was originally intended to supplement rather than replace. The advantage of the 9P110 launch vehicle was the number of mis-

siles carried in the ready-to-launch position and the number of reloads which could be transported within the vehicle.

The 9M14 Malyutka as deployed with the 9P110 ATGM vehicle, was developed in 1961, within a year of the 3M11 Fleyta on its 2P27 ATGM vehicle. The 9M14 was developed by the KBM OKB in Kolomna as an

BRDM 9P110s in Soviet parade colors. The 9P110 was used concurrently with the 2P32. It mounted six 9M14 Malyutka missiles, which were less capable in both range and armor piercing capability than the 3M11 missile used with the 2P32. However, the 9P110 vehicle mounted six 9M14 missiles and was more economical to mass-produce.

BRDM 9P110 located at the Artillery, Engineer, and Communications Forces Museum in St. Petersburg, Russia.

BRDM 9P110; the same as pictured in the top photograph.

BRDM 9P110 ATGM vehicle at the Artillery, Engineer, and Communications Forces Museum, St. Petersburg, Russia.

BRDM 9P110 ATGM vehicle. This vehicle, in excellent condition, is located at the military museum, Fort IX Czerniakowski, Sadyba, Warsaw, Poland.

BRDM 9P110 ATGM vehicle.

Close-up of the 9M14 missile launch rails under their overhead armor.

The 9M14 missiles on their launch rails.

BRDM 9P110 ATGM vehicle providing close support to T-62 MBTs.

economy missile, intended to be deployed in larger numbers than the earlier system and intended to be deployed alongside the other system. The 9M14 was a shorter range missile (500-3,000m effective range) than the 3M11 and had less armor piercing capability (410mm, as against 500mm for the 3M11).

The 9M14 (AT-3A Sagger A) was deployed with the 9P110 system from 1963. The later 9M14M (AT-3B Sagger B) was usually found only on helicopters.

The 9P110 still employed MCLOS missile guidance but with a trailing wire rather than radio command. This was cheaper to produce and suffered less from electronic interference.

The 9P110 offered a range and control advantage over its predecessors, but the main advantage of the system was the smaller missile size with folding flight control surfaces. This allowed eight reload missiles to be stowed on racks within the fighting compartment, which was a considerable advantage over previous systems.

The 9P110 was built and deployed in far larger numbers than either of the previous vehicle types.

The 9P110 fighting compartment superstructure did not extend to the rear of the hull as on the 2P32 and the armored roof section lifted with the missile system as a single piece.

A third production series BRDM-2. This vehicle is pictured at Aberdeen Proving Grounds, Maryland, USA. Note the six domed vent intakes and four rear vents on the engine deck. (Steven J. Zaloga)

BRDM-RKh NBC Reconnaissance Vehicle

In 1966 the BRDM was latterly modified as a chemical warfare scout vehicle. The BRDM-RKh carried more on-board survey and sensing devices than the base model BRDM. Measuring devices included a DP-3 nuclear survey meter, DP-5A radiation meter, KPO-1 sampling unit, GSP-1M and GSP-11 nerve gas alarms, and a radiation alarm. The vehicles carried forty flares or "sound stars" (signalnie raketi) onboard. Two flag dispensing boxes were mounted at the rear of the vehicle. Each contained twenty pole-mounted warning flags which were emplaced by small charges as the vehicle progressed. The yellow flags were marked "zarazheno" (contaminated), denoting clear paths through contaminated ground. The boxes were swung 180° and covered in canvas when the vehicle was in transit.

Rkh versions of the BRDM were widely used in MRDs and TDs, with a scale of deployment of four Rkh vehicles in a Tank Regiment, four per Motorised Rifle Regiment, four per Divisional Reconnaissance Battalion, and nine in the Chemical Defense Battalion, for a total of twenty-nine in a Motorized Rifle Division.

BRDM-2 crew transferring documents to a helicopter, September 1970. (TASS)

BRDM-RKh. A rare photograph of the BRDM-RKh based on the original BRDM chassis.

BRDM-RKh NBC scout vehicle.

SPECIFICATIONS BRDM-2

Design bureau: Dedkov OKB
Crew: 2 + 2 to 3
Manufacturing plant: GAZ
Service date: 1966 series production
Combat weight: 7,000kg

Dimensions: (m)
Length: 5.75
Width: 2.35
Height: 2.31
Wheelbase: 3.10
Track: 1.84
Ground clearance: 0.43

Armor: (mm)
Hull front: 7-14 mm
Hull sides: 7mm @ 0°
Hull roof: 7mm
Hull floor: 2-3mm
Turret front: 7mm
Turret sides: 7mm

Armament: (All armament controls are manual)
Main armament: 14.5mm KPVT/500
Secondary armament: 7.62mm PKT/2,000
Firing height: 2.13m
Elevation/depression: +30°/-5° manual

Automotive:
Type: GAZ-41
Capacity: 5250cm^3
Power output: 140hp (105kW) @ 3,200rpm
Fuel type/capcity: Petrol/290 liters
Fuel consumption: 0.35-0.45 liters/km
Transmission: 4 F 1R Hyd assisted.Synch on 3+4
Clutch: Single plate
Steering: Air/hydraulic assisted. Turn radius 9.0m
Tires: 13.00-18
Brakes: Hydraulic assisted
Electrical system: 24v
Radio: R-123 (R-123M from 1971) 5m antenna
Night vision: IR lights (driver, commander)

Performance:
Maximum road speed (km/h): 95-100
Maximum terrain speed (km/h): 50
Road range (km): 750
Terrain range (km): 450
Power/weight ratio: 20hp (14.9kW)/tonne
Ground pressure: 2.7kg/cm^2
Gradient: 30°
Trench :1.20m
Vertical obstacle: 0.4m
Fording: Amphibious @ 10km/h
Water range: 180km

BRDM-2 Armored Car

In 1962 V.K. Rubtsov and his engineers within the Dedkov OKB at GAZ began work on a replacement for the original BRDM, under the project designation Izdeliye 41 (article 41). The design team was the same group which had produced the original BRDM and they worked on the BRDM-2 using the earlier BRDM design as a basis.

The new design specification called for a vehicle with improved road and terrain performance, full amphibious capability, and heavier, turret-mounted armament. The new vehicle was also to have a full NBC system and night vision capability as standard and was required to have good radio command and communictions facilities. On this basis, the original prototype Izdeliye 41 was developed in 1962. On successful completion of field trials, the vehicle entered series production in 1963 as the GAZ-41 or BRDM-2. Its first public appearance was in 1966 and though production ceased in 1989, the vehicle remains in service with the Russian Army today and no direct replacement is likely to be fielded in the forseeable

future.

In response to the original directive on the requirements for the next generation armored car there were several significant design improvements incorporated into the BRDM-2. The most significant was the new turret, as used on the BTR-60PB wheeled APC, which provided armored protection for the gunner and manually operated 360° traverse. The increase in armament caliber to 14.5mm gave the vehicle limited anti-armor capability. Vehicle performance was improved by the replacement of the six cylinder 67kW (90hp) GAZ-40P engine used in the original BRDM with a new GAZ-41 V-8 petrol engine developing 105kW (140hp). The engine was moved to the rear of the vehicle, where it was less vulnerable. This configuration moved the fighting compartment forward, which provided better crew space and allowed the turret to be centrally positioned, so maintaining vehicle trim in water. In consideration of the increased role of AFVs on an NBC battlefield, the fully enclosed BRDM-2 was provided with an NBC overpressure and sensor system as standard.

When introduced into service, the BRDM-2 had bet-

A first production series BRDM-2. This BRDM, in Soviet parade colors, has the guard's symbol placed on the front superstructure rather than the hull side, which was more common. The triangular rear deck vents (raised here) were used on the first series production model BRDM-2.

Early production model BRDM-2. This vehicle is displayed at the Central Armed Forces Museum in Moscow.

BRDM-2 turret. Central Armed Forces Museum, Moscow.

BRDM-2. Central Armed Forces Museum, Moscow.

ter road speed and range than the original BRDM, with all-terrain and amphibious performance also improved. One major failing of the orginal BRDM was retained, however, namely the lack of access doors in the hull, forcing the crew to climb onto the vehicle over the sides and rear.

The BRDM-2 has been a highly successful design, having served in the Soviet and Russian Armies from 1963 to the present day. During its thirty-six years of service, the BRDM-2's wheeled APC contemporaries have gone through several generation changes. Between 1963 and the end of production in 1989, some 19,000 BRDM-2 vehicles were manufactured, of which nearly fifty percent were specialized types. The BRDM-2 was widely exported to former Warsaw Pact countries and Soviet client states in standard, ATGM, and NBC reconnaissance variants, with approximately 6,000 vehicles being exported in total. Some countries adopted their own name for the BRDM-2. For instance, former East Germany designated the BRDM-2 as the SPW-40P2. Hungary produced its own FUG-65 (OT-65) and FUG-70 (OT-70) armored cars on the basis of the BRDM-2. The BRDM-2 continues in military service worldwide today.

Each Russian MRD has twenty-eight BRDM-2s, twelve in the Reconnaissance Battalion and four in each tank regiment, BMP equipped MRR, and in each of the two BTR-80 (and formerly BTR-60/70) equipped MRR. Each Tank Division also has twenty-eight BRDM-2s, twelve in the Reconnaissance Battalion, four in the MRR and four in each of the three Tank Regiments.

Description

There were three distinct versions of the BRDM produced over the years, differing primarily in the layout of the engine deck air intakes. The first observed variant (plant designation GAZ-41), had two small triangular hatches over the air intakes behind the turret. The sec-

BRDM-2 crew transferring documents to a BTR-70 APC.

ond production model (plant designation GAZ-4106), had a double slatted grille air intake arrangement, while the third and final BRDM-2 variant introduced in the 1970s (plant designation GAZ-4108), had six domed baleen-type engine air intakes, correcting earlier design faults which made the engine intakes vulnerable to bullet-splash and frequently allowed water into the engine compartment. This third and final production model of the

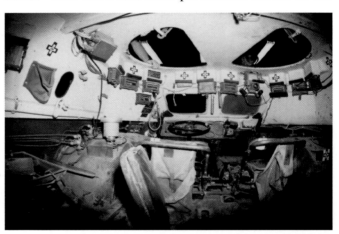

Interior view, BRDM-2. The driver's position is on the left, with the vehicle commander or missile controller's position on the right. (Steven J. Zaloga)

BRDM-2 was originally known in the West as the BRDM-3, but in Russia it remained designated BRDM-2, or was more rarely known by the plant number GAZ-4108.

The crew of the BRDM-2 usually consists of commander, driver, and two reconnaisance crew, one of whom acts as the gunner when the commander requires. The driver sits at the front left with the vehicle commander to his right. Both are provided with bulletproof windscreens and top hinged armored shutters which can be closed down in combat. A total of eight vision periscopes are provided for the commander and driver. Entry and exit is via two semi-circular roof hatches in the front of the fighting compartment roof. The BRDM-2's driver has a

Side view of a BRDM-2 at Aberdeen Proving Grounds, Maryland, USA. (Steven J. Zaloga)

BRDM-2 rear view.

marginally easier life than previous, with labor-saving devices including hydraulic-assisted steering and air-assisted brakes. There is a single firing port for the driver and commander in each side of the fighting compartment. In the middle of each side of the sloped upper fighting compartment is a projecting multiple vision port with three blocks set forward, sideways and rearward for maximum (180°) vision.

The turret is located in the center of the vehicle and is the same as used in the BTR-60/70/80 wheeled APCs. Traverse and elevation controls are all manually operated. The gunner or commander/gunner sits on a seat suspended from the turret sides. The turret is too small to have a roof hatch and so the gunner must exit the vehicle through the forward roof hatches.

The BRDM-2 is armed with a 14.5mm KPVT heavy machine gun, with a co-axial 7.62mm PKT machine gun mounted to the right of the main armament. The KPVT provides the BRDM with a light anti-armor capability sufficient to engage APCs and light AFVs to a range of 2,000m. The KPVT has a cyclic rate of fire of 600rpm and 500 rounds of 14.5mm ammunition for the weapon are carried on board. The PKT has an effective range of 1,500m and a cyclic rate of fire of 700rpm, with 2,500 rounds of 7.62mm ammunition being carried within the vehicle as standard.

The BRDM-2's armor is of welded construction

throughout, with a maximum armor thickness of 14mm on the hull front. This is insufficient to prevent penetration by US/NATO 0.50 caliber weapons at short range, and the vehicle is vulnerable to shrapnel from nearby artillery explosions.

The BRDM-2 is, like the original BRDM, fully amphibious. It has a single hydrojet propulsion system. Water is drawn into the system from under the vehicle hull and then driven out through the single rear hydrojet. Steering is by rudders set in the hydrojet tunnel and connected to the steering wheel. A single piece hatch covers the hydrojet when not in use. Before entering the water preparations are limited to manually erecting the trim vane and switching the bilge pump system on. When not required, the trim vane is stowed under the vehicle nose. The BRDM-2 can swim at speeds of up to seven km/hour with an endurance of approximately twenty-four hours.

Like the original BRDM, the BRDM-2 is fitted with a driver-operated CTPRS which can adjust the pressure on all tires or any selected tire to compensate for ground conditions or battle damage to any wheel. The air compressor maintains air pressure in the event of wheel damage on the battlefield and the system can be operated while the vehicle is on the move. The four chain-driven auxiliary wheels with 700 x 250mm aviation tires as used on the original BRDM are also used on the BRDM-2, preventing the vehicle from bottoming out while traversing uneven terrain.

The BRDM-2 is fitted with a winch as standard, mounted behind the front nose armor on the right side of the vehicle. When not in use, the winch opening is covered by a small hatch. The winch has thiry meters of cable and has a 4,000kg load capacity.

FG-125 infra-red driving lights are standard on the BRDM-2 and the commander is provided with an OU-3GK infra-red searchlight. The main armament is provided with a PPN-2 infra-red night sight with a range of 400m. The BRDM-2 is provided with a TNA-2 land navigation system as standard.

The base model BRDM-2 has a basic NBC overpressure system, with the air intake located on the left side of the hull roof behind the turret. Limited NBC detection equipment, consisting of a DP-3B roentgenmeter (with a range of 0-500 R/hour) and VPKhR portable chemical reconnaissance meter, is carried aboard the vehicle.

Suspension consists of semi-elliptical springs all round, with telescopic dual action hydraulic shock absorbers. The vehicle transmission is installed within the hull armor.

9P122 (AT-3 Sagger) ATGM Vehicle

The 9P122 ATGM system was developed in 1968 and became the definitive ATGM version of the BRDM-2 armored car series. The 9P122 launch vehicle entered service with the Soviet Army at the end of 1968 as a replacement for the 2P32, which was based on the original BRDM vehicle.

The 9P122 was fitted with a retractable firing mecha-

Interior view, BRDM-2 9P122 ATGM vehicle. The right seat on the 9P122 ATGM is occupied by the missile controller. Note the joystick control and raised superstructure for the sight.

nism, the overhead roof of which also formed the roof armor of the launch vehicle. Six missiles were mounted under the roof, and when not in use the mechanism was hydraulically lowered into the fighting compartment. In an emergency, the launcher mechanism could be manually raised. Eight reload missiles were stowed within the fighting compartment, which was a major improvement over previous ATGM systems. The missile operator sat in the front right of the vehicle with a small fire control panel in front of his position.

The 9P122 was armed with six 9M14M Malyutka M missiles, better known in the West for many years as the AT-3 Sagger. The 9M14M Malyutka M (AT-3b Sagger

Missile controller's station. Note the missile launch control box and joystick controller. (Steven J. Zaloga)

B) missile was developed specifically for use with the 9P122 launch vehicle and for infantry use with a "suitcase" container/launcher. The system was developed by the KBM Bureau at Kolomna, which had also developed the first generation 3M6 Schmel (AT-1 Snapper) ATGM system.

The 9M14M had an effective anti-armor range from 500m to 3,000m, with the capability to defeat 410mm of armor at 0° incidence. The missiles were controlled in flight by a trailing wire which was both more economical and less vulnerable to interference than its predecessors.

The 9M14M missiles were launched from within the 9P122 by the vehicle missile operator/commander, using a tracking sight in the front right of the fighting compartment roof. An experienced operator and crew could expect to achieve a maximum rate of fire of three missiles per minute. A remote control unit also allowed the missiles to be fired and tracked remotely at a distance of up to eighty meters from the vehicle. This resulted in difficulties in tracking the missiles, increasing the minimum range to 800m. This would have proved particularly difficult in any combat against NATO in Europe, where tank engagement ranges would have been in general at

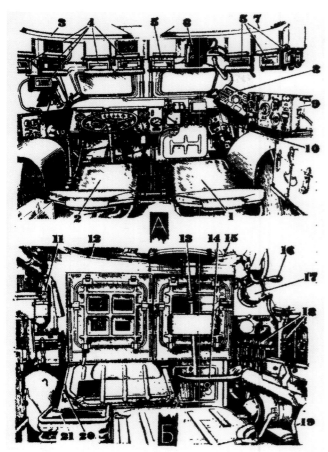

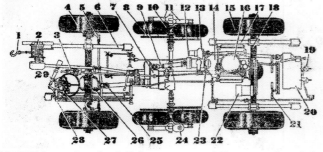

Fighting compartment layout, BRDM-2. The two views here; looking forward (A) and rearward (B), are from the BRDM's operator's manual.

BRDM mechanical drive system. The complex drive arrangement of the BRDM-2 is evident here, with four-wheel drive, auxiliary drive, hydrojet propulsion, and the front-mounted winch.

BRDM-2 in two-tone camouflage. Khantymirovskaya Tank Division, Moscow, 1998. (Alexandr Koshavtsev)

BRDM-2 third production model engine deck. The third production model (GAZ-4108) of the BRDM-2 has the distinctive air intakes shown here, designed to ensure that the engine remains dry under all conditions.

or under 1,000m. In defensive overwatch roles, the 9P122 was emplaced in scrapes built by BAT/BAT-M tracked engineering vehicles some 500m behind the forward engagement line. With its inability to fire on the move and relatively thin armor, the 9P122 was not designed for direct engagements with tanks but rather to provide long range ATGM support to Soviet Tank Divisions and Motorized Rifle Divisions.

The 9P122 was first used in combat during the 1973 Arab-Israeli conflict (The Yom Kippur War), where it served with Egyptian and Syrian forces. The system,

9P122 ATGM vehicle in firing position, June 1967. This frontal view shows clearly that the missiles are not inline, the central missile of each group of the three being raised slightly. (Yagudin)

BRDM-2 on display at the Officer's Club, Yuzhno-Sakhalinsk, Sakhalin Island, Russia.

This unusual photograph of a BRDM-2 (a 9P122 ATGM vehicle) in Polish army service gives a good view of the vehicle undercarriage.

9P122 ATGM vehicle at the Imperial War Museum, Duxford, UK, 1998. (Peter Plume, courtesy of IWM Duxford)

BRDM-2 9P122 ATGM vehicle. This vehicle was first displayed at the Artillery, Engineering, and Communications Troops Museum in St. Petersburg, Russia.

BRDM-2 9P122 launch mechanism. The launch rails are not sequentially numbered. (Steven J. Zaloga)

BRDM-2 9P122 ATGM vehicle, side view.

Rear view of a 9P122 launch mechanism. Note that four launch rails are in line and two are raised. (Steven J. Zaloga)

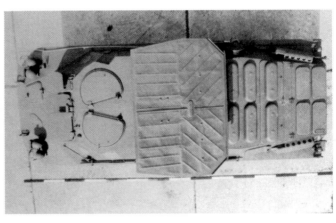

BRDM-2 9P122 ATGM vehicle, overhead view. Most 9P122 ATGM vehicles were built on the second production series BRDM-2. This vehicle is a rarer third production series vehicle.

BRDM-2 9P122 ATGM vehicle. The twin doors on the missile control sight are open in this view.

BRDM-2 9P122 ATGM with remote missile control. The 9M14 Sagger missiles could be fired remotely from the vehicle by means of a portable control box linked to the vehicle by a cable.

BRDM-2 9P122 ATGM vehicles on exercise. These are painted in Guards parade markings.

9P122 ATGM vehicles during winter exercises in the 1970s. They are painted in a whitewash paint sheme with the base green left on the front and sides as exercise identification markings.

BRDM-2 9P122. Note the trim vane stowed position and the small firing port on the fighting compartment side.

BRDM-2 9P122. The auxiliary wheels are lowered on this vehicle.

BRDM-2 9P122. Note the sight, which differs from that used on the 9P124.

along with its "suitcase"-launched infantry version, caused havoc with Israeli tank formations when first encountered in an ambush engagement on 6th October 1973. It led to press reports signalling that the weapon meant the end of the tank in modern warfare. The Israelis quickly recovered from the initial encounters with the missile system, however, and among later discoveries about the system were that its first launch hit probability was only twenty-five percent with trained crews, far less than the U.S. Army and NATO had earlier predicted. The vehicle-mounted 9P122 did, however, provide the capability to rapidly establish and relocate an anti-tank defense line and was well suited to its designed role, where several vehicles provided combined fire and thereby increased the overall effectiveness despite the low hit probability of each individual vehicle mounted system. The relatively small number of reserve missiles carried within the 9P122 launch vehicle remained a limiting factor. The launch vehicles, being lightly armored, were also very vulnerable to artillery counter-fire and relied on movement for survival.

In addition to the ATGM system, the 9P122 vehicle carried an 7.62mm RPK machine gun with 1,000 rounds of ammunition and an RPG-7 anti-tank rocket launcher with eight PG-7 anti-tank rockets.

The 9P122 retained the amphibious capability of the base model BRDM-2. The powered auxiliary wheels were also retained, giving the 9P122 ATGM vehicle performance close to the standard BRDM-2 reconnaissance vehicle.

There were thirty-six BRDM ATGM vehicles in each Soviet MRD, nine in the Anti-tank Battalion, nine in the BMP equipped MRR, and nine in each BTR-70/80 equipped MRR. A Soviet Tank Division had nine BRDM ATGM vehicles in its BMP equipped MRR.

The 9P122 was a relatively cheap and simple mobile anti-tank system compared to other missile systems in contemporary Russian service. As such, it was also widely exported, being sold to many countries including Afghanistan, Ethiopia, Iraq, Libya, Syria, and Yugoslavia, in addition to the usual Warsaw Pact clientele of the Soviet Union.

9P124 (AT-2) ATGM Vehicle

BRDM-2 9P124 ATGM vehicle, overhead view.

The 9P124 is a rare vehicle, which was first publicly observed in 1973 after the introduction of the 9P122. The 9P124 mounted four 9M17M Skorpion P (AT-2c Swatter, Falanga-M) missiles under a fully retractable overhead roof in an almost identical arrangement to the 9P122 system. The 9P124 was fielded as a more accu-

rate long range ATGM system to be used for selective overwatch roles while the less capable, but cheaper to produce 9P122 remained the standard Soviet Army wheeled ATGM system. The 9P124 vehicle effectively replaced the older 2P32 on the original BRDM chassis.

Four missiles were transported in the ready-to-fire position, attached to their under armor launching points, another four missiles being stored within the fighting compartment, providing a total of eight missiles carried on the vehicle. With the missile system retracted, the 9P124 vehicle can be differentiated from the 9P122 by the modified missile sight on the fighting compartment roof and small door in the left side of the fighting com-

Soviet Army BRDM-2 9P124 ATGM vehicles on parade. The quadruple mount 9P124 was introduced in 1973, five years after the 9P122 entered service with the Soviet Army. It fired the 9M17M Skorpion P (AT-2c Swatter) missile, a much improved version of the 3M11 (AT-2a) missile used on the original model BRDM 2P32 ATGM vehicle.

BRDM-2 9P124 ATGM vehicle. This second series production model BRDM-2 based 9P124 is about to enter Red Square during an annual 7th November military parade.

BRDM-2 9P124 displayed at the Artillery Museum, St. Petersburg.

9P124 front detail.

Left side view of the 9P124. Note the small hatch on the fighting compartment side, which is one of the few recognition features that distinguish the 9P124 from the 9P122 with the missile launcher platform stowed.

9P124 sight detail. Compare the sight shape and its armored door with that used on the 9P122.

partment superstructure forward of the missile launcher.

The 9M17M Skorpion P missile used with the 9P124 had a range of 3,500m, increased from 3,000m for the 9M17 Fleyta (AT-2a), with an armor defeating capability of 560mm @ 0° incidence. The 9M17M Skorpion P missiles were provided with infra-red SACLOS (Semi-Active Command Line of Sight) guidance rather than the radio controlled MCLOS of the earlier 2P32 Fleyta (AT-2a) system mounted on the BRDM-1. The SACLOS system employed still involved conventional wire guidance for the missiles but with a semi-active command link. The operator was required only to keep the target within his sight with the missile following the target designation rather than the operator trying to first find the missile in flight and then track it to its target, as with earlier MCLOS systems. The result was improved minimum range required to accurately acquire the target.

9P133 (AT-3c) ATGM Vehicle

In 1969 the BRDM-2 (usually the GAZ-4106 variant) was fitted with the upgraded 9M14P Malyutka-P (AT-3c Sagger C) missile system. So equipped, the vehicle was designated 9P133. The vehicle is externally almost identical to the 9P122.

The principal improvement of the 9M14P over the earlier 9M14M missile system was the use of a second generation SACLOS guidance system with resultant far higher first hit probability, and an improvement in minimum range.

Further improvements and upgrades of ATGM systems mounted on the BRDM-2 chassis included the provision of infra-red SACLOS guidance in 1977, and the later modification of the 9P122 to fire the improved 9M14P1 (Matyutka P1) and 9M14P2 (Malyutka P2) missiles.

9P137 (AT-2) ATGM Vehicle

The designation 9P137 was originally thought in the West to classify the first vehicles to mount the 9M113 Konkurs missile with its distinctive five tube launcher. It was usually referred to in the West as the AT-5 Spandrel. The thinking was that the later, almost identical 9P148 introduced the capability to fire both the 9M113 (AT-5) and the smaller 9M111 (AT-4) missiles. It is now understood from original Russian sources that the 9P148 system was developed as having such a dual capability from its conception and that the system was always known in Soviet Army service as the 9P148.

Though as yet unconfirmed (the BRDM-2 mounted ATGM missile system designations still not being declassified in Russia), reliable Russian sources indicate that the designation 9P137 is believed to have been used for the 9P124 vehicle firing the 9M17M Skorpion P (AT-2c (Swatter), (AT-2c (Swatter)/Falanga-M) when used with a SACLOS guidance system.

9P148 (AT-5 Spandrel) ATGM Vehicle

The replacement for the 9P122 and 9P133 Sagger systems in Soviet Army service was the 9P148 system firing the 9M113 Konkurs missile. The missile entered service in 1974, though it was not publicly observed on its 9P148 launcher until the 7th November military parade on Red Square in 1977. The 9P148 ATGM system quickly replaced earlier ATGM systems in the Soviet Army and the Group of Soviet Forces in Germany

BRDM-2 9P148 ATGM vehicles parade in Red Square, Moscow. The 9P148 ATGM vehicle entered service with the Soviet Army in 1974, but was first publicly displayed in Red Square, Moscow, on 7th November 1977. It was originally known in the West as the 9P137.

(GSFG), with all Russian Category 1 units being equipped with the new system by 1980. In Western terms, the BRDM-2 mounted 9P148 ATGM system was originally known as the BRDM-3, firing the AT-5 Spandrel missile.

The 9M113 Konkurs missile was developed by the KBP OKB at Tula under the direction of A. Shipunov. The 9M113 missile was developed as an upgraded version of the 9M111 (AT-4 Fagot) missile with better anti-tank capability than the 9M111, which entered service with the Soviet Army in 1973, slightly earlier than the 9P148 vehicle mounted version. The 9M113 Konkurs

missile has better range (75-4,000m) and armor defeating capability (600mm) than the 9M14M missile. It also travels at 208m/s; the significantly faster flight time reducing the likelihood of detection and consequent destruction or interference in flight. The 9M113 missile was bulky and heavy (28.5kg) compared to the 8kg 9M111 and 12.9kg 9M111M missiles, so internal stowage was compromised. The 9M113 missile used with the 9P148 was later replaced by the 9M113M Konkurs M. The systems were designated 9K113 and 9K113M respectively.

Frontal view of a 9P148 ATGM vehicle. The five 9M113 Konkurs launch tubes are mounted on a 360° traverse turntable. Note the missile operator's sight, turned to the right in this photograph.

The 9P148 launch vehicle used the later version of the BRDM-2 (GAZ-4108) with the balleen type air intakes on the rear deck. This model is often designated BRDM-3 in the West, though the Russians adopted no such designation for the improved vehicle. The 9P148 launch vehicle has a crew of two, the driver and commander/ATGM system operator.

The 9P148 fired five 9M113 Konkurs missiles, each mounted within its own tube launcher on a central launch assembly. The 9P148 vehicle/9M113 missile system was

9P148 ATGM vehicle. These 9P148s are on parade in Red Square, Moscow in the mid-1970s.

Overhead view of the 9P148 ATGM vehicle.

9P148 ATGM vehicles on Red Square, Moscow, during a 7th November parade.

Side view of a former East German army 9P148 ATGM vehicle.

Overhead view of a former East German army 9P148 ATGM vehicle.

9P148 launcher with five 9M113 Konkurs (AT-5 Spandrel) missiles attached.

9P148 ATGM vehicle. A rare view of a 9P148 with the launch mechanism stowed and the launcher hatch in the open position. With the launcher stowed, the 9P148 can, at a distance, be misidentified as a turretless BRDM-2U command vehicle.

9P148 ATGM vehicle. This vehicle is on display at the Artillery, Engineering, and Communications Forces Museum in St. Petersburg.

Sight and radio dashpot detail on the 9P148 ATGM vehicle.

9P148 M-1996 ATGM vehicle. The 9P148 ATGM is capable of firing both the 9M113 Konkurs and the 9M111 Fagot missiles. In Soviet Army service, five 9M113 missiles are usually mounted in the launcher. The use of smaller 9M111 missiles alongside the larger 9M113 missiles allows the stowage of twenty missiles within the vehicle. This is the latest version of the 9P148, with a thermal image system operator's sight. (Andrey Aksenov)

9P148 M-1996 ATGM vehicle. First displayed at the Defense Manufacturer's Exhibition at Tula, Russia, in October 1996, this latest version of the 9P148 probably uses the modified 9M113M Konkurs M missile. Note the size of the thermal sight. (Andrey Aksenov)

Rear view of the 9P148 M-1996 ATGM vehicle. This is the same vehicle as shown in the top picture. Note the biological hazard warnings on the vehicle sides. The vehicle to the left is a new version of the BTR-80 APC, introduced at the same exhibition, with 30mm 2A72 cannon and anti-tank missile armament. (Andrey Aksenov)

a second generation system, with much improved SACLOS tracking and fire control. The SACLOS sight had an ability to track missiles in a frontal arc of 180°. The electro-optical tracking system is mounted on the front right of the fighting compartment, with the sight mechanism projecting through the hull roof. The SACLOS system is fitted with a manual override for use as required, such as when optical jamming is encountered (the SACLOS system used on the 9P148 can detect such interference and warn the operator).

The 9P148 has a five-rail launcher system to which the 9M113 Konkurs missiles are attached within their individual launch tubes. Reload is achieved by means of a rectangular hatch directly behind the launch mechanism,

9P148 missile launch system. The 9P148 launch mechanism is rarely observed without the missile launch tubes attached. The launch system is traversed to the rear in this photograph.

through which the launcher is retracted at 90°, allowing the missiles to be reloaded by the operator from within the armored fighting compartment. Reload takes around thirty seconds for a trained crew and ten reload rounds are stowed within the fighting compartment. When not required, the launcher is retracted down through the small hatch on the fighting compartment roof. When travelling with the launcher retracted the 9P148 is, at a distance, almost identical in appearance to the BRDM-2U command vehicle.

The 7kg HEAT warhead, used with the 9M113 Konkurs missiles, has an armor penetration of 500-600mm @ 0° incidence. Flight time to target is normally fifteen to twenty seconds.

The 9P148 can accomodate a total of fourteen missiles, including five mounted ready to launch.

The 9P148 launch vehicle allowed the use of 9M113 Konkurs (AT-5 Spandrel) and 9M111 Fagot (NATO AT-4 Spigot) or, latterly 9M111-2 and 9M111M missiles in any combination on the same launcher assembly. In

Soviet service, five 9M113 missiles were normally carried. Three larger 9M113 and two smaller 9M111 missiles was a standard configuration in the East German Army and other former export clients such as Iraq. The main reason for mounting the primarily infantry-used 9M111-2 alongside the larger 9M113 was that it saved stowage space, thereby allowing the vehicle to carry a total of twenty missiles, with ten of each type being carried on board.

A modified version of the 9P148 was revealed for the first time during a military exhibition in Tula, near Moscow in the summer of 1996. The new version has a large thermal sight on the right side of the fighting compartment roof. At the time of writing the vehicle has not entered service with the Russian Army.

BRDM-2U Command Vehicle

Two distinct command versions of the BRDM-2 were produced for Battalion and Regimental HQ functions in Motorized Rifle Regiments, one retaining the original turret and the other being turretless. Both vehicles served the same function.

The turretless BRDM-U has a small forward opening hatch located centrally in the roof armor where the turret would otherwise be. Behind the hatch, a generator is located on the vehicle roof. There are two radio antennae on the BRDM-2U, one on either side of the vehicle in front of the side viewing ports. The turreted BRDM-U has four radio antennae, one on each side of the hull and two at the hull rear. East Germany and Poland used turretless BRDM-Us which differed from the Russian models in detail, most having a single rail antenna mounted on the hull roof.

BRDM-2U command vehicle. This overhead view of a standard, turretless BRDM-2U shows the distinguishing features of the vehicle. Note the twin radio antennae and the third roof hatch with a generator mounted behind on the vehicle roof. This BRDM-2 is based on a second series production model BRDM-2.

BRDM-2U command vehicles in Russian Army service, 1993. These turreted BRDM-2U command vehicles are pictured at Khodinka Airfield, Moscow, after use by the Russian Army on the streets of Moscow during the failed coup attempt in October 1993. (Alexsei Mikheev)

BRDM-2RKh NBC Reconnaissance Vehicle

There are two chemical scout versions of the BRDM-2, the original RKhA and the modernized RKhB. Both versions are fitted with two warning flag emplacing units at the rear, which fire flags into the ground to mark clear lanes through contaminated areas. The yellow flags are marked "Zarazheno" (contaminated). When not in use, the dispensers are swung 180° and sit on the rear of the vehicle under canvas covers.

There were twenty-nine chemical scout vehicles in each Soviet MRD, nine in the Chemical Defence Battalion, four in the Divisional Reconnaissance Battalion, four in the single Tank Regiment, four in the BMP-equipped MRR and four in each of the two MRRs. Tank Regiments also had around twenty-nine vehicles, four in the BMP-equipped MRR and four in each Tank Regiment.

BRDM-2 Rkh NBC reconnaissance vehicles were in some instances replaced in the Soviet Army during the 1980s by the tracked RKhM.

Preparing the flag dispenser units on a BRDM-2 Rkh vehicle. BRDM-2 Rkh vehicles carry two flag emplacer boxes, each containing twenty flags. These are electrically fired from within the vehicle, a small explosive charge embeding the flags into the ground. The boxes are swung 180° for transport.

BRDM-2 RKhA

The first chemical reconnaissance version of the BRDM-2 was the BRDM-2 RKhA. This version is easily distinguished from the later, definitive model as it retains the original 4.5mm KPVT heavy machine gun in the turret. The original BRDM-2 RKhA was used in relatively small numbers in comparison with the later BRDM-2 RKhB model.

BRDM-2 RKhA overhead view. This vehicle is based on the second production series BRDM-2, as can be identified by the engine deck with modified air intakes.

BRDM-2 RKhB

The second, modernized version of the BRDM-RKh, designated RKhB, is easily distinguished as it is armed with a 7.62mm PKT machine gun, centrally located in the turret in place of the earlier 14.5mm KPVT and co-axial 7.62mm PKT arrangement of the earlier model. The additional space provided by not installing the KPVT weapon is used for mounting additional sensor equipment. Air is drawn into the vehicle via vents in the turret mantlet and expelled through the turret roof, with an additional two vents in front of the driver's position. Within the hull, air samples are analyzed by vehicle-mounted versions of the VPKhR-54 system installed on the earlier BRDM and other on-board and portable measuring equipment.

On most vehicles three flare launchers, which launch signal rockets (signalnie raketi) or "sound stars", are mounted alongside the machine gun on the mantlet. These sound stars give warning to ground forces of a chemical contaminated environment being entered. The RKhB was a modernization and upgrade of the RkhA rather than a separate version. The RKhB has a combat weight of 7,090kg and a crew of three.

BRDM-2 RKhA chemical reconnaissance vehicle. The original RKhA version of the BRDM-2 retained the original turret and armament of the standard BRDM-2. All BRDM-2 RKhAs were eventually modified to RKhB standard with the deletion of the 14.5mm KPVT heavy machine gun and provision of additional sensor equipment.

BRDM-2 RKhB in Soviet Army service. The BRDM-2 RKhB has a new turret with only the 7.62mm PKT machine gun retained, with three "sound star" flare launcher tubes mounted alongside.

BRDM-2 RKhB in service with a Polish marine reconnaissance unit.

Polish army BRDM-2 RKhBs being decontaminated in the field.

Russian BRDM-2 RKhB in rail transit. Note the flag emplacer units in their stowed position, the mounting of the spare wheel, and other stowage on the vehicle.

BRDM-2 RKhB on display in Moscow, 1993. Note the single 7.62mm PKT machine gun installation. (Andrey Aksenov)

Flag emplacer units on the BRDM-2 RKhB. Note the additional fuel cans mounted on the superstructure side. (Andrey Aksenov)

BRDM-2 RKhB front fighting compartment and night vision equipment. (Andrey Aksenov)

BRDM-2 RKhB rear engine deck and flag emplacer units. The engine deck shows this vehicle to be a third production series (GAZ-4108) model BRDM-2. (Andrey Aksenov)

BRDM-2 RKhB. This rear view shows the marking flags in their emplacer units.

Close-up of a Czech BRDM-2 RKhB being decontaminated.

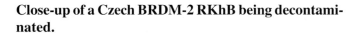

BRDM-2 RKhB at the Tank Museum, Bovington, UK. This ex-Iraqi BRDM-2 RKhB NBC reconnaissance vehicle is displayed in its original color scheme, as captured during the Gulf War.

BRDM-2 RKhB at Aberdeen Proving Ground, Maryland, USA. This vehicle is an ex-Iraqi BRDM-2 RKhB, with the rear flag dispenser frames still evident on the rear of the vehicle. The turret is traversed to the rear.

BRDM-2 RKhB, Omsk Military Show, June 1999. (Andrey Aksenov)

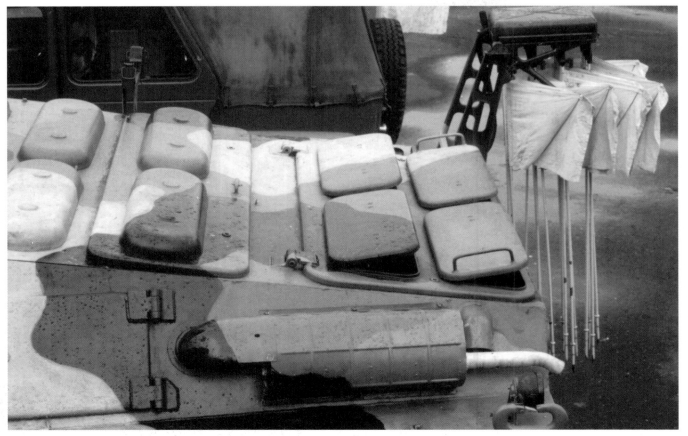

BRDM-2 RKhB flag dispenser with yellow marking pennants. (Andrey Aksenov)

Rear view of a BRDM-2 RKhB. (Andrey Aksenov)

BRDM-2 RKhB turret. (Andrey Aksenov)

BRDM-2 RKhB at Aberdeen Proving Grounds, Maryland, USA. This front view shows the small winch door on the hull nose.

BRDM-2 ZRK 9K31 STRELA-1 (SA-9) SAM System

In the immediate post-war era, the Soviet Army was provided with considerable numbers of anti-aircraft guns, making up for a recognized lack of anti-aircraft cover (particularly mobile systems) during World War II. As technology advanced, missile systems were subsequently introduced alongside conventional anti-aircraft guns, and in 1960, work began on a light sirface-to-air missle (SAM) system which was to be mounted on the BRDM-2 chassis. The system was later to be designated as the ZRK 9K31 Strela-1 anti-aircraft missile system, better known in the West by the name SA-9 "Gaskin".

Work on the ZRK system began in 1960, with initial design carried out at the NTK (Nauchno Tekhnicheskiy Komitet) GRAU bureau under G.V. Kartsev, and NII-3 led by B.F. Lazarev. Later development of the 9K31 system was split between several bureaus, including KBTM (Konstruktorskoye Bureau Tochnovo Mashinostroeniya - Precision Machine Building Bureau) which was responsible for developing the overall 9K31 complex, GKOT (Gosudarstvenny Komitet po Oboronnoy Tekhnike - State Committee for Military Equipment), under the direction

of A.Ye Nudelman as senior engineer, and with design of the missile guidance and homing systems being undertaken at the TsKB (Tsentralnoe Konstruktorskoe Bureau - Central Construction Bureau) "Geofizika" under senior engineer D.M. Khorol.

A.Ye Nudelman was ultimately responsible for the entire 9K31 project. 9K31 is the system designation, 9M31 is the missile designation, and 9P31 is the designation for the TEL vehicle.

The 9K31 Strela-1 was developed concurrently with the man-portable 9K32 Strela-2 (SA-7 Grail) system and was not, as often detailed in Western publications, an enlarged version of the man-portable system. The 9K32 entered service in 1967, a year earlier than the vehicle-mounted 9K31 system, which led to the assumption that the former was an enlarged vehicle mounted version of the latter. There have been persistent unverified rumors as to a quad version of the 9K32 (SA-7) having been trialled on the BRDM-2 chassis. Though unconfirmed, it would seem likely that some trials might logically had been conducted to test the basic vehicle configuration for such a SAM system. The 9M31 missile which was eventually introduced into service on its BRDM-2 chassis in 1968 as the 9K31 ZRK Strela-1 was, however, considerably larger than the 9K32 (SA-7) Grail system and had

SPECIFICATIONS ZRK 9K31 SAM System
(9P31 TEL Vehicle)

Vehicle data:
Length: 5.9m
Width: 2.4m
Height: 2.3m (travelling)

Missile data:
Weight: 30kg (Strela-1) 30.6kg (Strela-1M)
Warhead: 2.6kg
Length: 1.80m
Diameter: 120mm
Missile Speed: 420m/s
Reaction time from target location: 8.5 seconds

Control system:
GSN Infra - Red

man turret with a glass operator's window and elevating arm for the four 9M31 missiles in their containers, two of which are mounted each side of the central elevating tower on a light gantry frame. Elevation and traverse are manually operated.

No reserve missiles are carried internally, but two spare missiles in their containers are often mounted on specialized racks on either side of the vehicle fighting compartment.

The 9M31 missiles are infra-red tracking "fire and forget" systems. The early missiles had a range of 50-3,000m, with a maximum altitude of 3,000m. The later Strela-1M, introduced in 1970, has an improved lock-on capability and an anti-aircraft range of 560-8,000m, with

9P31 TEL vehicle, overhead view.

little commonality with the earlier man-portable system.

State proving trials were conducted in 1968 at the Dongusk Polygon, after which the system was accepted for service with the Soviet Army and Soviet Naval Marine forces.

Preparation for series production of the 9K31 system on its BRDM-2 based 9P31 transporter, erector, launcher (TEL) chassis was carried out at the Saratovskiy Agregatny Zavod (Saratov parts plant), while the 9M31 rocket was prepared for production at the Kovrovsky Mechanical Zavod.

When it was introduced into Soviet Army service in 1968, the 9K31 Strela-1 was the first Soviet wheeled self-propelled anti-aircraft defense system (SPAADS) to enter service since the BTR-40A and BTR-152A. The system had a long service life with the Soviet Army and was widely exported. The 9K31 was replaced in Soviet Army service during the 1980s by the tracked ZRK Strela 10 (SA-13 Gopher) and its later Strela 10M, 10M2, and 10M3 modifications on the MT-LB derived 9A34/9A35 TEL vehicle.

The BRDM-2 chassis was significantly modified for service use as the TEL vehicle for the 9K31 (SA-9) SAM. To accomodate the additional weight and improve the internal space requirements of the missile control systems, the auxiliary belly wheels of the standard BRDM-2 were removed though CTPRS and amphibious capability was retained. The 9K31 was primarily built on the second production model BRDM-2 (GAZ-4106) chassis with the system later also being fitted on the modified GAZ-4108 chassis.

The 9P31 TEL vehicle is easily recognized by its one-

an altitude cover of 30-3,500m. The missiles are fitted with Frag-HE warheads. The 9K31 system was in Soviet Army service located in defensive positions 500-2,500m behind the ZSU-23-4 self-propelled anti-aircraft gun system (SPAAGS), with which they were deployed to form a combined defensive shield.

The 9K31 underwent a rapid continuous improve-

Crew exiting a 9P31 TEL vehicle.

9P31 TEL vehicle, 9K31 Strela-1 SAM system. This vehicle, in service with the former East German Army, is shown in transit mode, with missile boxes removed and the launcher folded to the rear. Note the rack on the vehicle side for attaching an additional missile container.

BRDM-2 9P31 TEL vehicles on Red Square, Moscow, 7th November 1997.

ZRK 9K31 Strela-1 (NATO: SA-9 Gaskin) SAM TEL vehicles on exercise.

ZRK 9K31 Strela-1s on parade, Red Square, Moscow. 7th November 1977.

ZRK 9K31 Strela-1 four-way drawing.

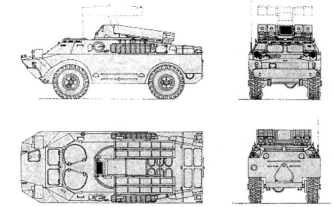

9P31 TEL vehicles in service with the Polish Army.

9P31 TEL vehicle on display at the military museum, Lesany, Czech Republic. (Roland Seifert)

Ex-Iraqi 9P31 located at the Tank Museum, Bovington, UK, in 1991. Note the side rack for accomodating a containerized missile and the distinctive metal guards fitted over the driving lights on 9P31 vehicles.

9P31 TEL vehicle in 1996. This vehicle is displayed at the Air Defence Training Center at Eisk in southern Russia. (Aleksei Mikheev)

ment program throughout its service life. Soon after its introduction into service, the original Strela-1 system was replaced by the Strela-1M, which was tested at the Dongusk polygon in 1969 and entered service with the Soviet Army in 1970. The original 9P31 launch vehicle was modified several times during its service life to accomodate the changes required by continuous upgrading of the missile system. Later modifications of the launch vehicle are the 9P31M Strela-1M introduced into service in 1970, the 9P-31M2 Strela-1M2, 9P-31MR Stela-1MR, and 9P31R Strela-1R.

In transit, the missile launch system is lowered to the rear, with the missile boxes sitting on the TEL vehicle's engine deck.

The 9P31 is normally deployed in batteries of four TEL vehicles, one of which is fitted with the 9S12 (NATO: Flat Box) warning system, which detects radar emissions from incoming aircraft. This vehicle passes this target information to the other three TEL vehicles. The 9S12 Flat Box antenna system consists of four detectors, mounted one above each front wheel arch, one behind the turret, and one to the left of the turret window.

Each Soviet Tank Regiment and Motorized Rifle Regiment was provided with two anti-aircraft battalions, one having two sections with two 9K31 systems, the other being equipped with the tracked ZSU-23-4 SPAADS. Command in Soviet Army service was provided via the PU-12 and PU-12M command link stations based on the wheeled BTR-60 chassis.

The 9K31 system first saw combat in the Middle East with Egypt, Syria, and Iraq. It was provided to all Warsaw Pact countries and was also widely exported to other countries including Angola, Benin, Cuba, Egypt, Guineau, Guinea-Bissau, India, Iran, Iraq, Libya, Madagascar, Mali, Mozambique, Nicaragua, North Yemen, the former Yugoslavia, and Vietnam.

BRDM-2 ATM-1

The ATM-1 "Ingul" is a turretless general load carrier and recovery vehicle version of the BRDM-2, developed in the the early 1990s after defense industry manufacturing in Russia slowed dramatically. The vehicle is intended for use with Russian emergency services, though it saw service in Chechyna in 1999.

The ATM-1 has a flatbed work platform on the vehicle roof which can carry a 1,500kg load. The front windows of the standard BRDM-2 are retained, however, an additional six windows are located in the front quarters and sides of the fighting compartment.

The chain-driven auxiliary wheels are not fitted and the space used for tool stowage. Doors are located in the vehicle sides for tool access.

GAZ-3934 Armored Car

As early as the mid 1980s, the GAZ OKB had begun work on a possible successor for the BRDM-2, which had been in service with the Soviet Army since 1966. The bureau also began work on diversifying the types of vehicles produced for the military in response to demands for specialist armored vehicles for internal security and border guard roles. The collapse of the Soviet Union in 1991 and subsequent drastic reduction in defense spending accelerated this requirement. The Gorkiy Avtomobile Zavod (GAZ) and its affiliated Arzamas Engineering Plant at Arzamas (which had been producing APCs since 1980) had, as with all other military manufacturers, had used to the best of technology, finance, and personnel was now expected to modify its output in a market where the Soviet Army and Soviet government-sponsored export sales had previously been the customers for all its light AFV production.

The GAZ-3934 series was originally developed as an attempt by GAZ to diversify and enter the markets with vehicles which have a wider appeal to military, para-military, and police forces. These vehicles, though developed in response to a need for non-military applications, were eventually to be used in conventional military roles, particularly during the conflict in the breakaway Republic of Chechnya.

The GAZ-3934 armored vehicle was developed from the orignal GAZ-47 (4701) all-terrain vehicle in an attempt, as with the GAZ-3937, to produce a small number of specialized AFVs primarily intended for internal security roles rather than conventional military operations. The GAZ-3934 series was developed in an effort to develop a civilian market for production lines geared to producing armored cars and armored personnel carriers. The development mechanisms and philosophy behind the two vehicle series may have been slightly different, but as the operations in Chechnya during 1996 demonstrated, the military application of both types in modern internal security roles has secured a continued requirement for the new vehicles now being produced by the Arzamas division of GAZ.

The base model in the GAZ-3934 series was developed in 1993 as an armored security vehicle. It was developed concurrently with the GAZ-3937 and is based on the same chassis. Generically called SIAM or SIAM-001, the base model GAZ-3934 was originally conceived as a delivery vehicle for money and valuables on Russia's

Ingul recovery vehicle. This vehicle is displayed at the NIIBT museum in Kubinka, Moscow in 1996. This vehicle type was used during the fighting in Chechnya in late 1999.

Turretless BRDM-2 in Moscow suburbs during the first Chechnyan war. During the first war with Chechnya, Russian militia and MVD units used a variety of AFVs as road check posts. This particular vehicle has been converted from a 9P148 ATGM vehicle. (Andrey Aksenov)

streets. The GAZ-3934 has all-welded armor which provides protection against small arms fire and the cab glass is armored and bulletproof. The original GAZ-3934 entered production in 1994.

From the GAZ-3934 base model, the GAZ-39344 military variant has now been developed, fitted with a modified BTR-80 turret and armament. Interestingly, however, the original GAZ-3934 security vehicle was introduced into service with the internal security forces of the Russian Federation, having served with MVD forces in Chechnya during 1996, painted in standard Russian three-color AFV camouflage scheme. The GAZ-3934 is an interesting illustration of where a vehicle originally designed to widen the market potential of an AFV type into civilian roles during a difficult time for military vehicle manufacturers has actually found a military niche for which it was not originally intended.

GAZ-39344 Armored Car

In 1994, the GAZ OKB developed a purpose-designed military modification of the GAZ-3934 designated GAZ-39344. The new vehicle is manufactured by the Arzamas Engineering Plant and is aimed at the internal security and paramilitary market. It is not intended as a replacement for the BRDM-2, for which no produc-

tion replacement has yet been seen. Originally known simply as the "SIAM 002", the new vehicle was first publicly demonstrated at a military exhibition in Nizhny Novgorod, Russia in September 1994, then internationally during the IDEF Turkey exhibition in 1995.

The GAZ-39344 is a modification of the GAZ-3934 "SIAM" or "SIAM-001" security vehicle, which was originally developed from the chassis and automotive components of the GAZ-3937 series to fulfill bank security and other civilian roles.

Description

The GAZ-39344 has the hull of the base model GAZ-3934 but is, like the GAZ-3937-10, fitted with a new turret derived from that employed on the BTR-80. It is complete with its manually operated 14.5mm KPVT and co-axial 7.62mm PKT armament with high angle fire capability, giving the vehicle an offensive fire range of 2,000m with the 14.5mm weapon and 1,500m with the 7.62mm machine gun. Turret traverse is manual. The vehicle's armament is intended to engage ground and air targets, though the potential success in the latter role must be limited. 500 rounds of 14.5mm ammunition (ten boxes) and 2,000 rounds of 7.62mm ammunition (eight boxes) are carried within the vehicle.

The GAZ-39344 has all-welded armor which pro-

GAZ-3934 "SIAM". The base model GAZ-3934 "SIAM" was originally developed as a bank security vehicle, but was later used by MVD forces during the first war in Chechnya. This vehicle is at a military exhibition in Nizhny Novgorod. (Steven J. Zaloga)

GAZ-3934 SIAM armored delivery vehicle. Omsk Military Show, June 1999. (Andrey Aksenov)

GAZ-3934 SIAM armored delivery vehicle. Omsk Military Show, June 1999. (Andrey Aksenov)

SPECIFICATIONS GAZ-39344

Design bureau: GAZ OKB
Crew: 2 + 6 (2+4?)
Manufacturing plant: Arzamas (GAZ)
Service date: 1995
Combat weight: 7,000kg
Vehicle weight: 5,000kg
Payload: 2,000kg

Dimensions: (m)
Length: 5.64
Width: 2.32
Height: 2.65 (including turret)
Wheelbase: 2.84
Track: 1.74
Wheelbase: 2.84
Ground clearance: 0.5

Armor: (mm)
Hull front: NA
Hull sides: NA
Turret front: NA
Turret sides: NA

Armament:
Main armament: 14.5mm KPVT/500
Secondary armament: 7.62mm PKT/2,000
Firing height: NA
Elevation/depression: -5° /+60°

Automotive:
Type: GAZ-5423
Cylinders: 6 in line
Power output: 175hp (129kW)
Fuel type/capacity: NA
Cooling: Air
Transmission: Manual
Steering: Turning radius 9.5m
Tires: 13.00 - 18
Wheels: 9.00 - 18
Brakes: Mechanical. Hydraulic assisted
Electrical system: 24v
Radio: Standard

Performance:
Maximum road speed (km/h): 95
Maximum terrain speed (km/h): NA
Road range (km): 700
Terrain range (km): NA
Power/weight ratio: 17.9hp (13.4kW)/tonne
Ground pressure: NA
Gradient: 24.5°
Trench: NA
Fording: NA
Angle of Approach: 24.5°
Angle of Departure: 30.5°

vides protection against small arms fire. The cab glass is armored and bulletproof.

The driver sits at the front left of the vehicle with the commander to his right, though this may be reversed for export versions. The commander also serves as gunner as required, and when in this role sits behind in the fighting compartment, seated on a suspended turret seat. Though the crew is normally two people (driver and commander/gunner), a separate gunner can be carried if required. The total combat crew is eight, including the infantry desant complement, who sit in two rows of seats facing each other.

Access and exit from the vehicle is by large doors on each side of the vehicle. These doors open forward, allowing a degree of crew protection during exit from the vehicle. The doors are fitted with windows of bulletproof glass and a firing port is located in the right door.

In total there are four firing ports, two on the left side of the fighting compartment on either side of the door, and two in the right side; one located in the hull and the other in the door behind the window.

The GAZ-39344 is powered by the same six cylinder in-line GAZ-5423 turbo-diesel engine as other vehicles in the GAZ-3937/3934 series, with options available from both the GAZ and Yaroslavl plants.

The wheels and tires used on the GAZ-39344 are from the BRDM-2. The tires are bulletproof and protected from damage by extended wheel arches. The vehicle is fitted with a driver-operated CTPRS, which can be adjusted with the vehicle on the move.

The vehicle has a combat weight of 7,000kg and has a payload capability of 2,000kg. The GAZ-39344 is also fitted with a land navigation system as standard, in addition to a radio transmitter/receiver.

Interestingly for a Russian AFV, crew comfort has been given considerable attention in the design of the GAZ-39344, which is fitted with an air conditioning system as standard.

The GAZ-39344 was used operationally during the first war in Chechnya by the Sofrino MVD brigade.

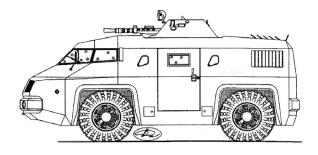

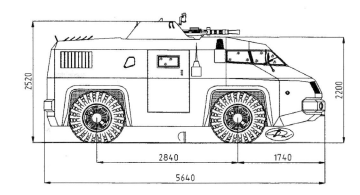

GAZ-39344 drawings. (Valery Dmitriev)

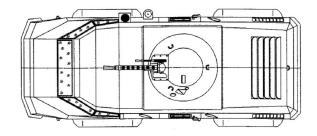

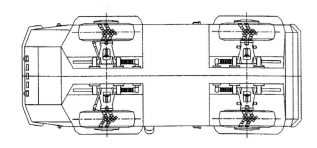

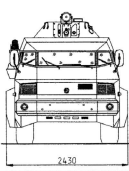

GAZ-39344.

GAZ-39344. The internal security vehicle was introduced in 1995, and has been seen in several international exhibitions during 1996 as part of a major Russian arms export drive. It was originally known as the SIAM-002.

GAZ-3937

The origins of the GAZ-3937 vehicle series began in 1984 with a border troops requirement for a high mobility lightly armored general purpose carrier similar in concept to the U.S. HMMWV "Hummer".

Attempts to produce such a vehicle using BRDM components were undertaken by NAMI, the state automobile design institute, resulting in the experimental NAMI-0281, which was developed to prototype stage. The GAZ OKB developed the concept further, resulting in a vehicle series with the generic factory designation GAZ-47. There were originally at least two variants of the GAZ-47 series; the GAZ-4701 4x4 wheeled vehicle and the tracked GAZ-4707. Both types were produced in small numbers and competitively field trialled at the NII-21 proving grounds at Bronnitsy near Moscow. The trials resulted in development of the tracked GAZ-4707 being terminated in favor of the less complex wheeled GAZ-4701, which evolved into the GAZ-3937 series.

In 1993, almost ten years after the initial requirement for a light multi-purpose vehicle for border troops had been issued, a small number of GAZ-3937 light armored vehicles were produced at GAZ, based on the BRDM-2

chassis and utilizing BRDM-2 and BTR-80 vehicle components. The base model GAZ-3937 was produced in very small numbers only (possibly as few as three vehicles) primarily for evaluation trials, exhibition, and development purposes, though the vehicle is significant in being the base model for a whole series of lightly armored military vehicles.

The GAZ-3937 was developed as a completely new

The original GAZ-3937 multi-purpose vehicle. The base model GAZ-3937 was designed for border guard, internal security vehicle, and APC roles. The base model shown here has since evolved into a whole family of specialized vehicles.

SPECIFICATIONS GAZ-3937

Design bureau: GAZ OKB
Crew: 2
Manufacturing plant: GAZ
Service date: Provng trials 1996-1999
Vehicle weight: 4,000kg
Cargo capacity: 2,500kg
Combat weight: 6,500kg

Dimensions: (m)
Length: 4.50
Width: 2.80
Height: 1.90 including tilt
Wheelbase: 3.05
Ground clearance: 0.475

Armor:
Base model unarmored

Armament:
Main armament: None on base model
Secondary armament: None on base model

Automotive:
Type: GAZ-5423 Turbo-diesel
Cylinders: 6 in-line
Power output: 175hp (129kW)
Fuel type: Diesel
Transmission: Manual
Tires: 13.00 - 18
Wheels: 9.00 - 18
Brakes: Mechanical Hydraulic assisted
Electrical system: 24v

Performance:
Maximum road speed (km/h): 120
Water speed (km/h): 5
Power/weight ratio: 26.9hp (20.1 kW)/tonne

class of vehicle, albeit utilizing components used by GAZ for the BRDM-2 and BTR-80 series. The most radical new development introduced on the GAZ-3937 and other vehicles in the series is the powerplant. The GAZ-3937 is powered by a completely new GAZ-5423 air-cooled turbo-diesel engine, developed specifically for ease and maintenance and its good performance at high altitudes, which was one of the original requirements for border

GAZ-3937 at Nizhny Novgorod. (Steven J. Zaloga)

GAZ-3937 on display at a military exhibition in Nizhny Novgorod. (Steven J. Zaloga)

guards use. The GAZ-3937 prototypes were extensively tested in the Pamir Mountains in Central Asia during evaluation trials, which proved the concept of using an air-cooled engine to power a modern military vehicle.

Although the base model GAZ-3937 has not entered series production, by 1996 the GAZ OKB had developed over twenty modifications of the GAZ-3937 series, including an anti-tank vehicle, SPAADS, and special forces variants, many of which are undergoing GABTU evalu-

GAZ-3937 at Nizhny Novgorod. (Steven J. Zaloga)

Front view of the GAZ-3937.

Rear view of the GAZ-3937.

GAZ-3937 on display at Nizhny Novgorod. (Steven J. Zaloga)

ation trials for acceptance into the Russian Army in 1999. The vehicle has also evolved into the related GAZ-3937-10 and GAZ-3934 series of armored cars.

Description

The base model GAZ-3937 has a small crew cab at the front left of the vehicle, with the engine at the right, leaving the rear of the vehicle clear as a cargo platform. The rear tilt does not exceed the cab height on what is overall a very low silhouette vehicle. The vehicle has been designed with all hatches well above the vehicle centerline in order to afford the vehicle good amphibious capability; the GAZ-3937 being fully amphibious with a water speed of 5km/hour.

The GAZ-3937 is powered by a unique air-cooled GAZ-5423 six cylinder in-line turbo charged diesel engine producing 175hp (129kW) and giving the vehicle a road speed of 120km/hour. The engine is standard to the GAZ-3937 family and was developed due to its very low maintenance requirements and its good performance at high altitudes, the latter requirement being of particular need in some border regions of Russia.

GAZ-3937-10 Armored Car

The GAZ-3937-10 was developed in 1995 and first publically displayed at the NII-21 proving grounds at Bronnitsy near Moscow in January of 1996. The GAZ-3937-10 is fitted with a rear-mounted turret modified from that used on the BTR-80 wheeled APC. The turret mounts the conventional 14.5mm KPVT HMG and a six barrel

902B "Tucha" (cloud) smoke grenade discharger on the turret rear. The GAZ-3938-10 is described as a dual purpose vehicle. It can operate as an armored car with a crew of three and a maximum payload of 2,500kg or as an APC with a crew of three and an infantry complement of seven men plus 1,500kg of cargo.

The GAZ-3937-10 is powered by the same 175hp (129kVT) GAZ-5423 air-cooled six cylinder in-line turbo diesel engine as the other vehicles in the series, providing the 7,000kg vehicle with a very considerable 105-120km/hour top speed and a claimed road range of 1,000km.

Access to the GAZ-3937-10 is by conventional armored side doors for the driver and vehicle commander. The vehicle crew are provided with large armored windshields and side windows, providing considerable visibility for an armored car. They are both also provided with roof access hatches with three forward facing vision blocks in each. Access for the infantry crew is by a small hatch in either side of the hull and two further hatches at the rear of the vehicle. As with the base model GAZ-3937, the hatches are mounted well above the vehicle centerline to afford the vehicle good amphibious capability. The vehicle can travel in water at speeds up to 4km/hour.

The GAZ-3937-10 is fitted with distinctive front bull bars which have also been fitted as standard on subsequent models in the GAZ-3937 series. The vehicle is provided with conventional and IR driving lights and a conventional spotlight on the vehicle roof.

All seven infantry accomodated in the GAZ-3937 are provided with a firing port. Two firing ports are located in the right hull side, three in the left side, and one in

GAZ-3937-10 armored car. This vehicle was first publicly displayed at the Bronnitsy Proving Grounds near Moscow in January 1996. It is armed with a new turret with 14.5mm KPVT main armament, 7.62mm PKT co-axial machine gun, and a six-barrel 902B "Tucha" (cloud) smoke launcher system.

Rear view, GAZ-3937-10. The twin rear hatches are, like all hatches on this vehicle, mounted above the vehicle water line.

Left side view, GAZ-3937-10.

Right side view, GAZ-3937-10.

GAZ-3937-10. The vehicle began evaluation trials at the NII-21 proving grounds at Bronnitsy during 1997 for acceptance into the Russian army. Note the raised fighting compartment roof and roof-mounted engine intakes and exhaust. (Aleksandr Koshavtsev)

GAZ-3937-10. Bronnitsy, January 1997. All the doors on the vehicle are mounted above its centerline for maximum amphibious capability. Close inspection shows the vehicle's modular construction; the cab and rear section being separate units.

GAZ-3937-10 negotiating a slope during field trials. (Aleksandr Koshavtsev)

GAZ-3937-10 on public display, Bronnitsy, January 1996.

GAZ-3937-10. This vehicle, pictured at the Bronnitsy polygon in February 1999, is shown with a Yaroslavl produced YaMZ series engine, offered as an alternative powerplant for the vehicle from 1999. (Andrey Aksenov)

each of the two rear doors. Two small vision blocks are mounted in each side of the the roof armor above the firing ports. The vehicle's armor and armored glass provides protection from small arms fire.

The GAZ-3937-10 is air transportable by the An-12, An-22, An-124, IL-76 aircraft, and the Mi-26 heavy lift helicopter.

At the end of 1996, the GAZ-3937-10 was also shown under the designation GAZ-39371, and in 1999 the vehicle was being offered with alternative YaMZ-460 series and GAZ-560 series powerplants.

GAZ-3937 Multi-purpose Vehicle

A new multi-purpose personnel carrier/command vehicle version of the GAZ-3937 was developed in 1995 on the base of the original vehicle. Somewhat confusingly, this model also retains the original GAZ-3937 designation without any suffix, despite major design modifications. The new vehicle was first publicly shown at the Bronnitsy Proving Grounds near Moscow in January of 1996, and is being offered by GAZ for military and para-military roles. The vehicle provides a significant

increase in capability over the BRDM-2U in the command vehicle role, as the vehicle has similar all-terrain performance but is better laid out internally in terms of crew space. The GAZ-3937 series is of modular construction, allowing the front vehicle crew and rear compartments to be matched to any required role.

The vehicle is described simply as multi-purpose but its arrangement is suited to command and communication vehicle roles. There are no firing ports or typical AFV modifications on this variant. The 3,500kg vehicle can accommodate a 1,500kg load when operating as a command vehicle or APC, with a vehicle crew of two plus seven infantry, and 2,500kg when functioning as an armored car with a reduced crew of two. The vehicle is not armored but is stated to provide limited protection from small arms fire.

The GAZ-3937 multi-purpose vehicle has an entirely new cab and personnel carrier bodywork. The driver and commander are located on the left side of the vehicle in a tandem seating arrangement as on the base model GAZ-3937, but with a higher cab roof line. The two crew both have their own access door on the left side of the vehicle, while the infantry complement are accommodated in a large box structure with two top opening access doors on

GAZ-3937 multi-purpose vehicle. This vehicle is unarmored. As with all vehicles in the series, it is built on a modular construction basis.

GAZ-3937 multi-purpose vehicle. This modified variant of the GAZ-3937 multipurpose vehicle was first demonstrated at the Bronnitsy polygon in early 1999. Note the modified panel lines where the modular cab section is joined to the hull, the new sidelights, and relocated spotlight.

Another view of the GAZ-3937 multi-purpose vehicle. The vehicle is parked between a DT-30 two-section tracked transporter and a GAZ-3937-11 APC. Bronnitsy polygon, February 1999.

GAZ-3937 multi-purpose vehicle. The vehicle was also first displayed at the Bronnitsy Proving Grounds in January 1996. The vehicle is, somewhat confusingly, also simply designated GAZ-3937 and not at the time of publication distinguished from other vehicles in the series.

Rear view, GAZ-3937 multi-purpose vehicle. As with the GAZ-3937-10 armored car, all hatches on the universal/command/transport variant are above the vehicle centerline.

GAZ-3937 multi-purpose vehicle.

GAZ-3937 multi-purpose vehicle. (Alexander Koshavtsev)

SPECIFICATIONS GAZ-3937 MULTI-PURPOSE VEHICLE

Design bureau: GAZ OKB
Crew: 2
Manufacturing plant: GAZ
Service date: NA
Vehicle weight: 4,750kg
Cargo capacity: 1,500 - 2,500kg
Combat weight: 6,250 - 7,250 kg

Dimensions: (m)
Length: 4.70
Width: 2.60
Height: 2.00
Wheelbase: 3.05
Ground clearance: 0.475

Armament:
Main armament: None

Automotive:
Type: GAZ-5423 Turbo - diesel
Cylinders: 6 in-line

Power output: 175hp (129kW)
Cooling: Air
Transmission: Manual
Steering: Turning radius 9.5m
Tires: 13.00 - 18
Wheels: 9.00 - 18
Brakes: Mechanical, Hydraulic assisted
Electrical system: 24v

Performance:
Maximum road speed: 112km/h
Maximum road range: 1,000km
Water speed: 4km/hour

each side and a further two doors at the rear. A large window in the front of the box superstructure can also be opened by its top hinges.

The GAZ-3937 multi-purpose vehicle is the only vehicle in the series publicly shown before 1999 which is unarmored. The vehicle is also unarmed and has no fixed mountings to allow crew weapons to be used from within the crew compartment.

The vehicle is powered by the same air-cooled 175hp (129kVT) GAZ-5423 six cylinder in-line turbo diesel engine as the base model GAZ-3937, mounted on the right side of the vehicle as with other vehicles in the series. The vehicle had an original quoted road speed of 120km/hour when first displayed in 1996, this figure now being reduced to 112km/hour with an ambitious road range of around 1,000km.

In early 1999, the vehicle was being offered with alternative engine powerplants, including the GAZ-560 unit and a new Yaroslavl sourced diesel engine.

The GAZ-3937 multi-purpose vehicle is described as amphibious for which purpose all access doors are above the vehicle centerline. The vehicle can travel in water at speeds of up to 4km/hour. The vehicle is air transportable by the IL-76, An-12, An-22, and An-124 fixed-wing aircraft and the Mi-26 helicopter.

The GAZ-3937 series is generically known as the "Vodnik", an amphibian.

GAZ-3937-11 Armored Personnel Carrier

Several new variants of the GAZ-3937 were developed during 1996, and first publicly demonstrated at the NII-21 polygon at Bronnitsy in December 1996. One such new variant is an armored personnel carrier, based on the original GAZ-3937-10 (GAZ-39371). This variant began undergoing GABTU acceptance trials for service in the Russian Army in early 1998, though by the end of 1999 no orders had been placed due to defense budget restrictions.

The new APC version of the GAZ-3937, designated GAZ-3937-11, is mechanically identical to other vehicles

GAZ-3937-11 APC. The GAZ-3937-11 APC version of the GAZ-3937 was first publicly displayed at the Bronnitsy Proving Grounds in December 1996, while undergoing GABTU evaluation trials for acceptance into military service. The vehicle is towing a 122mm D-30 gun. (Aleksandr Koshavtsev)

GAZ-3937-11 APC. The vehicle is shown during trials at Bronnitsy polygon, February 1999.

GAZ-3937-11 driver's compartment. The driver's controls on the GAZ-3937-11 are similar to a standard GAZ truck. Note the small side screen with its own windscreen wiper. A second crew member sits in tandem behind the driver.

Rear view of the GAZ-3937-11 APC. Each door on the vehicle is fitted with a firing port for personal weapons, while there are two pintle mounts on the vehicle roof for fitting squad light machine guns.

Rear view of the GAZ-3937-11 APC.

GAZ-3939-11 APC. These view shows the GAZ-3937-11 on display at the Omsk Military Show, June 1999. (Andrey Aksenov)

GAZ-3937-11 APC at the Omsk Military Show, June 1999. (Andrey Aksenov)

in the series but has a new cab and rear fighting compartment without a turret. The driver has a single cab and access is gained via a side door in the left side of the vehicle cab. A second crewman can sit in tandem behind the driver. The fighting compartment crew have access to the vehicle by means of a single door in each side of the vehicle; two rear access doors and two roof hatches. The roofline has a distinct chamfer in comparison with the earlier GAZ-3937-10.

The GAZ-3937-11 APC is armored and amphibious. The vehicle is of modular construction, the rear personnel carrier body being separate from the vehicle crew compartment and being interchangeable with other rear bodywork. The vehicle has firing ports in each side of the vehicle and the rear doors, with two brackets on the roof for mounting a section light machine gun.

The GAZ-3937-11 APC has a combat weight of 5,000kg and an additional load capacity of 1,700kg. The vehicle is powered by the same 175hp (129kW) GAZ-5423 turbo-diesel engine as other vehicles in the series, giving the vehicle a power/weight ratio of 26.1hp (19.4kW)/tonne, a quoted top speed of 110-120km/hour and a road range of 1,000km.

The vehicle is intended for multi-role operations as a reconnaissance vehicle, APC, and wheeled artillery tractor, taking the latter roles over from the tracked MT-LB.

GAZ-3937 120mm Self Propelled Mortar

In December 1996, a self propelled mortar version of the GAZ-3937 was publicly displayed for the first time at the NII-21 proving grounds at Bronnitsy, near Moscow. The new vehicle is based on the GAZ-3937-10 (GAZ-39371) armored car but with a shortened fighting compartment and a 120mm mortar system installed on a flat platform at the rear. The vehicle is similar in concept to the 2B11 mortar system mounted on the rear of the GAZ-66 4x4 truck, with the mortar firing over the rear of the vehicle. The official designation for the GAZ-3937 mortar carrier is not known at the time of publication.

The front crew compartment has two conventional doors for the vehicle crew and two hatches in the vehicle roof. An additional roof hatch is located behind the driver, fitted with three vision devices. A firing port is located in each side of the crew compartment.

GAZ-3937 120mm mortar carrier. The variant was first demonstrated at the Bronnitsy Proving Grounds near Moscow in December 1996.

GAZ-3937 120mm mortar carrier side view. (Andrey Aksenov)

GAZ-3937 120mm mortar carrier. (Andrey Aksenov)

GAZ-3937 mortar carrier. (Andrey Aksenov)

The right side of the closed compartment at the front of the vehicle is occupied by the six cylinder in-line GAZ-5423 air-cooled diesel engine, the air intake and engine exhaust being located on the right side of the vehicle roof.

At the rear of the vehicle the 120mm mortar is swivel-mounted immediately behind the crew compartment, firing over the vehicle rear. The 120mm mortar has an approximate indirect fire range of 8,900m and can fire several types of ammunition, including a rocket assisted mortar bomb with an extended range of 13,000m. The weapon has no direct fire capability.

The rear mortar platform is provided with four bows and a tarpaulin for inclement weather protection. With the tarpaulin fitted, the vehicle at a distance resembles a conventional truck.

Night vision equipment consists of four conventional driving lights and a white light searchlight mounted on the vehicle roof.

In early 1997 the vehicle began GABTU evaluation trials for acceptance in Russian Army service. At the time of writing these trials were not complete and funding for such vehicles was a bigger concern than the technical merits of the vehicles themselves.

GAZ-39371 Command Post Vehicle

A command post version of the GAZ-3937 series was demonstated at the NII-21 Polygon at Bronnitsy in Feb-ruary 1999. As with other vehicles in the GAZ-3937 series, this vehicle was undergoing acceptance trials for service in the Russian Army in 1998, though by early 2000 no orders had been placed for any vehicles in the series. This is due to defense budget restrictions and conflicts between the vehicle's manufacturer and the Russian government regarding funding for future AFV developments.

The new command post version of the GAZ-3937, designated GAZ-39371, is mechanically identical to other vehicles in the series but with a configuration consisting of the front modular section from the GAZ-3937-10 armored car and a rear container bodied command post.

The GAZ-39371"Shtabnoi" (command) variant is based on a modernization program within the Russian Army being undertaken in the late 1990s where command, communications, repair, and other vehicles are being increasingly built into modular container systems. They are then transported by a variety of vehicles which can drop the containers at the required site and then operate independently of the container. The containerized command post fitted to the rear of the armored GAZ-39371 transport vehicle is fitted with its own generator system and support legs. The vehicle can either operate as a mobile command post or the container can be dismounted from the vehicle and the command post crew can operate from a static position. The container is fitted with lifting hooks allowing the vehicle to be removed with a crane, though the container can also be jacked up and the

GAZ-39371 Shtabnoi (command) vehicle. The rear of the vehicle is fitted with a detachable box body which is fitted out as a command post, complete with its own NBC protection system mounted at the front of the body.

The GAZ-39371 Shtabnoi command vehicle on display at Bronnitsy, Moscow region, February 1999.

Rear view of the GAZ-39371 command vehicle. The bodywork has lifting points for offloading the command post with the aid of a crane.

Rear view of the GAZ-39371 command vehicle.

GAZ-39371 Shtabnoi command vehicle, Bronnitsy, Moscow, February 1999.

GAZ-39371 Shtabnoi command vehicle cab. This cab is the same as fitted to the GAZ-3937-10 armored car with its 14.5mm KPVT armed turret. The GAZ-3937 series was developed as a modular series of vehicles with interchangeable cab and rear sections on a common chassis. Whether this system will be practical in service remains to be seen.

vehicle driven out from under the container when supported on legs.

The GAZ-39371 Shtabnoi vehicle has a combat weight of 5,100kg with the loaded container itself weighing 2,400kg. The vehicle is powered by the six cylinder GAZ-5423 engine common to the GAZ-3937 series, which gives the vehicle a quoted maximum road speed of over 100km/hour and a range of 1,000km.

The GAZ-39371 command vehicle is being considered for service in the Russian Army in 1999.

BPM-97 Armored Car

In February 1999, a new armored car was displayed in public for the first time at the NII-21 military vehicle polygon at Bronnitsy near Moscow. The vehicle, designated only as the BPM-97 (Boevaya Pogranichnaya Mashina - military Border Patrol Vehicle -97) during its first public outing, was developed over a three year period by MGTV (Moscow Technical University) and built in cooperation with the KamAZ vehicle plant at Naberezhny Chelny, Tatarstan. The KamAZ plant is best known for its military and civilian truck manufacture, including the current military series KamAZ-4350, 5350, and 6350 "Mustang" family. The BPM-97 armored car is based on a shortened KamAZ-4326 4x4 chassis and slightly resembles the earlier BTR-40, though it is a considerably larger vehicle.

The BPM-97 was designed as a border guards vehicle (as was the original GAZ-3937 series) and has the capability to operate as an armored car or an armored personnel carrier. The vehicle may be a first attempt by the KamAZ plant to enter the armored vehicle market, which in 1999 is extremely competitive worldwide and particularly difficult in Russia. The Arzamas division of GAZ, as the primary Russian manufacturer of wheeled AFVs, has already encountered severe difficulties in gaining orders from the Russian government due to financing restrictions.

The BPM-97's main armament is a 12.7mm NSVT heavy machine gun, mounted in a turret adapted from that used on the BTR-80 series of wheeled APCs. In addition to the main armament, the vehicle carries an impressive array of additional firepower. An AGS-17 "Plamya" (flame) automatic grenade launcher is fitted on the turret, while a 9P135 launcher for the 9M111 Fagot missile can be pintle mounted on the vehicle roof, giving the vehicle significant ATGM capability. Alternative ATGM systems can also be mounted on the vehicle, as can a variety of camera and specialist night vision equipment. A six barrel 902B "Tucha" (smoke) smoke discharger system is also mounted on the right side of the turret.

As with the GAZ-3937 series, the vehicle is air-transportable by the An-22, An-124, and IL-76 heavy transport aircraft.

SPECIFICATIONS BPM-97 ARMORED CAR

Design bureau: N.Ye Bauman OKB
Crew: 3 + 7-9
Manufacturing plant: KamAZ
Service date: Prototype 1999
Combat weight: 10,500kg

Dimensions: (m)
Length: 6.82
Width: 2.585
Height: 2.50

Armament:
Main armament: 12.7mm NSVT
Secondary armament: AGS-17 "Plamya"
ATGM armament: Fagot, Metis or Kornet ATGM
systems, 902B Tucha smoke
dischargers

Automotive:
Type: NA

Cylinders: NA
Power output: 161kW (200hp)*

Armor:
During trials the upper hull armor was effective against 12.7mm B32 rounds fired from 300m, and the lower hull proved effective against 7.62mm B32 rounds fired at 10-30m from a Dragunov SVD rifle.

Performance:
Maximum road speed (km/h): 90
Maximum road range (km/h): 1,100
Wading depth (m): 1.5

Note:
*An alternative engine is available developing 190kW (260hp)

KamAZ BPM-97 armored car. The BPM-97 (as the vehicle was designated at its first public exhibition in February 1999) may be a developmental study only, or may represent KamAZ's first attempt to enter the wheeled AFV market dominated by GAZ and its affiliated Arzamas plant.

The KamAZ BPM-97 resembles an enlarged version of the original BTR-40 prototype which has similar sloped armor. Note the lower side and rear access doors and the three firing ports on each side of the vehicle, in addition to those in the rear doors. Crew access is considerably safer than in previous Russian armored car/APC designs.

BPM-97 armored car, Bronnitsy Proving Grounds, Moscow. Summer 1999. (Aleksandr Koshavtsev)

BPM-97. (Aleksandr Koshavtsev)

The well-sloped side armor of the BPM-97 is apparent in this view.

BPM-97. The turret armament package is impressive, with a 12.7mm NSVT, AGS-17 automatic grenade launcher, and 902B "Tucha" smoke mortars. This is in addition to the mountings on the roof for several optional ATGM systems.

BPM-97. Upper front hull and turret.

BPM-97 rear view.

BPM-97 side view.

BPM-97 turret with prominent 902B "Tucha" mortar package. The standard of welding varies considerably on this prototype, perhaps due to a lack of time to finish the vehicle before display.

KamAZ BPM-97 turret. These two views show the BPM-97's considerable armament package, including the mount for a 12.7mm NSVT heavy machine gun, 40mm grenade launcher with cartridge basket, 9P135 ATGM launcher for the 9M111 ATGM, and a 902B "Tucha" smoke mortar array.

Interior view of the BPM-97 with the driver's position to the left.

BPM-97 rear view with doors open. Note the single rear seats and small longitudinal bench, all facing the vehicle rear. A 9P135 launcher for the 9M111 "Fagot" (AT-4) ATGM system is mounted on the vehicle roof.

The 9P135 ATGM launcher on its turret mount.

Lavina Riot Control Vehicle

The MVD internal security service of the Russian Federation uses several specialized armored vehicles, the most common of which is the "Lavina", built by the Dmitrovski Experimental Zavod on the BAZ-69501 8x8 chassis produced at the Bryansk Avtomobil Zavod (BAZ).

The Lavina is a large vehicle, powered by two KamAZ-270 engines which are configured to allow the vehicle to maneuver with one engine disabled.

Armament consists of four water cannon which produce water pressure of twelve atmospheres and have a range of sixrt meters.

A later version of the Lavina, designated Lavina-M, is also now in service with the MVD. The Lavina-M differs only in being fitted with a front mounted, hydraulically operated dozer blade for obstacle removal and six B902 "Tucha" smoke dischargers which can fire several types of smoke and irritant gas to a range of 200m.

The Lavina and Lavina-M are commonly seen in major Russian cities during times of expected large gatherings and potential riot situations.

Front view of the BAZ-based Lavina-M. (Andrey Aksenov)

Lavina-M riot control vehicle. Note the turret-mounted controlled water cannon with the 902B "Tucha" smoke grenade launchers behind. (Andrey Aksenov)

Lavina-M riot control vehicle. The Lavina-M, on its BAZ-69501 8x8 chassis, is fitted as standard with a dozer blade, as seen here. (Andrey Aksenov)

Appendices

Specification Table —Notes

The metric system is used for all measurements with the exception of engine output figures, which are given in the more familiar horsepower rating in addition to kilowatts (kW). The notes below are provided to help the reader interpret the data tables that occur thorughout the book and in the appendices.

Dimensions:
All dimensions are measured in meters (m) and centimeters (cm).

Armament:
Weapon (caliber in millimeters) (mm) with number of rounds carried.

Armor:
Measured in millimeters (mm) with angles in degrees (°) where appropriate.

Engine:
Engine capacity in cubic centimeters (cm^3) (i.e. 3285cm^3 is 3.285 liters). Output is measured in horsepower (hp) and kilowatts (kW) at given engine revs per minute (rpm). Fuel is measured in liters with fuel consumption in liters per 100km. Where cylinder dimensions are given, the measurememts are bore diameter/stroke (mm).

Transmission:
Transmission is stated as number of forward/reverse gears with two speed transfer box where provided, e.g 4F/1R x 2.

Performance:
Speed in kilometers/hour (km/h)
Range in kilometers (km)

Power/weight ratio is measured in horsepower (hp) and kilowatts (kW) per metric tonne (1000kg).
Dimensions for obstacle crossing are given in meters.

Tires:
Tire size is usually indicated in millimeters (mm), though inches are used where this measurement was originally used.

Grammatical note:
Due to the complex nature of Russian grammar, plant names are sometimes modified according to the grammatical case in which they are used. Therefore the Vyksa plant may be described as Vyksa or Vyksinskiy, Izhorsk as Izhorsk or Izhorskiy and the Russo-Balt plant as the Russko-Baltiyskiy. In each case, only one plant is being described.

NOTE: The Vyksinskiy plant above, and throughout the book, is better spelled Vyksunskiy. This change was noted late in the production process.

LIGHT ARMORED CARS DATA TABLE

	D-8	D-12	FAI	FAI-M	BA-20	BA-20M	BA-64	BA-64B
							(BA-64-125)	
Crew:	2	2	2	2	2	3	2	2
Dimensions:								
Length:	3.540m	3.540m	3.75m	4.31m	4.10m	4.310m	3.67m	3.67m
Width:	1.705m	1.705m	1.68m	1.75m	1.80m	1.80m	1.52m	1.69m
Height:	1.680m	2.520m	2.24m	2.24m	2.30m	2.13m	1.875m	1.85m
Combat weight:	2000kg	2280kg	1990kg	2000kg	2340kg	2520kg	2360kg	2425kg
Armament:								
Main:	2x7.62mm	2x7.62mm	1x7.62mm	1x7.62mm	1x7.62mm	1x7.62mm	1x7.62mm	1x7.62mm
Secondary:	None	None	None	None	None	None	None	None
Ammunition:								
Main:	4158	2090/2079	1323	1323	1386	1386	1260	1260
Secondary:	None	None	None	None	None	None	None	None
Armor:	7mm	7mm	6mm	4-6mm	4-6mm	4-6mm	4-15mm	4-15mm
Automotive:								
Type:	Ford A	Ford A	GAZ- A	GAZ-M1	GAZ-M1	GAZ-M1	GAZ-MM	GAZ-MM
Cylinders / fuel:	4/petrol	4/petrol	4/petrol	4/petrol	4/petrol	4/petrol	4/petrol	4/petrol
Power output:	40hp (30kW)	40hp (30kW)	42hp (31kW)	50hp (38kW)	50hp (38kW)	50hp (38kW)	50hp (38kW)	54hp (41kW)
Maximum speed:	85km/h	85km/h	80km/h	90km/h	90km/h	70km/h	80km/h	85km/h
Maximum range:	270km	225km	225km	350km	350km	450km	560km	560km

MEDIUM & HEAVY ARMORED CARS DATA TABLE

	BA-27	BA-27M	BA-3	BA-6	BA-9	BA-10	BA-10M	BA-11	BA-11D
Crew:	4	4	4	4	4	4	4	4	4
Dimensions:									
Length:	4.617m	4.83m	4.77m	4.90m	4.635m	4.655m	4.65m	5.295m	5.295m
Width:	1.170m	1.93m	2.11m	2.07m	2.30m	2.07m	2.07m	2.390m	2.390m
Height:	2.520m	2.54m	2.35m	2.36m	2.15m	2.210m	2.19m	2.490m	2.490m
Combat weight:	4400kg	4500kg	6000kg	5120kg	4500kg	5140kg	5360kg	8130kg	8650kg
Armament:									
Main:	1x37mm	1x37mm	1x45mm	1x45mm	1x12.7mm	1x45mm	1x45mm	1x45mm	1x45mm
Secondary:	1x7.62mm	1x7.62mm	2x7.62mm	2x7.62mm	2x7.62mm	2x7.62mm	2x7.62mm	2x7.62mm	2x7.62mm
Ammunition:									
Main:	40	40	40	60	NA	49	49	114	114
Secondary:	2016	2016	3276	3276	NA	2079	2079	3087	3087
Armor:	8mm	8mm	6-8mm	6-9mm	6-10mm	6-10mm	6-10mm	13mm	13mm
Automotive:									
Type:	AMO F-15	GAZ	GAZ	GAZ	GAZ-M1	GAZ-M1	GAZ-M1	ZIS-16	ZIS-D-7
Cylinders/ fuel:	4/petrol	4/petrol	4/petrol	4/petrol	4/petrol	4/petrol	4/petrol	6/petrol	6/diesel
Power output:	35hp	40hp (30kW)	40hp (30kW)	40hp (30kW)	50hp (37kW)	52hp (38kW)	52hp (38kW)	99hp (74kW)	99hp(74kW)
Maximum speed:	35km/h	48km/h	63km/h	43km/h	55km/h	53km/h	55km/h	64km/h	48km/h
Maximum range:	300km	300km	260km	200km	230km	260-300km	300	316km	420km

SPECIALIZED ARMORED VEHICLES DATA TABLE

	BAD-2	PB-4	PB-7	BA-30	B-3	BA-22	KSP-76
Crew:	4	4	3	3	2	4	3
Type:	Amphibian	Amphibian	Amphibian	Half Track	Half Track	Ambulance	SPG
Dimensions:							
Length:	5.28m	5.30m	5.08m	4.94m	6.53	6.10m	6.36m
Width:	2.00m (est)	1.98m	2.15m	2.40m	2.35	1.98m	2.11m
Height:	2.36m (est)	2.255m	2.073m	2.34m	2.40	2.88m	1.65m
Combat weight:	4600kg	5280kg	4500kg	4600kg	7100kg	5240kg	5340kg
Armament:							
Main:	1x37mm	1x45mm	1x12.7mm	1x7.62mm	1x12.7	None	1x76.2mm ZiS-3
Secondary:	2x7.62mm	1x7.62mm	None	None	None	None	None
Ammunition:							
Main:	60	52	1000	1512	NA	None	54-58
Secondary:	3000	2268	NA	None	None	None	None
Armor:	6mm	7mm	8mm	6mm	15mm	6mm	16.5mm
Automotive:							
Type:	GAZ-AA	GAZ-AA	GAZ-M1	GAZ-M1	ZIS-16	GAZ-AA	GAZ-11
Cylinders / fuel:	4/petrol	4/petrol	4/petrol	4/petrol	6/petrol	4/petrol	6/petrol
Power output:	40hp (30kW)	40hp (30kW)	50hp (37kW)	50hp (37kW)	85hp (63kW)	40hp (30kW)	85hp (63kW)
Maximum speed:	50km/h	50km/h	60km/h	55km/h	40km/h	40km/h	70km/h
Maximum range:	NA	200km	120km	253km	150km	250km	300km
Amphibious speed:	6km/h	4km/h	NA	N/app	N/app	N/app	N/app

POST-WAR ARMORED CARS 1945-1997 DATA TABLE

	BTR-40	BRDM	BRDM-2	GAZ-3937 (Base Model)	GAZ-3937-10	GAZ-39344
Crew:	2 + 8	2+3	4	2	3	2/3 +4
Dimensions:						
Length:	5.00	5.70	5.75	4.50	NA	5.64
Width:	2.01	2.17	2.35	2.80	NA	2.32
Height:	1.83	2.25	2.31	1.90	NA	2.65
Combat weight:	5300kg	5600kg	7000kg	6500kg	NA	7000kg
Armament:						
Main:	1 x 7.62mm	1x7.62	1x14.5mm	None	1x14.5mm	1x14.5mm
Secondary:	None	None	1x7.62mm	None	1x7.62mm	1x7.62mm
Ammunition:						
Main:	1250	1250	500	NA	NA	500
Secondary:	None	None	2000	NA	NA	2000
Armor:	6-13mm	6-12mm	7-14mm	NA	NA	NA
Automotive:						
Type:	GAZ-40	GAZ-40P	GAZ-41	GAZ-5423	GAZ-5423	GAZ-5423
Cylinders/fuel:	L-6 petrol	L-6 petrol	V-8 petrol	L-6 Diesel	L-6 Diesel	L-6 Diesel
Power output:	78hp (58KW)	90hp (67kW)	140hp (104kW)	175hp (129kW)	175hp (129kW)	175hp (129kW)
Maximum speed:	78km/h	80km/h	95km/h	120km/h	NA	95km/h
Maximum range:	300 + km	500km	750km	1000km	1000km	700km
Amphibious speed:	N/app	9km/h	10km/h	5km/h	NA	NA

ARMORED CARS IN MUSEUMS
(BY LOCATION)

The information provided below is a list of armored cars and related vehicles which are preserved today in museums worldwide and known to the author at the time of publication. Post-World War Two Russian vehicles have been widely exported and are now to be found in military museums worldwide. Since the Gulf War, many Russian-supplied ex-Iraqi vehicles are now to be found in many museums and military bases in Europe, the Middle East, and the United States. A surprising number of modern wheeled AFV's are also now held in private collections. This listing is by no means intended to be all-inclusive and is a general reference as to where some of the Russian armored cars highlighted in this book may be seen today.

CZECH REPUBLIC
Prague
The Military Museum in Lesany, near Prague, has a small collection of Russian AFV's including a BA-64B, a standard reconnaissance model BRDM, and a BRDM-2. It also has a 9P31 launch vehicle for the ZRK 9K31 Strela-1 SAM system.

FINLAND
Parola Tank Museum, Parola
The Parola Tank Museum in Finland has a rare BA-20M with the frame antenna from the original BA-20 series and an equally interesting BA-10M. Both vehicles were captured in Finland during the Russo-Finnish "Winter War." The BA-10M is in running condition. Both vehicles have recently been moved inside the museum building after years of being subjected to the elements. The museum also has another BA-10 converted by the Finnish Army to a wheeled ARV.

FRANCE
Saumur Tank Museum
Saumur has a small number of Russian AFV's including at least one BRDM-2.

GERMANY
Military Museum, Dresden
The Military Museum in Dresden, former East Germany, has a BA-64B, a BTR-40, and an original BRDM. In West Germany there are numerous BRDM-2 versions in the museum collections of British, American, and German military bases, some of which are open to the public.

Munsterlager
The Military museum at Munsterlager in late 1997 trans-ferred an Iraqi BRDM-2 to the Tank Museum, Bovington, UK.

Sinsheim
The Sinsheim museum in Germany has a BRDM armored car.

HUNGARY
Budapest
The National Army Museum in Budapest has a BRDM 2P27 ATGM vehicle.

ISRAEL
Latrun Military Museum
The Latrun military museum in Israel has an extensive collection of Russian AFV's including several armored cars. These include a BTR-40, a standard BRDM-2, and at least two 9P122 ATGM vehicles.

POLAND
Polish Armed Forces Museum, Warsaw
The Polish Armed Forces Museum in Warsaw has a BTR-40, a BRDM, and a BRDM 2P27 ATGM vehicle.

Fort IX, Sadyba District, Warsaw
The military museum at Fort IX in the Sadyba district of Warsaw has a good collection of well restored wheeled AFV's including a BRDM, BRDM 2P27, and 9P110 ATGM vehicles, a BRDM-2, and a BRDM-2U (Polish variant). Other vehicles are at present in the reserve area of the museum.

RUSSIA
NIIBT Tank Museum, Kubinka, Moscow Oblast
The NIIBT Tank Museum collection at Kubinka, near Moscow, has a fine collection of armored cars, with many well preserved examples of service vehicles and several rare prototypes. Heavy armored cars in the collection include the BA-27M, a BA-6, and another vehicle which is identified by the museum as a BA-3. The BA-3, though featuring the rear door of that production model, also has features from the later BA-6 and may be a hybrid or prototype model. The museum also houses the original PB-4 amphibious armored car prototype. Few early light armored cars are represented; the collection including only the BA-21 prototype. Interestingly, even the once ubiquitous BA-64 series is not represented. The museum has a good collection of post war armored cars and APC's, represented by the BTR-40, BTR-40A 14.5mm SPAAMG, BTR-40A ZhD 14.5mm SPAAMG, BTR-40B with overhead armor, an original BTR-40V pro-

totype, BTR-40 ZPTU-2 7.62mm SPAAMG prototype, BRDM, and BRDM-2. Interestingly, no post-war ATGM versions of the BRDM and BRDM-2 armored cars are currently on display though several are held in the reserve collection. A KSP-76 wheeled SPG prototype is also to be found in the Kubinka Tank Museum.

Central Armed Forces Museum, Moscow

The Central Armed Forces Museum in Moscow has a BA-64B which underwent restoration in 1996 and is now back on display, and also a BTR-40 and BRDM-2. During 1996 the only known complete FAI-M armored car surviving today was temporarily displayed at the museum, after being restored by a Russian enthusiast, Anton Sholito and his "Ekipazh" (crew) group who in early 1999 also recovered a rare T-34 M-1943 OT-34 flamethrower tank from a lake within Moscow's city limits. The FAI-M hull and turret were mated to an available replacement GAZ-M1 "Emka" chassis. This vehicle was loaned to the Central Armed Forces Museum in Moscow in September 1996 where it was temporarily on display before being taken back into private hands in April of 1997. The vehicle is in running condition. In September 1997, the Central Armed Forces Museum sent their T-18 M-1928 light tank replica to the NIIBT collection at Kubinka and in return received Kubinka's BA-6 on loan, the vehicle now being located in the open and exposed to the elements. The vehicle's top paint coats have begun to peel after two Russian winters, showing the original paint to be a light khaki green in contrast to its present dark green.

Komsomolsk Na Amur

The military museum at Komsomolsk Na Amur has a small collection of wheeled AFV's including a rare BTR-40B with armored roof, a BRDM, and a BRDM-2.

Museum of Military Transport, Ryazan

The Museum of Military Transport at Ryazan has a large collection of wheeled and tracked military vehicles, including a BTR-40 and BTR-40B.

Nizhny Novgorod

A BA-64B is located outside the Kremlin in Nizhny Novgorod.

Artillery, Engineering, and Communications Museum, St.Petersburg

The Artillery, Engineering, and Communications Museum in St.Petersburg (also known as the Kronwerk Museum) has for many years had within the museum building two BRDM ATGM variants, the BRDM 2P27 (AT-1 Schmel (Bumble Bee)), and the BRDM 9P32 (AT-2 Fleyta (Flute)). In 1997 the museum's collection of BRDM based ATGM vehicles was significantly increased and now also includes a BRDM 9P110, together with BRDM-2 based 9P124, 9P133 and 9P148 ATGM vehicles, all of which are displayed outside the museum building.

SOUTH AFRICA
South African Armor Museum, Bloemfontein

The South African Armor Museum in Bloemfontein has a BRDM-2 captured in Angola with other vehicles held in reserve.

UKRAINE
Great Patriotic War Memorial Museum, Kiev

The Great Patriotic War Memorial Museum in Kiev has a BA-20M (designated by the museum as a BA-24), a BTR-40, BRDM (actually a BRDM 2P32 ATGM vehicle) and a BRDM-2.

UNITED KINGDOM
Bovington Tank Museum, Bovington, UK

The Bovington Tank Museum has a pristine BRDM provided by the NIIBT museum at Kubinka several years ago along with a BTR-60PK APC in exchange for two British armored vehicles.

The collection also has a BRDM-2 RKhB captured in Iraq which is on display and a further two BRDM-2 RKhBs vehicles in storage. The museum is currently restoring one 9P31 TEL vehicle for the 9K31 Strela-1 (SA-9) SAM system using another BRDM-2 for parts in order to have one complete and running example. There is also a BTR-40 in storage awaiting restoration.

Imperial War Museum, Duxford, Cambridge

The IWM at Duxford has a ex-Iraqi BRDM-2, captured by allied forces during the Gulf War and a BRDM-2 9P122 ATGM vehicle which is in private ownership.

Budge Collection, Retford, UK.

The Budge collection has a BTR-40, at least one BRDM-2, a BRDM-2 9P122 ATGM vehicle, and a BTR-40.

UNITED STATES
Aberdeen Proving Grounds, Maryland, USA

Aberdeen Proving Grounds has a BRDM-2 and a BRDM-2 RKhB, both captured from Iraq during the Gulf War.

New England Armor Museum, Danbury, Connecticut, USA

The New England Armor Museum now has the only known surviving BA-64B located in the U.S. It was originally captured by U.S. Forces in Korea and was subsequently shipped back to Aberdeen Proving Grounds (APG) for evaluation. For many years it was on display at APG before being moved to the New England Armor Museum.

Patton Museum, Fort Knox, Kentucky, USA

The Patton Museum in Fort Knox has a BRDM-2 reconnaissance vehicle.

ARMORED CARS IN MUSEUMS (BY TYPE)

FAI/FAI-M
A single FAI-M is known to remain today, restored in Moscow during 1996 by Russian enthusiast Anton Shalito. The vehicle is based on an FAI-M hull and turret mated to a restored GAZ-M1 chassis. The vehicle was briefly displayed at the Central Armed Forces Museum in Moscow during 1996 but is now back in private ownership. An FAI-M hull and turret was also recently located in Poland.

BA-20/BA-20M
There are two known BA-20s displayed in museums today, both BA-20Ms. One (a BA-20M with early frame aerial) is at the Parola Tank Museum in Finland, which after years outside has now been taken into the museum building for protection from the elements. The other is at the Great Patriotic War Memorial Museum in Kiev, Ukraine, and is nominally a BA-20M which has been poorly restored and is identified by the museum as a BA-24.

BA-21
The NIIBT collection of Kubinka has a BA-21 prototype on display.

BA-64/BA-64B
A small number of BA-64s are known to remain today, all being the BA-64B model. The best known is at the Central Armed Forces Museum in Moscow. This vehicle arrived at the museum in 1965 and was restored during the winter of 1996-97. Another BA-64B is located at the New England Armor Museum, Danbury, Connecticut in the U.S. This vehicle was captured by U.S. forces in Korea and was one of several returned to the U.S. This particular vehicle was formerly located at Aberdeen Proving Grounds in Maryland, USA. Another known example is displayed at the military museum in Dresden, Germany. Other examples can be found in Nizhny Novgorod in Russia (a BA-64B outside the city Kremlin), Lesany, near Prague, and in museums in Bulgaria, China, Korea, Poland, and former Yugoslavia, according to Russian sources.

BA-3
A BA-3 is located within the NIIBT collection at Kubinka, near Moscow. It is not entirely clear if the vehicle is an original BA-3, as represented, or an early prototype BA-6, as there was no distinct production model change and there are few external details which distinguish the two models, though the vehicle has the rear door which was deleted on series production BA-6 vehicles.

BA-6
A single BA-6 is known to have survived to the present day. Until 1998 the vehicle was also located at the NIIBT collection at Kubinka. It is currently on loan to the Central Armed Forces Museum in Moscow.

BA-10 / BA-10M
A BA-10M is preserved today at the Parola Tank Museum in Finland. The vehicle is unusual in that it is in running condition. It has recently been moved into the museum building after years of being subjected to the elements in the outside display area. A second example of a BA-10 converted by the Finnish Army to use as an ARV is also to be found in the museum. The museum also has two BA-10M turrets in its reserve collection. A BA-10M is also to be found standing on a low plinth on a battlefield in western Russia or Byelorussia. The vehicle was shown on Russian television on 9th May 1998, but its exact location is unknown.

BA-11 / BA-11D
No BA-11 series vehicles are known to have survived to the present day.

BTR-40
Many national military museums have BTR-40s in their collections. Several BTR-40s are to be found in the NIIBT Tank Museum at Kubinka, including some rare prototypes. The Central Armed Forces Museum in Moscow has an example of a standard BTR-40, while the Ryazan Militart Transport Museum has a BTR-40 and a BTR-40B. The Great Patriotic War Memorial Museum in Kiev, Ukraine has a BTR-40. BTR-40s are also common in Eastern Europe, with examples in many locations includ-

BTR-40 at the Great Patriotic War Memorial Museum, Kiev, Ukraine. (Jochen Vollert, via Armor Archive)

ing the military museums in Dresden, Germany and Warsaw, Skarzysko-Kamienna, and Kolobrzeg in Poland. Several museums worldwide have BTR-40s in their collections and some are also occasionally available for sale through companies such as Robert Fleming Associates in the UK.

BRDM

BRDMs are found in many Russian and former Warsaw Pact country military collections, though the original BRDM is rare in the West. The Bovington Tank Museum in the UK has a pristine example, delivered new by the Kubinka Tank Museum in a vehicle swap several years ago. In Eastern Europe, original BRDMs are located in the military museums in Dresden, Germany, the Polish Armed Forces Museum in Warsaw, the Warsaw Katyn Museum, Skarzysko-Kamienna, and Kolobrzeg in Poland, and the Sinsheim museum in Germany. In 1996, the Artillery, Engineering and Communications Museum in St. Petersburg took delivery of several pristine ATGM vehicles based on BRDM and BRDM-2 chassis. The collection now includes a BRDM 2P27 and BRDM 2P32 which have been located within the museum building for many years and the new outside display area collection, including an original BRDM 9P110 ATGM vehicle. Many museums in eastern Europe have examples of the 2P27 ATGM version of the BRDM-2, including the WPF museum in Warsaw, Poland and the museum at Fort X, Sadyba, Warsaw. The latter also has a 9P110 ATGM vehicle in excellent restored condition.

BRDM-2

Original Russian BRDM-2s are to be found in the Central Armed Forces Museum in Moscow and the Great Patriotic War Memorial Museum in Kiev. Other BRDM-2 vehicles are located at military museums in Omsk, Khabarovsk and the Officer's Club in Yuzhno-Sakhalinsk, Sakhalin Island and in many other museums in Russia. In Poland, the Polish Armed Forces Museum in Warsaw has two BRDM-2s, with an example also located at Skarzysko-Kamienna. There is a BRDM-2 in the military museum at Lesany, Czech republic. The Artillery, Engineering, and Communications Forces Museum in St. Petersburg also has a good collection of BRDM-2 based ATGM vehicles, including the 9P133, 9P137, and 9P148. Since the Gulf War, BRDM-2s are now also to be found in military collections worldwide, particularly in countries which participated in the war and brought back Iraqi army war trophies. BRDM-2s are to be found in many U.S. military collections, including Aberdeen Proving Grounds, Maryland, the Patton Armor Museum, Fort Knox, and Fort Stewart, Georgia, to name only a few. In

late 1997 an ex-Iraqi BRDM-2 was delivered to the Tank Museum at Bovington, UK from Munsterlager in Germany. A BRDM-2 9P122 ATGM version of the BRDM-2 can be found at the Imperial War Museum, Duxford. The BRDM-2 ATGM and RKhB NBC reconnaissance versions of the BRDM-2 are almost as common in museum collections as the base model, again due to being collected in large numbers as a result of the Gulf War. The Tank Museum in Bovington, UK has an example, as has Aberdeen Proving Grounds, Maryland, USA, and Fort Stewart, Georgia received one in 1991. The 9K31 Strela-1 (SA-9) SPADMS version of the BRDM-2 is also located in several museums worldwide, including the Tank Museum at Bovington, UK, and the Military Museum at Lesany, Prague in the Czech Republic. Interestingly, the only example known to be displayed in Russia is on a PVO military base at Eisk near the Azov Sea.

BRDM-2s at the Military Museum, Latrun, Israel. (Jochen Vollert, via Armor Archive)

BRDM-2 RKhB at the Tank Museum, Bovington, UK.

POST - WAR RUSSIAN ARMORED CARS IN FOREIGN SERVICE

This is not intended as a definitive list of the worldwide use of Russian armored cars but is a general guide to those countries where post-war Russian armored cars have been or are in service.

	BTR-40	BTR-40A	BRDM	BRDM-2	BRDM-9P122	9P137	BRDM9K31
Afghanistan	X			X			
Albania	X	X					
Algeria			X	X			X
Angola				X			X
Benin				X			X
Botswana				X			
Bulgaria	X		X	X			X
Burundi	X						
Central African Republic				X			
Chad				X			
China	X						
Congo			X	X			
Croatia				X			X
Cuba	X		X	X			X
Czech Republic					X		X
Egypt				X	X		X
Estonia				X			
Ethiopia	X		X	X	X	X	X
Guinea	X		X	X			
Guinea Bissau	X			X			
Hungary				X	X	X	X
India				X			X
Indonesia	X						
Iran	X						
Iraq				X	X	X	X
Kampuchea	X						
North Korea	X						
Laos	X						
Latvia				X			
Libya				X	X		X
Mongolia				X			
Morocco			X	X	X		
Mozambique	X		X	X	X		X
Malawi				X			
Namibia				X			
Nicaragua	X			X	X		X
Peru				X			
Poland				X	X		X
Romania				X	X		X
Russia/CIS countries	X	X	X	X	X	X	X
Rwanda	X						
Slovakia					X		
Somalia	X			X			
Sudan			X	X			
Syria	X			X	X	X	
Tanzania	X			X			X
Uganda	X					X	X
Vietnam	X	X		X			X
Yemen	X			X			X
Former Yugoslavia	X			X	X		X
Zaire	X						
Zambia			X	X			

Glossary of Terms and Abbreviations

AA	Anti-Aircraft		MRR	Motorized Rifle Regiment
AP	Armor Piercing		m/v	Muzzle Velocity
AP	Anti-Personnel			
APC	Armored Personnel Carrier		NA	Not Available
APDS	Armor Piercing Discarding Sabot		N/app	Not Appropriate
APHE	Armor Piercing High Explosive		NAMI	Nauchniy Avtomobilniy Moskovskiy Institute

AA   Anti-Aircraft
AP   Armor Piercing
AP   Anti-Personnel
APC   Armored Personnel Carrier
APDS   Armor Piercing Discarding Sabot
APHE   Armor Piercing High Explosive
AT   Anti-Tank
ATGM   Anti-Tank Guided Missile

bhp   Brake Horsepower
BRDM   Bronirovannaya Razvedivatelno
          Dozornaya Mashina (Armored Recce Vehicle)
B/S   Bore/stroke

CIS   Commonwealth of Independent States
          (Former Soviet Union)
CPSU   Communist Party of the Soviet Union
CTPRS   Central Tire Pressure Regulation System

DShK   Degtyarev-Shpagin Krupnokaliberniy
          (DS heavy caliber)
DT   Degtyarev Tank (Machine Gun)
DT   Dual tired

GABTU   Glavnoye Avto-Bronetankovoye Upravlenye
          (Main Auto Armor-Tank Command)
GAZ   Gorkovskiy Avtomobilniy Zavod (Gorkiy city
          1932-91, now Nizhny Novgorod)
GK   Gubchataya Kamera (Bulletproof tire)

HEAT   High Explosive Anti-Tank (ammunition)
hp   Horsepower

IR   Infra-Red

Kg/cm²   Kilograms per square centimeter
KB   Konstruktorskoye Bureau (design bureau)
KIM   Kommunisticheskiy Internatsional Molodozhi
          (International Young Communists)
km/h   Kilometers/hour
KPVT   Krupnokaliberniy Pulemyot Vladimirova
          Tankoviy (Vladimirov HMG)

MCLOS   Manual Command Line of Sight (missile
          guidance)
MG   Machine Gun
MICV   Mechanized Infantry Combat Vehicle
MRD   Motorized Rifle Division

MRR   Motorized Rifle Regiment
m/v   Muzzle Velocity

NA   Not Available
N/app   Not Appropriate
NAMI   Nauchniy Avtomobilniy Moskovskiy Institute
          (Scientific Automobile Institute)
NATI   Nauchniy Avto-Traktorniy Institut (Scientific
          Auto-Tractor Institute)
NBC   Nuclear Biological Chemical
NIIBT   Nauchno Issledovatelskiy Institut
          Bronetankovoy Tekhniki (AFV institute)

OKB   Opytno Konstruktorskoye Bureau
          (experimental design bureau)

PKT   Pulemyot Kalashnikova Tankoviy
          (Kalashnikov tank machine gun)
RKKA   Rabotche Krestyanskaya Krasnaya Armiya
          (Workers Red Army)

rpm   Revs per minute/rounds per minute

SACLOS   Semi-Active Command Line of Sight (missile
          guidance)
SAM   Surface to Air Missile
SGMB   Stankovy Goryunova Modernizirovaniy dlya
          Bronetransportera (APC MG)
SPAAG   Self Propelled Anti-Aircraft Gun
SPAADS   Self Propelled Anti-Aircraft Defense System
SPATG   Self Propelled Anti-Tank Gun
SPG   Self Propelled Gun
SPH   Self Propelled Howitzer

TD   Tank Division
TEL   Transporter, Erector, Launcher vehicle
TR   Tank Regiment

Zavod   Factory, plant
ZhD   Zheleznaya Doroga (railroad)
ZIL   Zavod imeni I.A. Likhacheva (Moscow, from
          1953)
ZIS   Zavod imeni Stalina (Moscow, to 1953)
ZPTU   Zenitno-Pulemyotnaya Tankovaya Ustanovka
          (tank anti-aircraft equipment)
ZRK   Zenitniy Raketniy Kompleks (Anti-aircraft
          rocket complex)

BIBLIOGRAPHY

Periodicals:
AFV News (Canada)
Armies & Weapons (UK)
ATOM (Former Czechoslovakia)
Avtomobilniy Transport (Russia)
Centurion (UK)
Defence (UK)
International Defence Review (UK)
Jane's Defence Weekly [JDW] (UK)
Jane's Intelligence Review ([JIR] UK)
Jane's Soviet Intelligence Review [JSIR] (UK)
Journal of Military Ordnance [JOMO] (US)
Krasnaya Zvezda (Russia)
M-Hobby (Russia)
Militartechnik (Germany)
Modell Bau Heute [MBH] (former East Germany)
Modelarz (Poland)
Modelist Konstruktor (Russia)
Modell Fan (Germany)
Nauka i Zhizn (Russia)
Red Star (Soviet Military Research Group, UK)
Soviet Military Review (Russia)
Tankette (MAFVA, UK)
Tekhnika Molodozhi (Russia)
Tekhnika i Vooruzhenie (Russia)
Voenniy Parad (Russia)
Zolnierz Polski (Poland)
Za Roulom (Russia)

Specific articles consulted:
"The BA-64 Armoured Cars". R.Harley. *Centurion,* №22, October 1978, pp4-7.

"BA-64 Bronevik Voennogo Vremeniy Bolshaya Pushechnaya Seriya". E.Prochko. *Tekhnika Molodezhi,* №4 1983, pp36-37.

"BA-64: Bronevik Voennogo Vremeniy". Nikolai Polikarpov. *M-Hobby* ,№1 (6) 1996, pp34-37.

"BRDM-2: Mashina dlya Razvedki". N.Aleshin, V.Sergeev. *Modelist Konstruktor,* №6 198?, pp8-11.

"BRDM Russian Scout Car". E.Groves. *Tankette,* Vol 5 №3 February 1970, pp4-5.

"BRDM-2 RKhB NBC Reconnaissance Vehicle". *Jane's Defence Weekly*, Vol 8 № 9,1987, pp445.

"Bronetankovaya Tekhnika Polygon". A. Romanov, ed. Moscow 1993.

"Bronierovannie Razvedchiki". E.Prochko. *Tekhnika Molodezhi* , №3 1983. pp28-29.

"Bronieford". E.Prochko. *Tekhnika Molodezhi.* Date unknown, pp28-29 (FAI).

"Bronevik Revolushi". Leonid Gogolev. *Tekhnika Molodezhi* № 1, 1983, pp28-29.

"Cherez Lobie Prepyatstviya". E.Prochko. *Tekhnika Molodezhi* , №11 1983, pp24-25.

"Chrzest-Bojowy Pod Lodzia". *Zolnierz Polski* , №4 1987, pp4, 25.1.87.

"Die Fahzeugfamilie SPW-40 (6)". *Modell Bau Heute* , №2 1979, pp26 (BRDM).

"GAZ Powers Russian Export Drive". Christopher F.Foss. *JDW* 14 Oct 1995, pp25-26.

"GAZ v Broni". E.Prochko. *Avtoshop*, June 1995, pp36-40.

"GAZ Vehicles Address Russia's Changing Security Needs." Jim Kinnear. *Jane's Intelligence Review*, Vol 11 №1, January 1999, pp 15-17.

"Gefechtsfahrzeuge der mot Schutzen". MTH, *Militarverlag*, East Berlin,DDR,1985

"Istoria Razvitia bronierovannikh plavayushikh mashin Rosii". Aleksei Stepanov. *Tekhnikai Vooruzhenie*, No. 2, 2000, pp 1-7.

"Legkiy Dvukhosni". E.Prochko. *Tekhnika Molodezhi,* №10 1983, pp26-27.

"Legkiy Samochod Pancerny BA-64". Bogdan Gabrysiak. *Modelarz*, Issue unknown, pp28.

"Oruzie Rossii". *Russia's Arms Catalogue.* Vol. 1 Moscow, 1996-1997

"Opancerzony Samochod Rozpoznawczy SPW-40P". *Modelarz* №3, 1984, pp29-30.

"Panzerwagen BA-10". A.Schmidt, E.Backer. *Modell Fan,* February 81, pp24, 26.

"Pervie Amfibyi". Evgenniy Prochko. *Tekhnika Molodezhi* , №6 1983, pp26-27.

"Pervie Sovietski". Leonid Gogolev. *Tekhnika Molodezhi* , №2, 1983, pp28-29.

"PB-4 Amphibious Armoured Car". Jim Kinnear. *Red Star,* №21, March-April 1986, pp4-5.

"Rosposnawcz Samochod Opancerzony BTR-40". *Zolnierz Polski,* №41,1988, pp22.

"Rossisky 'Hummer'". *Za Roulom*, №4, 1994, pp11 (GAZ-3937).

"Russian Armoured Car BA-10, 1935 Model". G.Dooley. *Tankette* , Vol 5 №3, Feb 1970, pp12.

"The Russian BA-64 Armored Car Series". Nikolai Polikarpov. *Journal of Military Ordnance* , Vol 6 №5, September 1996, pp4-7.

"Russian BA-64". Karl Rosenlof. *AFV News*, Vol 13 №4.

"Russian BA-64 Armoured Car". J.Steuard. *AFV, G2,*Vol 4 №5 1973, pp5.

"Russian Road-Rail Vehicle Conversions 1930-45". Jim Kinnear. *Red Star,* №21, March-April 1986, pp15.

"The SA-9 Gaskin: Surprisingly Sophisticated". Mark Daly. *JDW*, 20 Oct 1984, pp66-8.

"Samochod Pancerny BA-64". Janusz Magnuski. *Modelarz*, №3 1974, pp26-29.

"Samochodnaya na Kolesakh". E.Prochko. *Tekhnika Molodezhi* № 8 1983, pp36-37.

"Shtabnoi, Svyaznoi, Razvedivatelniy". E.Prochko. *Tekhnika Molodezhi*, №5 1983, pp24-25.

"Soviet BRDM-2 (Part 1)". E. Ashworth. *Military Modelling*, April 1985. pp258-259, 299.

"Soviet BRDM-2 (Part 2)". E. Ashworth. *Military Modelling*, May 1985, pp350-351, 367.

"Soviet BRDM-2 (Part 3)". E. Ashworth. *Military Modelling*, June 1985, pp424-5.

"SPW-40P". *Modelarz*, №3 1984, pp26-27.

"SPW-40P". Boris Lux. *Modell Bau Heute,* №10 1977, pp28-30.

"SPW-40P mit 3 PALR". Boris Lux. *Modell Bau Heute*, №2 1978, pp26-27.

"SPW-40P mit 4 PALR". Boris Lux. *Modell Bau Heute,* №3 1978, pp30-31.

"SPW-40P mit 6 PALR". Boris Lux. *Modell Bau Heute*, № 4 1978, pp28-30.

"SPW-40P2". Boris Lux. *Modell Bau Heute*, №1 1979, pp27-29.

"SPW-40P2 mit 6 PARL". Boris Lux. *Modell Bau Heute*, №3 1979, pp32-33.

"SPW-40P2 alb Motorisierte Strela". Boris Lux. *Modell Bau Heute*, №12 1981, pp17-20.

"Soviet BA-10 Armoured Car". James Steuard. *AFV G2*, Vol 4 №9, 1974. pp18-19.

"We Need Strong Armour and Army". Vladimir Tyurin. *Voenniy Parad*, July-Aug 1994, pp24-25.

Books:

Armoured Fighting Vehicles of the World. Christopher F.Foss. London,1971,1977,1982 editions.

Avtomobilniy Soldati. L.D.Gogolev. Moscow, 1990.

Avtomobiliy Stranyi Sovietov. L.M.Shugurov, V.L.Shirshov. DOSAAF, Moscow, 1983.

Avtomobiliy Rossii i SSSR, Part 1. L.M.Shugurov. Moscow, 1993.

Avtomobiliy Rossii I SSSR, Part 2. L.M.Shugurov. Moscow, 1993.

Bez Tain i Sekretov. N.S.Popov at al. St.Petersburg, 1996.

Boevaya Tekhnika . V.S.Knyazkov. DOSAAF,Moscow, 1986.

BRDM factory manual.

BRDM-2 factory manual.

Brone-Mashini. L.D.Gogolev. Moscow, 1986.

Bronetankovaya Sovietisch Vooruzhenie Sil. DOSAAF, Moscow, 1987.

Bronetankovaya Tekhnika. V.S.Voznyuk, P.N.Shapov. DOSAAF, Moscow, 1981

Bronetankovaya Tekhnika Fotoalbom. V.Brizgov, O.Ermolin
(editors). Gonchar, Moscow, 1993.

Bronierovannaya Razvedivatelno - Dozornaya Mashina BRDM:Tekhnicheskoe Opisanie i Instruktsiya po Expluatatsii. Russian MoD. Moscow,1984.

Bronietankovaya Tekhnika Sovietskiy Vooruzhenikh Sil. Moscow, 1990.

Czerwony Blitkrieg. Janusz Magnuski, Maxim Kolomietz. Pelta Publishing, Warsaw, Poland,1994.

Defence Intelligence Report: Warsaw Pact Ground Forces Equipment Handbook: AFV's. Paul Fein (editor). Defence Intelligence Agency, Washington, April 1980.

Die Roten Panzer. I.G.Andronikov, W.D.Moslovenko. Munich, 1963.

Early Armoured Cars. E.Bartholomew. Shire Publications. Aylesbury, UK, 1978.

FAI factory manual.

Fighting Vehicles of the Red Army. Bryan Perrett. London, 1979.

Godni k stroevoi. F. Lapshin. Autoreview No. 5 (215) 2000, pp 50-53.

Handbook on the Soviet Armed Forces. Defence Intelligence Agency, July 1969.

Handbook on Soviet Ground Forces FM30-40. U.S. Department of the Army, Washington, 1975.

Handbook on the USSR Military forces (TM-30-430). U.S. War Department, Washington, USA, 1945.

Historic Military Vehicles Directory. Bart Vanderveen. Wheels & Tracks, London, 1989.

Identification Handbook: Soviet Military Weapons & Equipment. HQ U.S. Army Europe. U.S. Army. 1972.

Istoriya Sozdaniya i Razvitiya Vooruzheniya i Voennoi Tekhniki PVO Sukhoputnikh Voisk Rossii. S.I.Petukhov, I.V.Shestov, S.A.Golovin (editor). Russian Academy of Rocket and Artillery Science. Moscow,1998. Parts 1 and 2.

Jane's AFV Recognition Handbook. Christopher F. Foss (Editor). 2nd edition, Jane's Information Group, London,1982.

Jane's Armour and Artillery. Christopher F. Foss (Editor). Jane's, London,1979-1998 editions.

Jane's Tank Recognition Guide. Christopher F. Foss. Harper Collins, Glasgow, 1996.

Jane's World Armoured Fighting Vehicles. Christopher F. Foss. London,1976.

L'Automobile en URSS - Chronologie de 1917 a 1990. A.Dupouy. Grenoble, France, 1991.

Les Engins Blindes A Roues Vol 3 Le BTR-40 et le BTR-152. A.Dupouy. Grenoble, France, 1997.

Modern Soviet Armor. Steven J. Zaloga. London, 1979.

Obozrenie Otechestvennoi Bronetankovoi Tekhniki (1905-1995). A.V.Karpenko. Nevsky Bastion Publishers, St. Petersburg, 1996.

Observers Military Vehicles Directory (from 1945). B.H.Vanderveen, London, 1972.

Observers Fighting Vehicles Directory (WW2). B.H.Vanderveen, London, 1972.

Observers Army Vehicles Directory (to 1940). B.H.Vanderveen, London, 1974.

Opancerzony Samochod Rozpoznawczy BRDM. Typi Broni 24 WMON, Warsaw, Poland, 1975.

Oruzhie Pobedi 1941-45. V.N. Novikova. Moscow, 1985.

Recognition Handbook, Foreign Weapons & Equipment (USSR) UK MoD,1964.

Rossiskoe Raketnoye Oruzhiy 1943-1993. A.V.Karpenko PIKA , St. Petersburg, 1993.

Russian Armoured Cars (to 1945). John Milsom. AFV Profile, №60. 1970

Russian Tanks 1900-70. John Milsom. Arms & Armour Press, London, 1970.

The Soviet Army: Troops, Organisation and Equipment. FM-100-2-3. U.S. Army, 1984.

Soviet Equipment Recognition Guide (TM30-3). U.S. Army Foreign Science & Technology Centre, USA, 1975.

Soviet Wheeled Armoured Vehicles. S. Zaloga. Concord Publishing. Hong Kong, 1990.

Soviet Tanks and Combat Vehicles of World War Two. Steven J. Zaloga and James Grandsen. Arms & Armour Press, London,1984.

Soviet Tanks and Combat Vehicles 1946 to the Present. Steven J. Zaloga, James W. Loop. Arms & Armour Press, London, 1987.

Suomalaiset Panssarivaunut 1918 - 1997. Esa Muikku, Jukka Purhonen. Apali, Tampere, Finland, 1998.

The Soviet Army: Troops. Organization and Equipment FM 100-2-3. Department of the Army, Washington Vezdekhodi RKKA. Evgenniy Prochko. Armada, Moscow, 1998.

Weapons & Tactics of the Soviet Army. David C. Isby. London, 1981.

Wozy Bojowe LWP 1943-1983. Janusz Magnuski. Wydawnickwo Ministerstwa Obrony Narodowey Warsaw 1985.

The World's Armoured Fighting Vehicles. Dr F.M.Von Senger und Utterlain. London, 1962.

Zenitnie Raketnie Kompleksi PVO Sukhoputnikh Voisk. G.N.Dmitriev (editor). Kiev, Ukraine, 1996.

INDEX